Move Beyond 5

TEACHER'S EDITION PACK

macmillan education

Anna Cole
Michael Terry

LISTENING & VOCABULARY	GRAMMAR (2)	LANGUAGE & BEYOND	SPEAKING	WRITING
Leaving home ***Recognize informal speech*** **Vocabulary (2):** Adjectives for describing objects	Past tenses review ***Talk about past actions***	Get organized ***Collaborate to organize a group activity***	Invitations ***Make and react to invitations***	A special object (description) ***Make a writing plan***
Around the world ***Listen for the information you need*** **Vocabulary (2):** Travel	The future ***Talk about events in the future***	Respect others ***Respect other people's personal space***	At the airport ***Check in at the airport***	Wish you were here (postcard) ***Use correct verb tenses***
Talking music ***Transfer spoken information to a table*** **Vocabulary (2):** Adverbs of degree	Comparison of adverbs ***Compare how people do things***	Get organized ***Stay on task and avoid distractions***	My sister thinks … ***Present other people's opinions***	My music profile (profile) ***Link contrasting ideas***
Back from the future ***Use stress and intonation to help you understand*** **Vocabulary (2):** Extreme adjectives	Second conditional ***Talk about imaginary situations in the present and future*** PRONOUNCE Stressed words and phrases	Know yourself ***Decide what's important to you***	Do you mind? ***Make and react to requests***	A poem about true friends (poem) ***Use a dictionary***
The power of color ***Follow a conversation*** **Vocabulary (2):** Color idioms	*(In order) to … , so (that) …* ***Talk about the purpose of doing things***	Communicate & cooperate ***Recognize nonverbal communication***	At the pharmacy ***Ask for help with words at the pharmacy***	A place I really like (description) ***Link similar ideas***

IRREGULAR VERBS page 74 EXTRAS pages 75–76

CONTENTS

WELCOME TO THE *MOVE BEYOND* TEACHER'S EDITION

Move Beyond is an exciting eight-level course for teenagers, covering CEFR levels from A1+ to B2. Its scope and sequence is meticulously mapped to the CEFR and international exams. The course offers comprehensive coverage of the four language skills through the incremental and cumulative development of subskills. It equips students with transferable linguistic strategies to use in the English classroom and beyond. The inclusion of age-appropriate 21st-century skills adds an inspiring new dimension to language teaching. The life skills lessons create a learning environment that's relevant and accessible to teenagers.

The course is flexible and works in a number of teaching contexts. Lessons are clearly labeled so that you can choose to prioritize material that's relevant in your teaching contexts. The extensive online materials present you with a variety of teaching and practice alternatives to enrich the learning experience.

With eight levels, your school's needs can be met with one single course – be it for streaming, multilevel entry or a program that takes your students from A1+ all the way up to B2.

The material has a creative and dynamic approach to topics that motivates students and makes language learning more meaningful and successful. Units provide constant opportunities for students to express themselves, while the pages are brought to life through a series of specially produced videos. Throughout the course, language is recycled and reviewed, allowing students to assess and consolidate their progress.

The course's combination of language skills, life skills, and motivating material prepares students for success in and beyond the classroom.

A message from the authors

Secondary teaching is a rewarding but demanding profession. With this course we have tried to make your role as a teacher as easy as possible. The material is clearly organized and can be taught with little or no preparation time. We have also provided resources to help you test and evaluate progress, review material, and work with mixed-ability classes.

Having enthusiastic and interested students also makes the teaching role easier, so throughout the creation of this series we have considered the teenagers' perspective on learning and come up with materials that teach them about the world and allow them to express their view of the world.

When producing the course, we used the following key principles to guide our writing.

10 KEY PRINCIPLES OF *MOVE BEYOND*

1 Subskills: learning how to read, listen, speak, and write

All reading, listening, speaking, and writing lessons have an integrated subskills focus that teaches students linguistic strategies to maximize their learning. This comprehensive subskills syllabus is a key part of the literacy development objective of *Move Beyond*.

2 Life skills: learning for life

To be successful at school and in life, students need to learn skills that go beyond pure academic knowledge. In order to thrive in today's global market, they need to become aware of and acquire a range of life skills, such as learning to deal with stress, communicating effectively, and understanding different cultures. One lesson in every unit is dedicated to developing a life skill under one of five umbrella headings: Get organized, Get thinking, Respect others, Know yourself, and Communicate & cooperate.

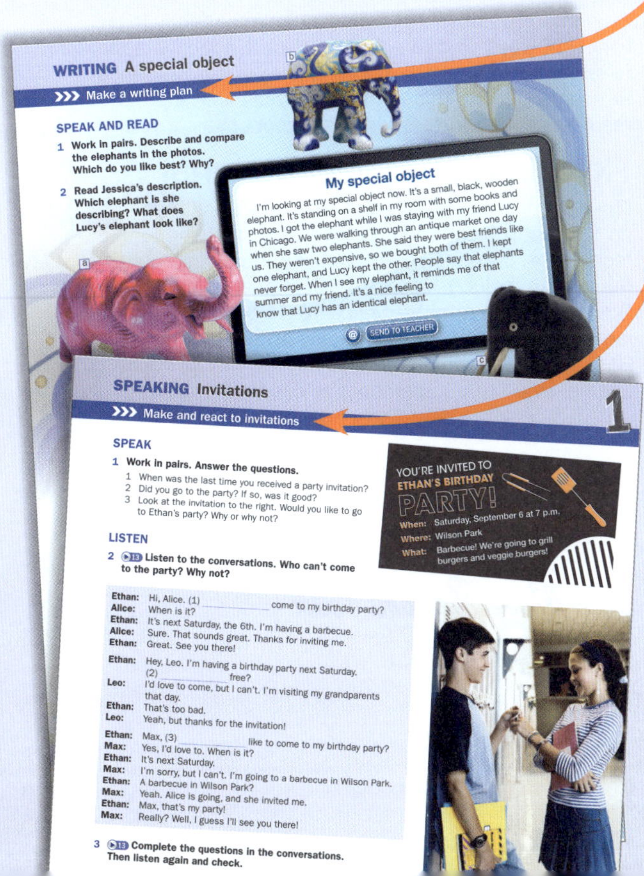

3 Original content and striking images

The cross-curricular focus of *Move Beyond* helps students learn about the world around them, and the original material sustains students' interest. The striking images create a strong visual impact and engage students with the content.

4 Varied and adaptable approach

Move Beyond has adaptations for students' differing learning styles and levels. There are ideas and prompts for students who need more help and a varied approach to dealing with topics and language. To help with differentiation in the classroom, the Teacher's Edition suggests alternative procedures for stronger or weaker students and for fast finishers.

5 Clear and easy to use

All lessons in *Move Beyond* are easy to teach directly from the page. Goals and stages are clearly marked so that teachers can quickly see the objectives and structure of each lesson.

6 Opportunities for personalization

Throughout the course, students are encouraged to relate what they have learned to their own experiences. This personal investment in the course is motivating and rewarding, and it makes the learning process more memorable and the content more relevant.

7 Strong communication focus

In *Move Beyond*, the pairwork discussions, functional speaking tasks, presentations, and variety of writing tasks all encourage students to engage in meaningful and real communication.

8 Language in context

All new language in *Move Beyond* is contextualized for students to see its functional purpose and a situation for use before it is studied.

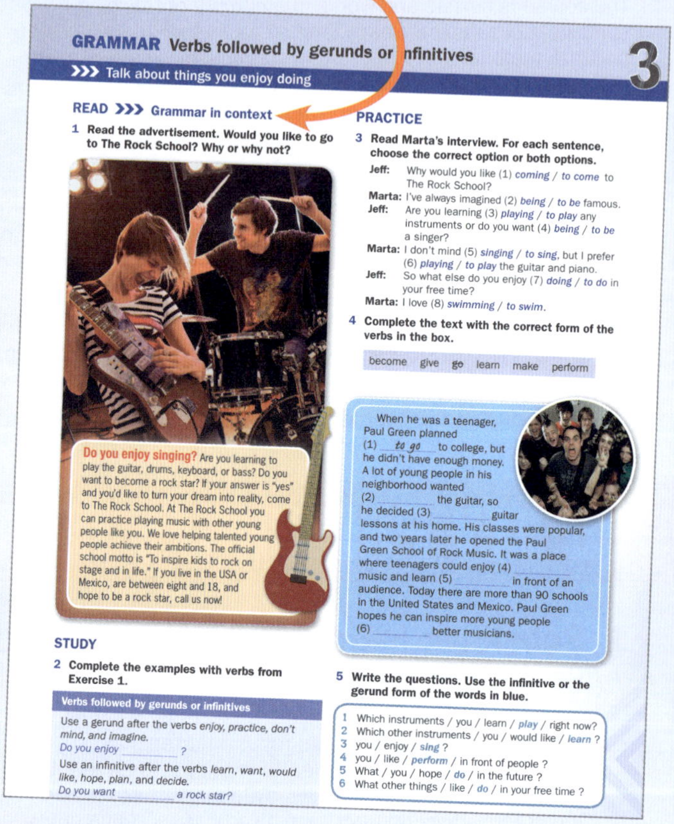

GRAMMAR Verbs followed by gerunds or infinitives **3**

››› Talk about things you enjoy doing

READ ››› Grammar in context

1 **Read the advertisement. Would you like to go to The Rock School? Why or why not?**

Do you enjoy singing? Are you learning to play the guitar, drums, keyboard, or bass? Do you want to become a rock star? If your answer is "yes" and you'd like to turn your dream into reality, come to The Rock School. At The Rock School you can practice playing music with other young people like you. We love helping talented young people achieve their ambitions. The official school motto is "To inspire kids to rock on stage and in life." If you live in the USA or Mexico, are between eight and 18, and hope to be a rock star, call us now!

STUDY

2 **Complete the examples with verbs from Exercise 1.**

Verbs followed by gerunds or infinitives

Use a gerund after the verbs *enjoy, practice, don't mind,* and *imagine.*
Do you enjoy ________ ?
Use an infinitive after the verbs *learn, want, would like, hope, plan,* and *decide.*
Do you want ________ a rock star?

PRACTICE

3 **Read Marta's interview. For each sentence, choose the correct option or both options.**

Jeff: Why would you like (1) *coming / to come* to The Rock School?
Marta: I've always imagined (2) *being / to be* famous.
Jeff: Are you learning (3) *playing / to play* any instruments or do you want (4) *being / to be* a singer?
Marta: I don't mind (5) *singing / to sing*, but I prefer (6) *playing / to play* the guitar and piano.
Jeff: So what else do you enjoy (7) *doing / to do* in your free time?
Marta: I love (8) *swimming / to swim*.

4 **Complete the text with the correct form of the verbs in the box.**

become give ~~go~~ learn make perform

When he was a teenager, Paul Green planned (1) *to go* to college, but he didn't have enough money. A lot of young people in his neighborhood wanted (2) ________ the guitar, so he decided (3) ________ guitar lessons at his home. His classes were popular, and two years later he opened the Paul Green School of Rock Music. It was a place where teenagers could enjoy (4) ________ music and learn (5) ________ in front of an audience. Today there are more than 90 schools in the United States and Mexico. Paul Green hopes he can inspire more young people (6) ________ better musicians.

5 **Write the questions. Use the infinitive or the gerund form of the words in blue.**

1 Which instruments / you / learn / play / right now?
2 Which other instruments / you / would like / learn ?
3 you / enjoy / sing ?
4 you / like / perform / in front of people ?
5 What / you / hope / do / in the future ?
6 What other things / like / do / in your free time ?

9 Learner autonomy

Students are encouraged to work independently in a variety of ways, from a carefully guided inductive approach to grammar to se lf-study worksheets in the Student's Resource Center. This approach makes learning more memorable and furthers learner autonomy.

10 Flexible multimedia material

Move Beyond can be used by teachers with limited or no access to technology. But for those wanting to use technology, both inside and outside the classroom, the course includes a projectable digital version of the Student's Book and the Online Workbook as well as a large bank of additional materials and tests in the Online Resource Centers. Every *Move Beyond* unit contains an original video to supplement the opening lesson.

> We hope you enjoy teaching with *Move Beyond* and that your students enjoy learning with it. We wish you a successful and productive academic year.
>
> *The Move Beyond Team*

> The first two pages are a single **vocabulary lesson** that serves as an introduction to the unit and its central theme.

Unit themes appeal to teenagers and provide interesting, unusual, and informative material.

1 The lesson starts with a Recall exercise that activates prior knowledge of vocabulary. Recall words are listed in the Words & Beyond section at the back of the book, where students learn and practice a related Vocabulary Tip.

2 New vocabulary is clearly visible in a word box and is presented and practiced with the support of the images on the pages. Lexical sets are recorded for ease of presentation. Once introduced, vocabulary is recycled throughout the unit and reviewed in the Unit Review and every two units in a Progress Check.

A pronunciation section focuses on misunderstandings that commonly occur when English is used between speakers of different first languages. Pronunciation sections can appear in any lesson, depending on the content, and focus on key sounds and stress patterns in words and sentences.

UNIT 2 PACK YOUR BAGS

IN THE PICTURE Travel

Talk about travel items

WORK WITH WORDS

1 RECALL **Work in pairs. Do the tasks. You have two minutes.**

a **Make a list of methods of transportation under the headings.**

Air	Rail	Road	Sea
plane	*train*	*bike*	*boat*

b **Complete the sentences with *by* or *to*.**

From Los Angeles ________ New York City, it takes five hours ________ plane or 42 hours ________ car.

c **Match the verbs in the box to the correct methods of transportation.**

drive fly ride sail

You can drive a bus, a ...

2 17 **Look at the pictures. Put the items (a–l) in the correct groups. Then listen and check.**

suitcase

luggage/ baggage

personal items

money and documents

3 a 18 PRONOUNCE **Listen and repeat the words. Pay attention to the /p/ and /b/ sounds.**

backpack brush bag passport shampoo toothpaste

b 19 **Listen and circle the word you hear. Then listen and repeat both words.**

1 back / pack 2 beach / peach 3 Ben / pen 4 bear / pear 5 bill / pill

14

The unit opener is supported by a video that brings the pages to life. Audio and video are located in the Presentation Kit for ease of access in the classroom and easily available for students on the DVD-ROM.

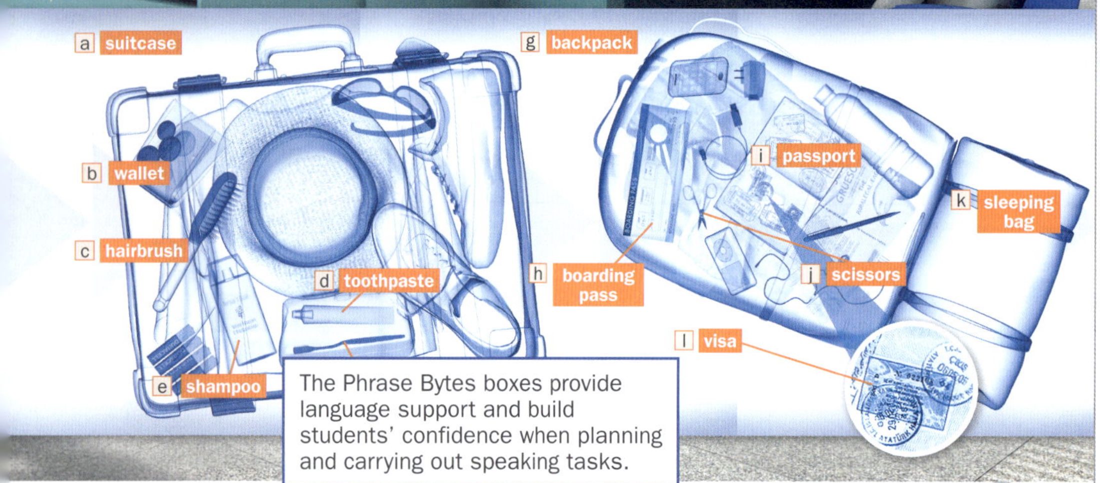

The Phrase Bytes boxes provide language support and build students' confidence when planning and carrying out speaking tasks.

4 Work in pairs. Describe and guess the objects in Exercise 2.

You use it to keep your hair neat. *A brush.*

5 Work in pairs. Look at the pictures again. What other objects are in the backpack and suitcase? Make a list.

6 THE MOVING PICTURE Watch the video of an airport scanner. Write the names of the items that you see.

PHRASE BYTES

What about taking / packing … ?
Let's take … / Why don't we take … ?
We definitely need …
I don't think / I'm not sure … is necessary / especially useful.

SPEAK

7 Work in pairs. You're going on a camping trip in your area.

- With your partner, decide on the five most important things to pack.
- Look at the pictures for ideas and think of other items.
- Compare your ideas with another pair.

MOVE BEYOND

Do the Words & Beyond exercise on page 70.

Workbook, page 92

15

5 The Move Beyond extras provide material for fast finishers, homework, or additional class activities. The Move Beyond extras refer students to the additional exercises on the Words & Beyond pages at the end of the Student's Book section.

3 The Moving Picture feature on the opening pages brings a dynamic element to the spread by introducing a video and an accompanying task connected to the lesson.

4 The final exercises consolidate language with communicative activities in a personalized context.

Lesson 2 – Reading

> After the double-page opening spread, each individual page is one complete lesson. The **reading** and **listening** lessons include an integrated but explicit subskills focus, designed to teach students how to read and listen successfully to a variety of text types over the course of a level.

1 The first exercise gives students the opportunity to say what they know or think about the topic of the lesson. This increases confidence and helps students to focus on the lesson.

2 The HOW TO box provides tips for applying the subskill. Students read the tips, carry out a related task, and then reflect on which tips they used to complete the task.

3 Students read a variety of text types and learn the subskills they need to deal successfully with each genre. Reading texts include unusual and original perspectives on familiar topics.

4 The React exercises encourage students to share opinions on the text and relate to it in a personal way.

5 The Move Beyond task provides a further activity related to the content of the reading text.

Subskills are clearly identified.

All texts are recorded to provide extra classroom and self-study opportunities.

Reading texts contain contextualized examples of the grammar point of the next lesson.

There are links to the corresponding Workbook pages (that can be found at the end of the Student's Book) at the bottom of each page.

READING Be a vacation vo[lunteer]

>>> Identify the purpose of a text

SPEAK AND READ

1 **Work in pairs. Talk about your best vacation. Answer these questions.**
1 Where did you go and who were you with?
2 What kind of vacation was it?
3 Why was it so good?

2 a **Read the tips in the HOW TO box.**

b 20 **Read the first part of the text and identify its purpose.**

3 **Which tips in the HOW TO box did you use for help with Exercise 2b? Check (✓) them.**

HOW TO
identify the purpose of a text
- ☐ Use the headings, layout, pictures, and weblinks to identify the **type of text**.
- ☐ Read the beginning of the text and decide who the readers might be.
- ☐ Identify the **writer** and the **writer's goal** – is it to give information, entertain, or persuade?

VACATION VOLUNTEERS: se[...]e it!

What's a voluntourist?
You know what a tourist is. And you've probably heard of volunteers (people who help others for free). Voluntourists are people who travel to a different place on their vacations to provide aid after a natural disaster or help a local community.

What's Vacation Volunteers?
Since 2001, *Vacation Volunteers* has offered voluntourist programs for 14- to 18 year old students at home and overseas. For two to four weeks, you can live with a host family and do a program of social or environmental work. All you need is a backpack, your toothbrush, and a positive attitude! We have programs in North and South America, Africa, Asia, Europe, and Australia.

Interested? Click here and read what some of our voluntourists have said.

4 20 **Read the voluntourists' stories. Complete the report form for Molly and Alex.**

Program report
Area: ______
Project: ______
Project length: ______
How the program has helped you: ______

REACT

5 **Work in pairs. Discuss the questions.**
1 What helps communities in need more: volunteers or donations of money?
2 As a voluntourist, what kind of program would you choose?
3 Which place, country, or continent would you most like to visit?

MOVE BEYOND
Underline the names of six continents in the text. Which continent is missing?

Molly, 15 (New Zealand)
I've just spent four weeks in South Africa. I've been home for a week now, and I haven't gotten used to it yet. I miss everything about South Africa, but especially the people. They were always cheerful and ready to share food or tell stories. I miss the children in the activity center where I worked too. The program gave me the opportunity to experience the world in a new way. I've learned that you don't need a lot of money or material things to enjoy life.

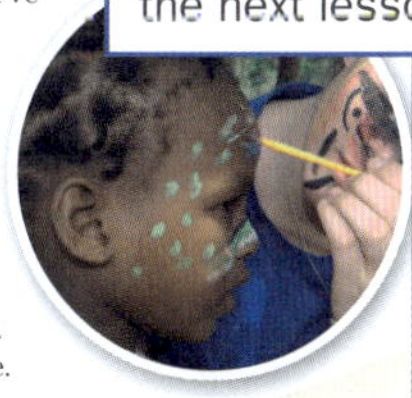

Alex, 16 (USA)
I've never been overseas, and I was a little nervous about traveling outside the USA, so I chose a two-week project in Boston. My team helped elderly people with housework and shopping. It was my first time away from home alone, but I wasn't homesick because I made so many new friends. I can really recommend programs like this. Since the trip, I've felt much more confident. Making a difference as a voluntourist is definitely better than sitting at home!

16

Workbook, page 93

Lesson 3 – Grammar (1)

> The target **grammar** is always presented in context, and students are encouraged to figure out rules from examples.

GRAMMAR Present perfect 2

»» Talk about how long something has happened

READ »» Grammar in context

1 **Read the article. What volunteer activity is the Rawlins family doing and why?**

Since 2006, thousands of voluntourists have traveled to New Orleans, USA, to rebuild the city. Hurricane Katrina destroyed 300,000 homes in 2005, and the city hasn't completed rebuilding work yet. The Rawlins family has been in New Orleans for one week.

"We've already finished a playground, and we've just started on a park project," explains Amy Rawlins. "I've never been on a trip like this before," says 16-year-old Elena. "Have you ever worked on vacation? Since we arrived, we've worked for eight hours every day. The weird thing is – I've had a fantastic time!"

STUDY

2 **Read the explanations. Then underline examples of the three different uses of the present perfect in Exercise 1.**

Present perfect

Use the present perfect for:
1 past actions when the exact time is not mentioned.
2 past actions with *ever/never.*
3 actions in the recent past with *just, yet,* and *already.*

Form the present perfect with *have/has* + *(not)* + past participle.

Irregular past participles change in form.
See page 74.

3 **Underline *for* and *since* in Exercise 1. Then complete the explanations.**

Present perfect: with *for* and *since*

Use *for* or *since* to answer the question *How long ...?*
Use ________ with specific dates, months, or years.
Use ________ with lengths of time.
See GRAMMAR DATABASE, page 65.

PRACTICE

4 a **Ben wants to be a voluntourist. Complete the interview with the present perfect form of the verbs and the adverbs.**

I: (1) ____________ (you / ever / be) to the USA?
Ben: Yes, I (2) ____________ (already / visit) Boston on a sight-seeing trip.
I: (3) ____________ (you / ever / stay) in a tent with 10 people?
Ben: Uh ... no, I (4) ____________ (never / be) camping. But I (5) ____________ (sleep) in a sleeping bag at my friend's house.
I: (6) ____________ (you / ever / work) eight hours in a day?
Ben: No, (7) I ____________ (not do / that / yet). Um, I think I (8) ____________ (just / change) my mind ...

b **Write your answers to the three questions in Exercise 4a. Use *already, not yet,* and *never.***

5 **Complete the visitor's form. Write the questions and complete the answers with *for* or *since.***

1 How many years ____________?
We've spent our vacations in Orlando *since* I can remember.
2 How many years ____________?
We've stayed at the Beach Campsite ________ 10 years.
3 How long ____________?
We've been here ________ Saturday.
4 How many days ____________?
We've had good weather ________ we came here.
5 How long ____________?
I've looked forward to this vacation ________ a long time!

WRITE AND SPEAK

6 a **Work in pairs. First write five activities you do regularly. Give your list to your partner.**
I eat toast for breakfast. I do gymnastics. I go to school with my brother.

b **Ask your partner how long he or she has done the activities on the list. Answer your partner's questions.**

How long have you eaten toast for breakfast?

For 10 years. / Since I was three.

c **Tell the class one interesting thing about your partner.**

»» Workbook, pages 94–95

17

1 Target grammar is always presented in context. Students either read or read and listen to a conversation or short text that expands on the theme of the unit.

2 In the Study section, students are guided to notice grammar structures from the text and then to complete explanations or examples in the Study box.

3 The target grammar is practiced in a controlled but meaningful context that often also provides opportunities for personalization.

4 Practice exercises start with more controlled task types and then become progressively freer, preparing students to talk about their own lives and experiences in the Speak or Write and Speak exercise at the end of the lesson.

5 The final tasks focus on speaking and/or writing for accuracy of the target structure within a communicative context.

Lesson 4 – Listening and vocabulary

> **Listening** comprehension tasks are designed to support understanding and not to test. They progress from a focus on global understanding to an understanding of specific details. The exercises are designed to give practice in a specific listening subskill. Students are always asked to react personally to what they hear.

1 As on the Reading page, the first exercise ensures that students access their relevant knowledge and experiences before they listen.

2 Listening texts contain contextualized examples of the grammar point of the next lesson, allowing students to hear the language in context before looking at it in depth.

3 The HOW TO box provides tips that help students focus on the subskill.

4 The React exercise encourages students to give their personal opinion on the listening text.

5 In the Work with Words section, students focus on the second lexical set of the unit. In some units the Work with Words section comes before the listening activity in order to introduce new target vocabulary first.

6 The Move Beyond task allows students to do a further task related to the new vocabulary set.

LISTENING AND VOCABULARY Around the world

>>> Listen for the information you need

SPEAK AND LISTEN

1 Work in pairs. Answer the questions.

1 What are your favorite ways to travel? Why?
2 What are the positive and negative aspects of traveling by boat?

2 Read the beginning of Oscar's blog. Why is he writing a blog?

3 a Read the tips in the HOW TO box.

b 21 Listen to Oscar's video blog. First listen for the main ideas only and answer the questions. Then listen again and add some details to your answers.

1 What's the family doing now?
2 How does Oscar feel about the trip?
3 At sea, what does he do in the morning?
4 What does he do in the afternoon?
5 Who's Oscar meeting in Brisbane?
6 What are they going to do?

4 Which tips in the HOW TO box did you use for help with Exercise 3b? Check (✓) them.

Hi, I'm Oscar. My family and I are sailing around the world on a two-year voyage in our boat, *Dolphin*. Check me out with the rest of the crew (that's my mom, dad, and my sister, Poppy), and follow our voyage on this blog. I'll probably post some videos too. Enjoy!

HOW TO

listen for the information you need

First listen for the main ideas.

- ☐ Don't worry if you can't understand everything.
- ☐ Listen for words you know. They can help you understand important ideas.

Then listen for specific information.

- ☐ Decide what you want to know.
- ☐ Think about the words you might hear.

REACT

5 Work in pairs. What do you think? Tell your partner.

1 What are the good things about living on a boat?
2 What problems are there living in a small space on a boat?
3 Would you like to be homeschooled? Why or why not?
4 Would you like to take a trip around the world? Why or why not?

WORK WITH WORDS

6 22 Complete the map and online ticket with the travel words in the box. Listen and check.

arrival connection delay departure destination fare passenger reservation ~~route~~ seat

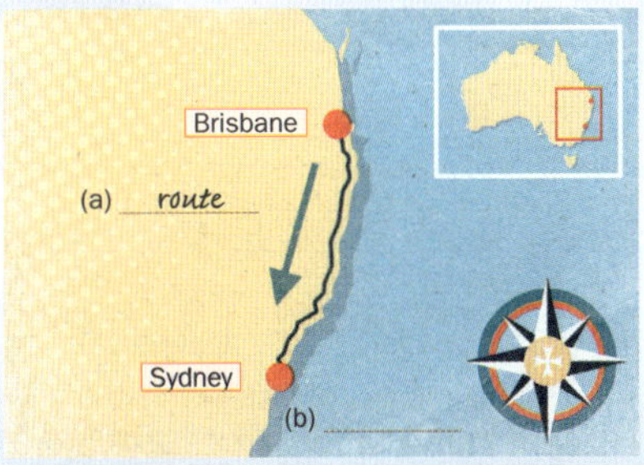

(c) ________: Brisbane, October 5, 7:30 a.m.
(d) ________: Sydney, October 5, 9:06 p.m.
(e) ________s: none (direct train)
Please note that there may be a possible
(f) ________ because of work at Sydney Central Station.
(g) 4 ________s (2 adults, 2 children under 16)
(h) 4 ________s, (i) ________s: 21, 22, 23, 24 in coach G
Total (j) ________: $289.52

7 a Make an online ticket like the one in Exercise 6. Change the trip details (destination, arrival and departure times, and the connections). Don't show your ticket to anybody.

b Work in pairs. Ask your partner questions to find out the details of his or her trip and make notes.

MOVE BEYOND

Do the Words & Beyond exercise on page 70.

Workbook, pages 96–97

Lesson 5 – Grammar (2)

> The second **grammar** lesson follows the same structure as the first **grammar** lesson of the unit – see page 13.

GRAMMAR The future

2

»» Talk about events in the future

READ »» Grammar in context

1 **Read the chat message. What's an InterRail trip?**

DAN: My big sister's starting her InterRail trip on Saturday. Her train to Paris leaves at twelve o'clock, and then she's going to travel around Europe by train for a month.

JUAN: Wow, that'll be amazing. Will she be OK?

DAN: Well, she isn't traveling alone, and my parents will definitely call her every day. So she isn't likely to have any problems.

JUAN: What countries are they going to visit?

DAN: They don't know their final route yet – but it's likely to be a lot! You can travel to 30 countries with an InterRail ticket. They probably won't remember which countries they went to!

STUDY

2 **Read the explanations. Then underline an example of each form in Exercise 1.**

The future

Form	Use
present progressive	future arrangements
simple present	events on a timetable
be + *going to* + base verb	future plans/intentions
will/won't + base verb + *definitely* = 100% sure + *probably* = 75% sure	predictions
be + *likely to* + base verb	probable events

Place *definitely* and *probably* after *will*, but before *won't*.

My parents will ________ call her every day.

They ________ won't remember which countries they went to!

See GRAMMAR DATABASE, page 65.

»» Workbook, page 98

PRACTICE

3 (23) **Felipe and his parents are going on their dream trip on the Ecuador railway from Quito to Guayaquil. Choose the correct options. Then listen and check.**

Felipe: We (1) *'ll go* / *'re going* on our trip tomorrow.
Sam: When (2) *does your train leave* / *is your train likely to leave*?
Felipe: In the morning. It (3) *'s arriving* / *arrives* in Cotopaxi National Park for lunch. On the second day, we (4) *'re going to travel* / *'re traveling* through the Avenue of the Volcanoes – the train climbs to over 3,600 meters!
Sam: It sounds exciting. Is it (5) *likely to be* / *being* dangerous?
Felipe: No, it's very safe – well, pretty safe. Only one volcano is active.
Sam: (6) *Are you going to sleep* / *Do you sleep* on the train?
Felipe: No, we aren't. We (7) *'re staying* / *likely to stay* in hotels.

4 **Read quotes by students about their plans and dreams. Write the correct future forms.**

1 Tomorrow I *'m doing* (do) an audition for a theater school.
2 My judo course ________ (start) next week.
3 Next year I ________ (learn) Japanese.
4 In 10 years I ________ (definitely / be) a pilot.
5 My dream is to be a famous singer, but it ________ (not / likely / come) true.
6 I ________ (probably / get) my driver's license and a car when I'm 17.

WRITE AND SPEAK

5 a **Work in pairs. Write three sentences about your plans and dreams using these time phrases. (Don't show your partner.)**

1 Next week … 2 In 10 years … 3 Next year …

b **Try and predict your partner's future. Write three sentences using your own ideas.**

Next week you'll definitely get a good grade on your English test.
In 10 years you'll probably be a musician.
You're not likely to be a teacher.

c **Tell your partner your ideas. Then look at your partner's sentences from Exercise 5a. Were any of your predictions correct?**

This year you'll make the soccer team.

Yes, I'm definitely going to do that. / Maybe I'll do that. / I'm not sure.

No, I'm not going to do that. / I'm not likely to do that. / No, I probably won't do that.

19

Target vocabulary is recycled throughout the unit.

There are frequent opportunities for students to talk about themselves and to express their views.

The Grammar Database is a useful reference section where all the grammar points of the level are covered in further detail. You can find additional tips and suggestions for using the Grammar Database in the Teacher's Resource Center.

Lesson 6 – Language & Beyond

> The **Language & Beyond** page is the life skills lesson. The goal of these lessons is to equip students with the necessary transferable skills for life beyond the classroom, especially in college and in the workplace. The life skills lessons are grouped under five umbrella headings: Know yourself, Get organized, Get thinking, Respect others, and Communicate & cooperate.

1 A wide range of texts and images is used to raise students' awareness of a particular issue or challenge in their everyday lives. In the first stage, they read or read and listen to texts or conversations about situations that are common among teenagers everywhere.

2 Students are then directed to carry out a practical task in the Do stage. Often working in small groups, they put themselves in the situation described and think about what they would do.

3 The Reflection Point feature encourages students to pause and think about what they've just done and guides them toward drawing their own conclusions.

4 The life skills in *Move Beyond* are transferable to other situations and contexts. The exercises in the Extend section enable students to apply the skills they have learned to a realistic situation, which builds a classroom-to-real-life bridge.

Working with other students is a key part of the life skills lesson.

Useful phrases help students to discuss issues and carry out tasks in English.

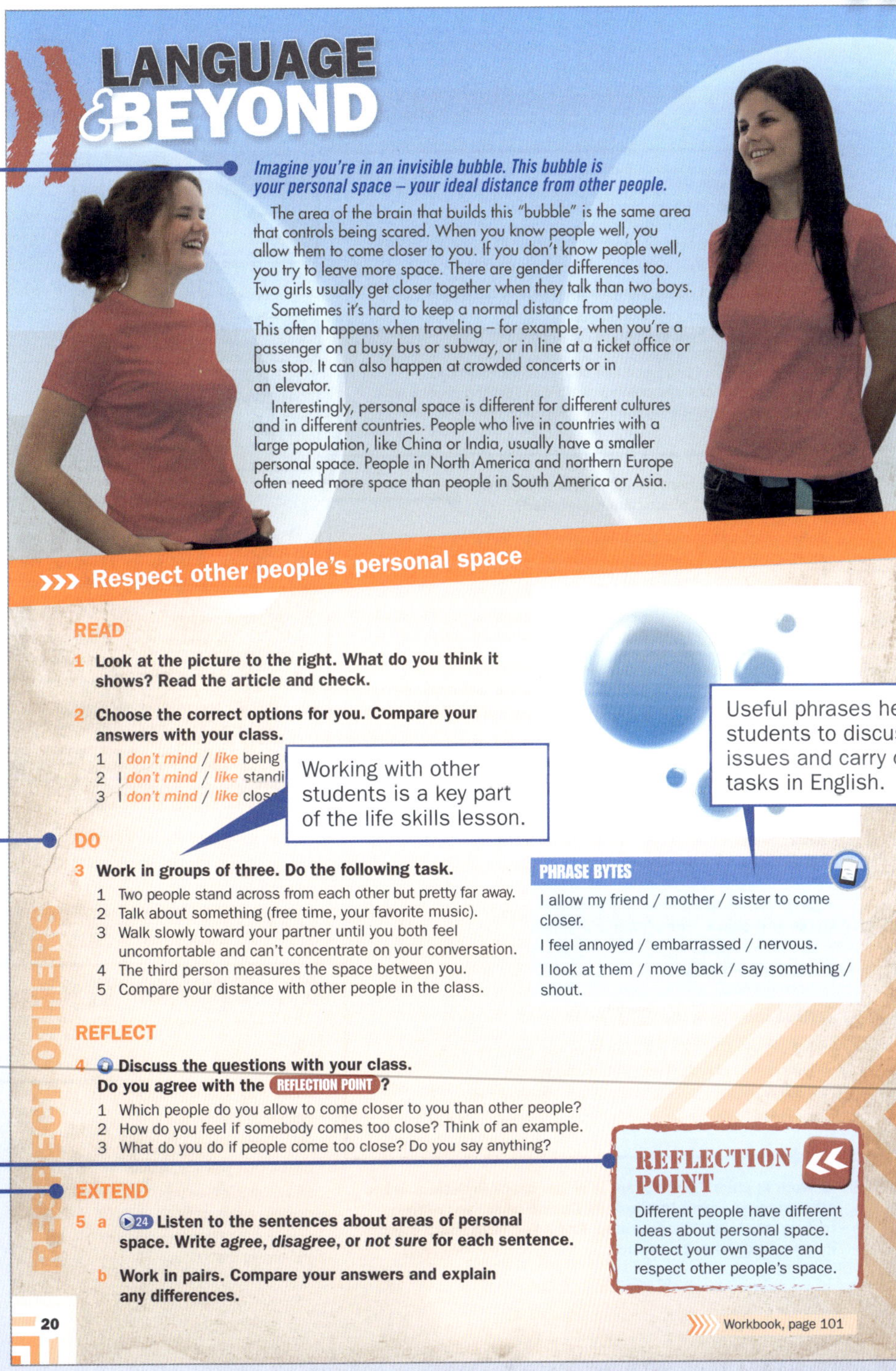

LANGUAGE & BEYOND

Imagine you're in an invisible bubble. This bubble is your personal space – your ideal distance from other people.

The area of the brain that builds this "bubble" is the same area that controls being scared. When you know people well, you allow them to come closer to you. If you don't know people well, you try to leave more space. There are gender differences too. Two girls usually get closer together when they talk than two boys.

Sometimes it's hard to keep a normal distance from people. This often happens when traveling – for example, when you're a passenger on a busy bus or subway, or in line at a ticket office or bus stop. It can also happen at crowded concerts or in an elevator.

Interestingly, personal space is different for different cultures and in different countries. People who live in countries with a large population, like China or India, usually have a smaller personal space. People in North America and northern Europe often need more space than people in South America or Asia.

»» Respect other people's personal space

RESPECT OTHERS

READ

1 **Look at the picture to the right. What do you think it shows? Read the article and check.**

2 **Choose the correct options for you. Compare your answers with your class.**

1 I *don't mind* / *like* being
2 I *don't mind* / *like* standi
3 I *don't mind* / *like* clos

DO

3 **Work in groups of three. Do the following task.**

1 Two people stand across from each other but pretty far away.
2 Talk about something (free time, your favorite music).
3 Walk slowly toward your partner until you both feel uncomfortable and can't concentrate on your conversation.
4 The third person measures the space between you.
5 Compare your distance with other people in the class.

PHRASE BYTES

I allow my friend / mother / sister to come closer.

I feel annoyed / embarrassed / nervous.

I look at them / move back / say something / shout.

REFLECT

4 **Discuss the questions with your class. Do you agree with the REFLECTION POINT?**

1 Which people do you allow to come closer to you than other people?
2 How do you feel if somebody comes too close? Think of an example.
3 What do you do if people come too close? Do you say anything?

REFLECTION POINT

Different people have different ideas about personal space. Protect your own space and respect other people's space.

EXTEND

5 a **24 Listen to the sentences about areas of personal space. Write *agree*, *disagree*, or *not sure* for each sentence.**

b **Work in pairs. Compare your answers and explain any differences.**

20

Workbook, page 101

Lesson 7 – Speaking

> Using real-life scenarios, the **speaking** page provides students with the language they need to communicate effectively in a range of everyday situations. Each speaking lesson helps students develop a specific speaking subskill. Every speaking page includes an audio track of teens using the new language in context.

SPEAKING At the airport 2

»» Check in at the airport

SPEAK

1 **Answer these questions.**

1 What's the closest airport to your town or area?
2 What's the best way to get to the airport from your home?
3 How many times have you been to an airport? Did you go there to meet people or fly?

2 **Match the airport signs (a–f) to the correct activities (1–6).**

1 Planes land at this part of the airport. e
2 Planes take off from this part of the airport. ......
3 You board the plane here. ......
4 You get your boarding pass here and/or check your bags. ......
5 Somebody checks your passport before you enter a country here. ......
6 Somebody sometimes checks your bags after your flight here. ......

LISTEN

3 **(25) Listen to the conversation. Where's Bella? What other airport places are mentioned?**

Bella: Hello, I'd like to check in for the flight to Rome.
Agent: Can I have your passport, please?
Bella: Yes. Here you go.
Agent: How many bags are you checking?
Bella: One suitcase.
Agent: Do you have any carry-on bags?
Bella: I have a backpack.
Agent: OK, that's fine. Do you have any sharp objects in there?
Bella: Sorry, I don't understand. Could you repeat that, please?
Agent: Do you have any sharp objects in your carry-on bag? Scissors, knives, anything like that?
Bella: Uh, yes, I have some scissors.
Agent: I'm sorry, you'll have to put those in your suitcase. Here's your boarding pass. Departures are upstairs.
Bella: Which gate number is it?
Agent: You board at Gate 30.
Bella: Sorry, I didn't hear that. Can you say that again, please?
Agent: Gate 30. Have a good flight.

4 **(26) Underline sentences in the conversation for 1–4 below. Listen and check. Then listen and repeat.**

1 you want to check in
2 you give something to somebody
3 you talk about carry-on bags
4 you ask about the gate

5 a **Read the tips in the HOW TO box.**

b **(27) Complete the phrases from the conversation. Listen and check. Then listen and repeat.**

1 Sorry, I don't …
2 Sorry, I didn't …
3 Could you … ?
4 Can you say … ?

HOW TO
check that you understand
- Say you didn't hear or don't understand.
- Ask the other person to repeat the information.
- Be polite: use *sorry* and *please*.

ACT

6 **Work in pairs. One student is at the check-in desk, and the other student wants to check in. Decide where you're flying to, how much luggage you have, and if you have sharp objects. Prepare and act out a scene.**

PHRASEBOOK (28)
Check in at the airport
I'd like to check in (for) …
Here you go.
I have a backpack / suitcase.
Where are Departures?
Which gate number is it?
Check that you understand
Sorry, I didn't hear that. Can you say that again, please?
Sorry, I don't understand. Could you repeat that, please?

»» Workbook, page 99

21

1 The lesson starts with speaking exercises, which give students the opportunity to describe pictures and speculate about a situation. New vocabulary is often introduced.

2 Audio tracks of conversations provide students with the context for key functional language. Students listen to the conversation and complete an initial gist exercise before focusing on the speaking function or subskill.

3 A variety of exercise types focuses students' attention on the speaking subskill.

4 Each lesson ends with an Act section in which students prepare a scene of their own to present in groups or to the rest of the class.

5 A **PHRASEBOOK** with relevant functional phrases is provided for use with the Act section of the lesson. This is part of the audio material provided and also serves as a review for speaking functions.

Lesson 8 – Writing

> The **writing** lesson in each unit allows students to put everything they've learned in the unit into practice. Each writing lesson also develops a specific writing subskill. Students are systematically guided to discuss, write, and share their writing.

1 The lesson opens with a short speaking and reading exercise to introduce the topic. Students read a model text and complete a task to check that they have understood the text.

2 The HOW TO feature focuses on a writing subskill and offers tips about the lesson objective.

3 After practicing the subskill, students are given a topic for a writing task and instructed to discuss their ideas in pairs or groups first to help them prepare for writing.

4 Students follow a three-step writing plan that guides them to organize their ideas, use the grammar from the unit, and follow the tips in the HOW TO box.

5 In the final exercise, students share their work with each other and either write a reply or discuss what they have written.

WRITING Wish you were here

>>> Use correct verb tenses

SPEAK AND READ

1 Work in groups. Answer the questions.

1 Why do people usually write postcards?
2 Who do you receive postcards from?
3 Who do you send postcards to?

2 Read Vicky's postcard. Check (✓) the correct pictures on the front.

Dear Marco,
We've been in Spain for three days now, and I'm having a fantastic time! The trip was terrible – our flight had a three-hour delay. I was getting really tired of waiting in the airport. Then we missed our connection, of course, because of the late departure.
But our campsite is fantastic! There's a huge swimming pool, a game room, and a lot of sports like mini golf and table tennis. The weather isn't bad, but it's a little cloudy. Yesterday we rented bikes and rode along the coast. Then we went to an excellent restaurant. The food here is so delicious! Tomorrow we're taking the train into Barcelona, and we're going to do some sightseeing. I think it'll be exciting.
Wish you were here!
Vicky

3 a Read the tips in the HOW TO box.

HOW TO
use correct verb tenses

- Decide if the action is past, present, or future.
- Look at the rules for past, present, and future tenses in Units 1 and 2.
- Use the correct tense with the correct time words (*yesterday*, *tomorrow*, *right now*, *for two years*, *always*).

b Underline examples of seven different tenses in the postcard.

PRACTICE

4 Write the sentences in another postcard in the correct tense. Use the HOW TO box to help you.

1 We ________ (get) here five days ago.
2 I ________ (play) tennis here every day.
3 I ________ (not play) computer games since we got here.
4 We ________ (watch) a show later tonight.
5 It ________ (rain) today.
6 I hope it ________ (stop) later.

DISCUSS

5 Imagine you're on vacation now. Talk about the fun activities you've done already and the activities you plan to do.

WRITE

6 Write a postcard to a friend while you're on your imaginary vacation.

1 Describe where you're staying and what you're doing. Use the simple present or present progressive to describe your actions.
2 Use the simple past or past progressive to describe what you did previously on vacation. Use the future with *will* or *be going to* to say what you're planning for the next day.
3 Use the present perfect to describe how long you've been doing an action or an action you've already done. Use the tips in the HOW TO box.

SHARE

7 Take turns reading your postcards to the class. Whose trip sounds the most interesting? Why?

22

Workbook, pages 100–101

Lesson 9 – Unit Review

> The **Unit Review** page allows students to check and assess their own progress in vocabulary and grammar.

UNIT REVIEW 2

VOCABULARY Travel items

1 **Complete the conversation with the correct words.**

Teacher: How many bags do you have, Luke?
Luke: Uh, just two big (1) s__________ with my clothes and shoes.
Teacher: That's a lot for five days in Lima! Your (2) b__________ looks heavy too.
Luke: I have my (3) s__________ b__________ so I can sleep on the plane. And my (4) t__________ and (5) t__________ so I can brush my teeth after lunch, my (6) h__________, of course, for my hair. Oh, and (7) s__________, to wash my hair later. I like to be prepared!
Teacher: OK, everybody, did you all check in online? Good, get your (8) b__________ p__________ ready. Ping, do you have your (9) v__________ for Peru? All right, let's take our baggage to the desk. Remember, no sharp items like (10) s__________ in your carry-on bags. Yes, Luke?
Luke: Um, I think I've forgotten my (11) p__________ and my (12) w__________ with all my money in it.

___ /12

Travel

2 **Choose the correct options to complete the travel plan.**

Tuesday

Our flight is at 2:25 p.m. Hopefully there will be no (1) delays / fares. Please check in online with your (2) connection / reservation number and choose a (3) seat / destination. We'll meet at the airport an hour before (4) arrival / departure. Please remember not to disturb other (5) seats / passe... during the flight. After our (6) ... departure in Lima, we'll ... (7) passenger / ...ection to our hotel, which is ...nal (8) delay / destination. We'll take a private bus, which is the quickest and cheapest (9) passenger / route. The (10) reservation / fare for the bus is included in the price of the trip.

Wednesday

Visit to the famous Archeological Museum.

___ /10

GRAMMAR
Present perfect

3 **Write the verbs in the present perfect and choose *for* or *since*.**

Guide: This vase is the museum's most expensive item. It (1) __________ (be) in the museum (2) for / since I started working here. I (3) __________ (work) here (4) for / since 30 years. (5) For / Since the last two years a rich collector (6) __________ (want) to buy the vase. We (7) __________ (just / decide) to sell it, but the collector (8) __________ (not take) it away yet. Don't touch it, young man!
Luke: Oh, uh … sorry.

___ /16

The future

4 **Choose the teacher's next sentence (A or B).**

1 It's our last day today.
 A We're flying back home.
 B We're likely to fly back home.
2 We need to be at the airport at 5:00 p.m.
 A The plane leaves at 6:00 p.m.
 B The plane is leaving at 6:00 p.m.
3 You have a free afternoon.
 A You're enjoying it. B I hope you'll enjoy it.
4 I've checked the weather for later today.
 A It doesn't rain. B It isn't likely to rain.
5 Let's meet at the hotel at 4:00 p.m.
 A We're going to travel to the airport by bus.
 B We travel to the airport by bus.
6 Luke, please make sure you're on time.
 A We aren't waiting for you.
 B We won't wait for you.

___ /12

Your score: ___ /50

SKILLS CHECK

✓✓✓ Yes, I can. No problem!
✓✓ Yes, I can. But I need a little help.
✓ Yes, I can. But I need a lot of help.

I can identify the purpose of a text. ______
I can listen for the information I need. ______
I can respect other people's personal space. ______
I can check in at the airport. ______
I can use correct verb tenses. ______

Workbook, pages 102–103

23

1 The Unit Review starts with two exercises to test both lexical sets covered in the unit. Each exercise has a space for students to record their score.

The exercises in the Unit Review are all set in a single context and reflect the way language is used in real life.

2 Two grammar exercises test the two grammar points covered in the unit.

3 After completing all the exercises, students calculate their total score. Each review has the same overall score so that students can assess their progress across units.

4 Students are encouraged to self-assess their progress using CEFR "can do" statements that refer directly back to the objectives of the skills pages.

> After every two units there is a two-page skills-based **Progress Check** that allows students and teachers to see how well the learning objectives in the preceding two units have been met. Tasks on these pages reflect those that students will see on standardized English tests. The Progress Checks also include tips on how to deal successfully with the various tasks.

1 Progress Check tasks consolidate the language from the preceding two units.

2 The Test-Taking Tips help students prepare for standard test-style tasks.

PROGRESS CHECK

READ

1 Read the article and decide if the sentences are correct (*C*) or incorrect (*I*).

1 Woolton was part of Liverpool in 1957. ____
2 Paul McCartney met John Lennon after a concert. ____
3 The Beatles were more popular in the past. ____
4 Lennon lived in Mendips when he was an art student. ____
5 Lennon lived in Mendips for a short time with his first wife. ____
6 People have had the opportunity to visit Mendips since 2003. ____
7 McCartney met Lennon before he moved to Forthlin Road. ____
8 Lennon and McCartney met at Paul's house to practice their first songs. ____
9 The tour guides for the two houses live in the houses. ____
10 You can only go into the houses if you're on a National Trust tour. ____

TEST-TAKING TIPS

do a true/false activity

- Read the sentences carefully before you read.
- Look at any pictures that can help you understand the text.
- Read the text carefully and choose the correct answers.
- Check details: if any part of the sentence is false, then it's incorrect.

LIVERPOOL HIGHLIGHTS:

The Beatles' childhood homes

On a summer afternoon in 1957, a group called The Quarrymen gave a concert in a field behind a church in Woolton. Now a suburb of Liverpool, Woolton was a separate village at that time. The same evening, The Quarrymen played again, this time in the church hall. A boy named Paul was in the audience for both performances. While they were setting up for the evening concert, a friend of his introduced him to John, the group's singer. It was the moment when John Lennon and Paul McCartney met for the first time.

Over half a century has passed since that first meeting, but interest in the Beatles, the group they formed together, has not decreased. People from all over the world still come to Liverpool to see where the Beatles lived and played. Two of the most popular destinations are the houses where Lennon and McCartney grew up.

Mendips is the house on Menlove Avenue where Lennon lived from the age of five until he left home to study at Liverpool Art College in the late 1950s. He briefly moved back into the house in the early 1960s with his first wife. Lennon's second wife, Yoko Ono, bought the house in 2003. It was restored and opened to the public the same year. The highlight for Beatles fans is a trip upstairs to the tiny bedroom in the front where Lennon slept.

Paul McCartney's childhood home on Forthlin Road is smaller and simpler. The McCartney family moved into the house in 1955 when Paul was in middle school. It's often referred to as "the birthplace of the Beatles" because this is where Lennon and McCartney practiced their earliest songs. Like Mendips, the house has been restored. Visitors can stand in the McCartney sitting room, with its colorful curtains, antique television, and old-fashioned wallpaper, and imagine how the teenage McCartney lived.

Today custodians live in both houses. Their job is to care for the houses and to show groups of visitors around when they arrive four times a day, five days a week.

If you want to see inside the houses, you have to go on a minibus tour organized by the National Trust. It's important to reserve a place online in advance, because visits are limited to 15 people at a time. It's also important to be punctual. Passengers need to arrive 15 minutes before the minibus departs, and the tour doesn't wait for people who arrive late.

Reading: ______ /10

24

PROGRESS CHECK 1&2

LISTEN

2 29 **You'll hear an adventure camp organizer talking to a group of teenagers. Listen and write the missing information in the blanks.**

"Goodbye talk" to group

About Adventure Weeks:
- The first Adventure Week was (1) ________ ago.
- Two main objectives for campers:
  Personal: to keep in touch with new friends
  Skills: to learn about (2) ________

Practical things:
- Bus leaves for the airport at 10 a.m.
- We can't wait if you're late.
- Alternative transportation: taxi fare is (3) ________.
- Print your (4) ________ before you leave.
- Bus to (5) ________ leaves at 11 a.m.

Listening: ______ /10

TEST-TAKING TIPS

listen and complete notes

- Read the information carefully before you listen.
- Decide what kind of information is missing.
- Listen for the words before the missing information.
- Write the exact words that you hear.

WRITE

3 For each question, complete the second sentence so that it means the same as the first. Use no more than three words.

1 We met when we were in math class in college.
We met while we __________ math in college.
2 Can you come to our housewarming party?
Would __________ to come to our housewarming party?
3 We moved into our new house two weeks ago.
We've lived in our new house __________ .
4 We're still waiting for John to answer our email.
John __________ our email yet.

______ /4

TEST-TAKING TIPS

do sentence transformations

- Read the instructions. How many words can you use?
- Read both sentences carefully.
- Decide if the missing words are nouns, verbs, or other parts of speech.
- Check that the meaning is the same and your spelling is correct.

4 You decide to send a short message to an Australian friend named Neil. Write your message (35–45 words).

- Say if you are having a good week and say why or why not.
- Say what you have done.
- Tell him what you plan to do on the weekend or next week.

______ /6

Writing: ______ /10

TEST-TAKING TIPS

write a short message or blog post

- Read the task carefully.
- Answer all the questions in the task.
- Use the correct tense(s): past, present, or future.
- Use the correct number of words – count them.

Progress check score ______ **/30**

25

Other features

At the end of the Student's Book material, you'll find the following resources:

Grammar Database
The Grammar Database provides detailed additional explanations of the grammar points of each unit, as well as grammar tables and common errors to watch out for. It is a valuable reference section for students.

Words & Beyond
These pages contain lists of the main lexical sets from each unit, as well as other important vocabulary from the unit, vocabulary tips, and additional tasks.

Irregular verbs
A list of common irregular verbs is provided for students' reference.

Extras
The material for pairwork activities (with Student A and Student B) from the units is provided here, as well as answers to quiz questions.

3 Overall scoring is the same in every Progress Check, so students can monitor both their overall progress and their progress in specific skills.

USING THE *MOVE BEYOND* WORKBOOK

The *Move Beyond* Workbook lessons recontextualize, review, and recycle target items from the corresponding lesson pages of the Student's Book, and offer comprehensive practice for homework and class use.

- Two vocabulary pages per unit practice the target vocabulary in new contexts.
- Intuitive instructions make it easier to complete each exercise.
- Puzzles and games add an element of fun and variety.

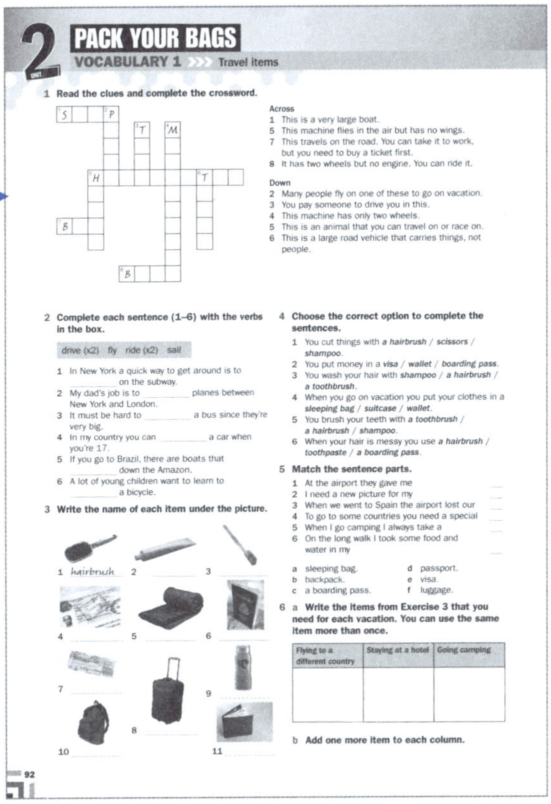

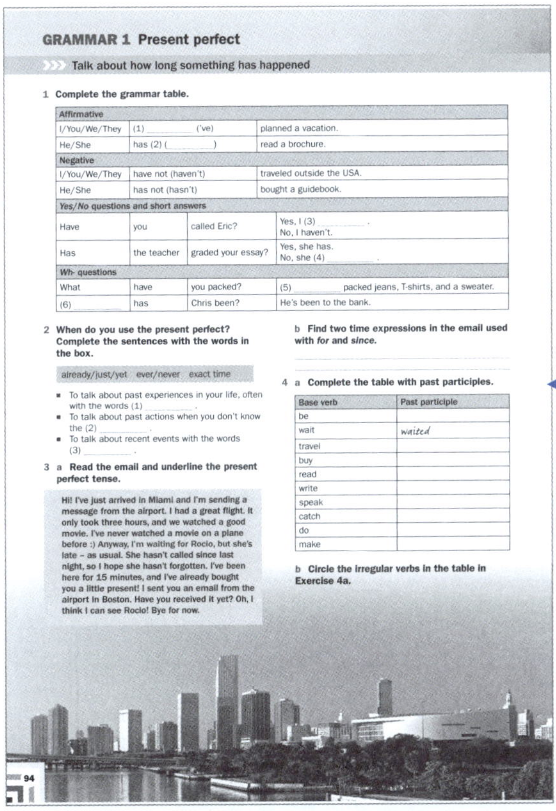

- The Workbook contains three pages per unit for practicing target grammar.
- Grammar Study boxes review the form and use of key grammar.
- Students then practice through contextualized grammar exercises.
- Exercises on the Grammar pages are presented in order of difficulty, shown by chevrons (› = easiest, ›› = medium challenge, ››› = most difficult).

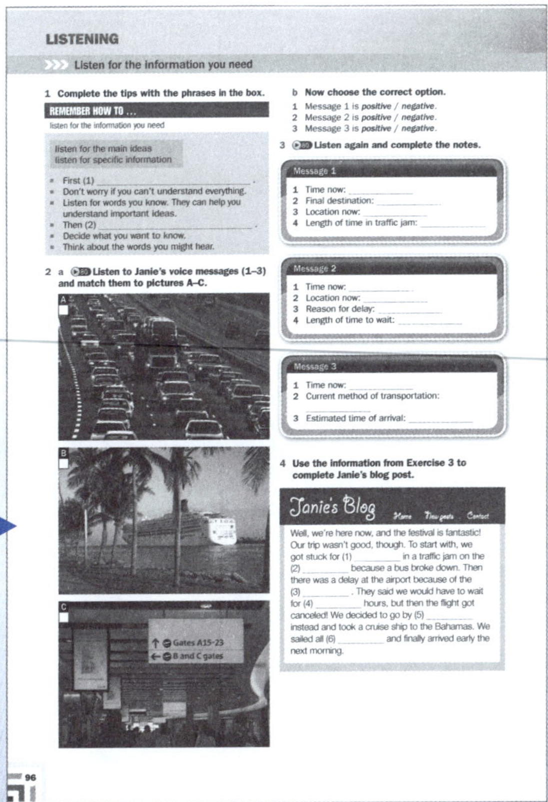

- Key listening subskills from the Student's Book are reintroduced and reexamined.
- Exercises put these skills into practice and review target language.
- Additional listening exercises focus on the theme of the unit, often through test-style tasks related to the subskill in the lesson.

USING THE *MOVE BEYOND* WORKBOOK

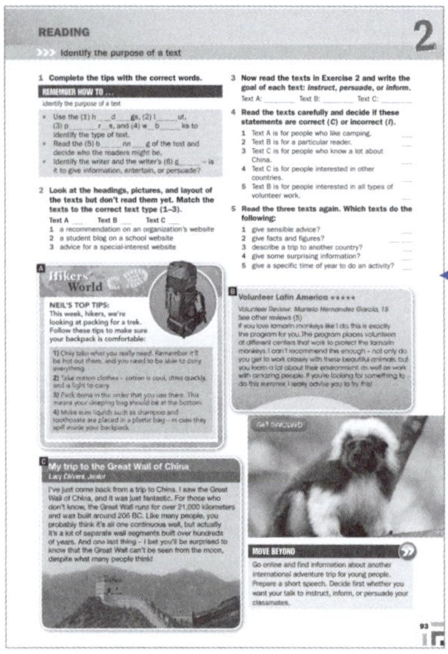

- REMEMBER HOW TO boxes focus on key subskills from the Student's Book lesson.
- Texts build on the themes introduced in the Student's Book.
- Tasks focus on putting reading subskills into practice, recycling key language, and exposing students to test-style tasks.

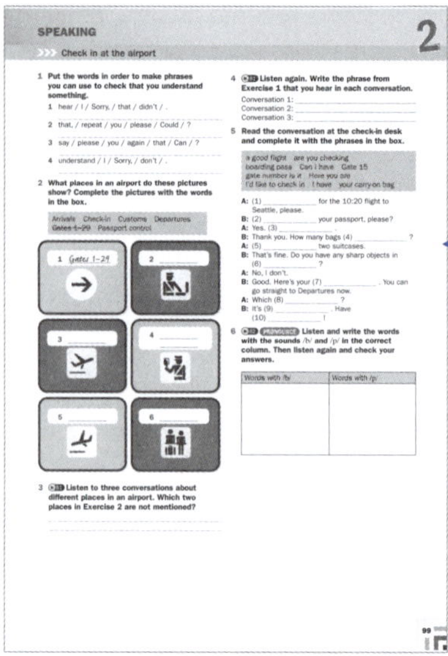

- The Speaking lesson focuses on reviewing key lexical items.
- Target items are presented in context, and recordings are frequently used to focus on important aspects of speaking, such as register, stress, and intonation.

- Key writing subskills from the Student's Book are developed in exercises carefully designed to practice the skill.
- Emphasis is put on the planning and structuring of texts, and students are guided through final test-type writing tasks.

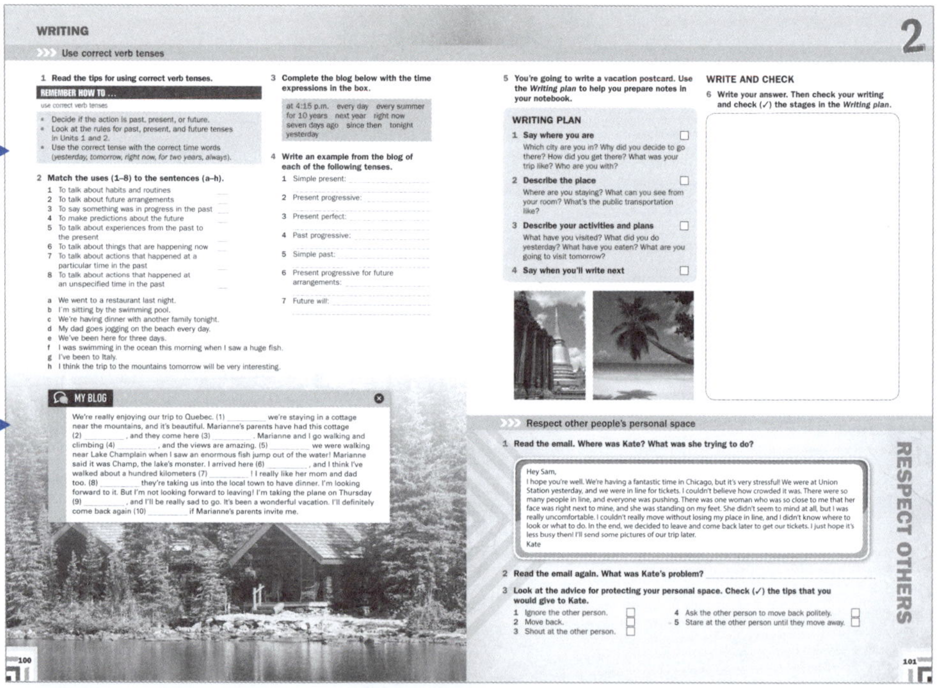

- The unit life skill is revisited, and students are challenged to apply the skill in a personalized new context.

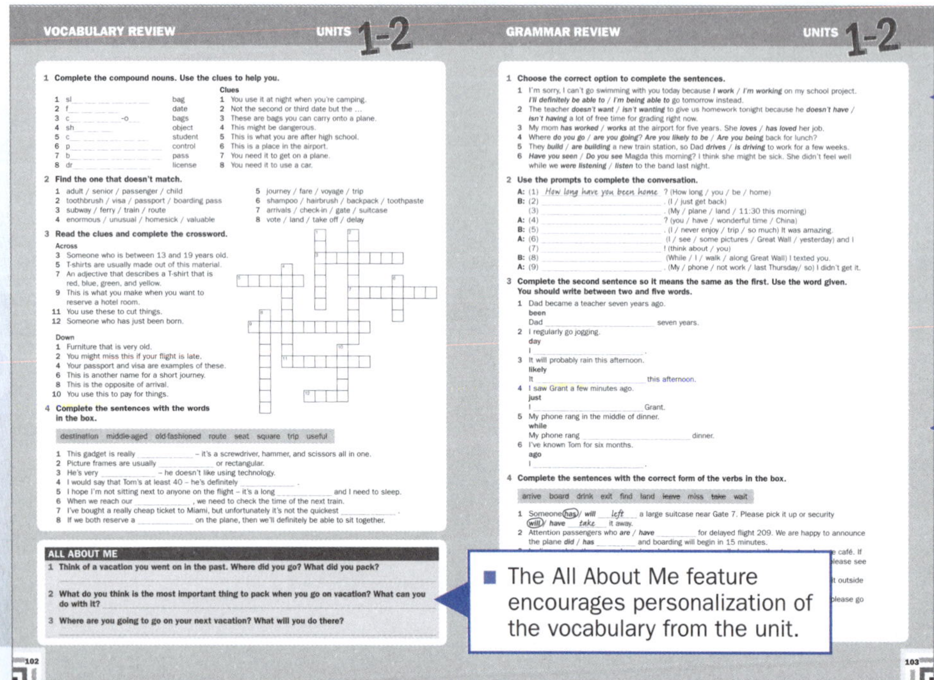

- Target vocabulary and grammar taken from any units of the Student's Book covered to date are recontextualized and reviewed here, allowing students to monitor their own progress.
- The review pages offer cumulative assessment, with exercises combining two or more grammar points or vocabulary sets.
- The All About Me feature encourages personalization of the vocabulary from the unit.

MOVE BEYOND DIGITAL

The digital components of *Move Beyond* are easy to integrate into your regular classroom activities. The range of multimedia resources gives teachers an excellent opportunity to digitize their lessons and present the material in different ways, which varies the pace and dynamics in the classroom. Classwork, homework, and testing are all accommodated in the *Move Beyond* Teacher's Resource Center, where plenty of flexible additional materials for both online and offline use can be found.

Go to mee2.macmillaneducation.com to access:

- *Move Beyond Level 5* Presentation Kit, consisting of a digital Student's Book designed for classroom presentation
- *Move Beyond Level 5* Teacher's Resource Center, for extra materials, tests, videos, and downloadable audio

Teacher's Resource Center

The Teacher's Resource Center provides teachers with downloadable extra grammar and vocabulary worksheets, tips, and testing materials to support the course. It contains a whole range of additional *Move Beyond* materials to be used in the classroom or assigned for homework, as well as access to everything in the Student's Resource Center.

Full answer keys and scripts for all course components.

Extra Grammar and Vocabulary worksheets.

Further ideas and activities for exploring the *Move Beyond* videos.

Teacher's notes to accompany the worksheets.

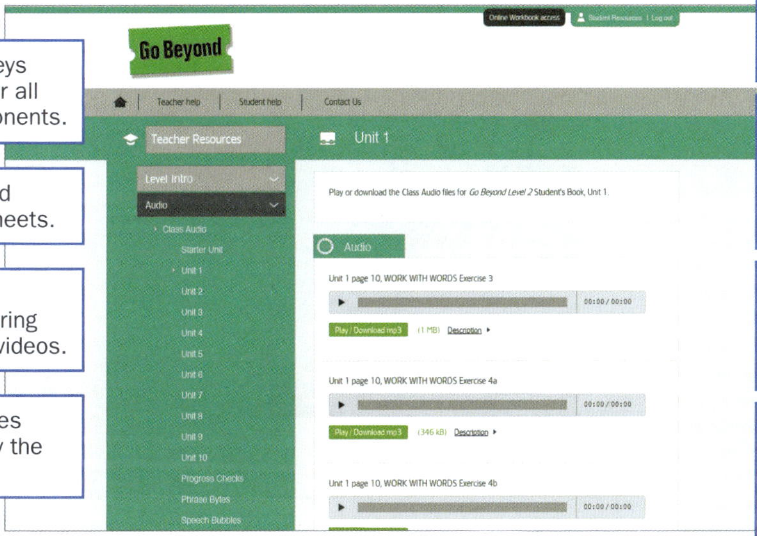

Tips and model answers to accompany the Student's Book and Workbook writing tasks.

A teacher-delivered speaking section to accompany every Student's Book Progress Check.

Static PDF tests for each unit and for the beginning, middle, and end of each level.

A link to special *Move Beyond* materials on www.onestopenglish.com, as well as access to other useful onestopenglish resources.

Presentation Kit

The Presentation Kit includes a projectable digital version of the ***Move Beyond*** Student's Book for teachers to use in class to promote "eyes-up" learning and student interaction. Easily downloadable to multiple devices from mee2.macmillaneducation.com, the Presentation Kit can also be used for lesson preparation at home.

Once downloaded, the Presentation Kit can be used offline. Audio recordings, videos, and answer keys are embedded in the pages for easy reference along with optional pop-up audio scripts and video subtitles, which are synched to the content. There are also fully interactive exercises to work through as a class.

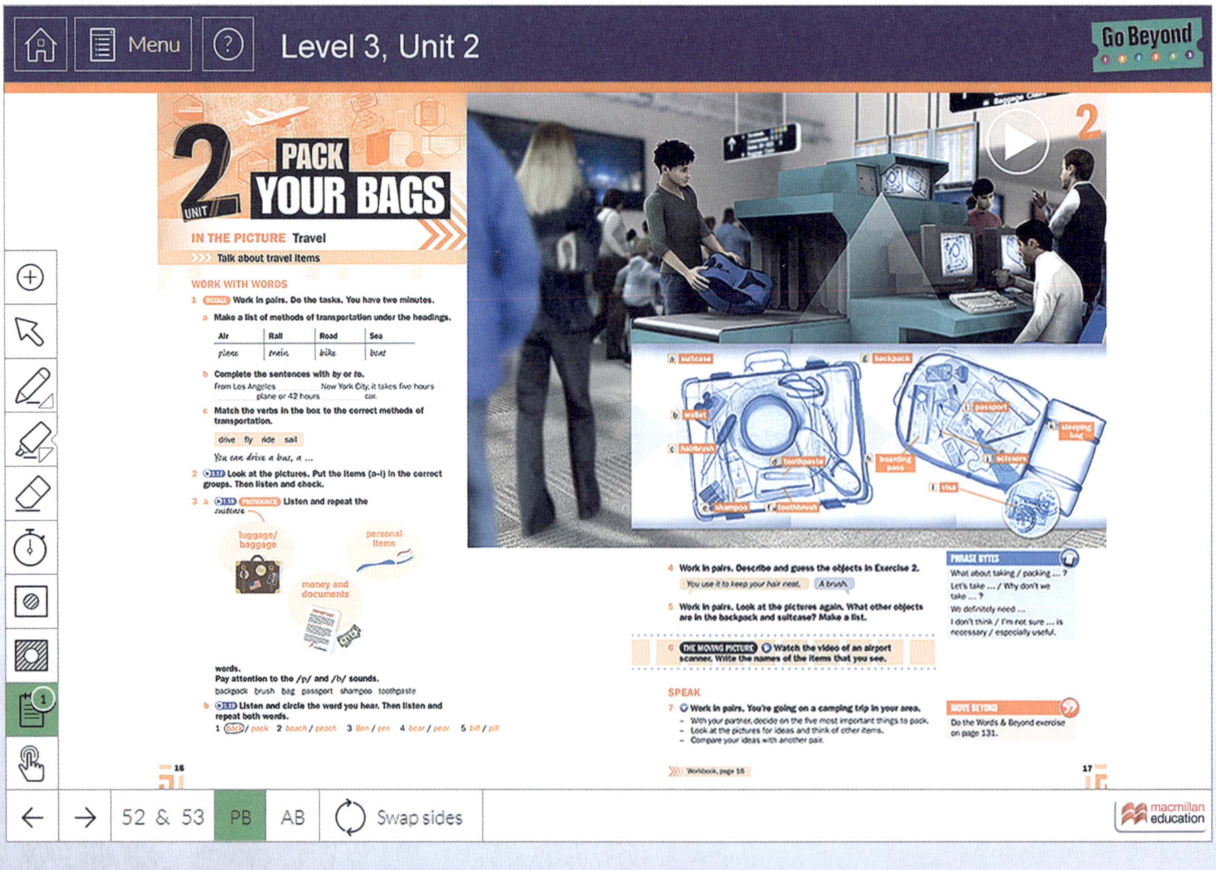

MOVE BEYOND DIGITAL

Move Beyond videos

There is a video for each *Move Beyond* unit, adding richness and variety to the material. The Moving Picture videos from the opening spreads bring global experiences into the classroom. The videos include documentary clips, vox pops, slideshows, digital animation, and YouTube-style videos. These engaging visuals support listening skills and act as conversation starters.

The *Move Beyond* videos are embedded in the Presentation Kit and supplied on a DVD-ROM at the back of the combined Student's Book/Workbook. Teachers can also access them at home via the Teacher's Resource Center.

From The Moving Picture video, Unit 2.

Video tips

You can extend the activities or use the videos separately by using some of these video tips.

From The Moving Picture video, Unit 9.

Before you watch

Students can predict what they'll see and hear in the video.

- Show students the title of the video or give them the topic and ask them to brainstorm vocabulary they think will come up.
- Show the video using the "Fast forward" option or show one or two stills from the video and ask students to predict what is happening or what people are saying.
- Show the first few seconds of the video and ask students to predict what will happen next.

While you watch

You can ask students to watch the videos normally or use just the picture or audio.

A Picture with no sound

- In pairs, one student watches and describes what he or she sees to a partner, who takes notes. They then watch together and discuss differences.
- Make a worksheet with screen shots from scenes in the video. Students write their own dialog or complete speech bubbles.
- Students write their own script for what they see. They then speak over the video, providing the narration or character voices. Finally, they compare their version to the original.

B Sound with no picture

- Students listen to the sound only and speculate in pairs/groups about what they hear. They then watch to see if they were right.

C Picture and sound

- Students make notes as they watch and then compare notes with a partner or in groups.
- After showing the video a first time, give students cards with key words or phrases from the video. As students watch the video a second time, ask them to hold up their cards each time they hear the key word or phrase from their cards in the video.

After you watch

Use these activities in conjunction with the before/while you watch activities or as your main activity.

- Students create a fictional story, write a news story, or do a role-play based on the video or part of it.
- Students write an email or a text message to somebody in the video. They can also make a brochure, ad, fact file, or poster related to a topic or place in the video.
- Show students still photos of people from the video and ask them to make a brief biography for that person – name, age, nationality, family, likes and dislikes, hobbies, and favorite food.

TEACHING TIPS

To optimize your teaching experience with ***Move Beyond***, we've put together some tips for the following key areas:

- Classroom management
- Teaching vocabulary and grammar
- Teaching skills
- Teaching pronunciation

Classroom management

Managing a classroom of teenagers is not always easy, and good classroom management, including organizing resources, creating an effective learning environment, monitoring student progress, and anticipating potential obstacles to learning, is crucial for keeping students on track. The following tips will help you maximize the time in the classroom and ensure a productive learning environment.

Set time limits

Realistic time limits challenge students and engage them in the task. They are less likely to be disruptive. Use the as a guide for what proportion of the lesson you should spend on each task. Set the time limit after you have explained the task and checked students understand the instructions. You can give regular updates on the time remaining for a task. For example, during a three-minute task you might give a *One minute to go* warning, then *Only thirty seconds left …* , etc.

Encourage peer checking

Students appreciate the opportunity to look at a partner's answers to make sure they have the right idea. If students are allowed to compare their answers, they'll have more confidence in them and therefore will be more likely to volunteer them. It also gives students an opportunity to develop their ability to compare and explain in English why they chose their answers.

At this age, students are often frightened of making mistakes in front of their peers. Point out to students, whenever possible, that making mistakes is positive, reminding them that the most successful learners are usually the ones who are not afraid to experiment and make mistakes.

Vary selection techniques

Keep students alert by varying the ways you select them to answer questions. Alternate between selecting students to give answers and asking for volunteers in order to involve all students in the process of checking answers.

Another option is to select a student and let him or her decide which question to answer. This is good for less confident students, as it allows them to answer questions that they are more likely to have right. This student can then choose who will answer the next question. Alternatively, if you have closely monitored students while they were doing the exercise, "randomly" call on students who have the correct answers. Both of these techniques are good for giving students confidence to speak and offer up their answers in class.

Correct errors effectively

It is important not to overcorrect, as this can make students lose confidence. However, undercorrecting leads to students developing bad language habits and decreases their ability to communicate in the long term. When students are carrying out pairwork exercises, the focus is on fluency, and it's better not to correct errors. However, monitor students and note important errors and good use of language to go over at the end of the exercise in a feedback session. Allow a few minutes of class time for error correction. Write the errors on the board without saying who made the mistake and elicit correct answers from the class.

Reward students

You can reward students for good answers or improvement with instant feedback, but it's also useful to create a system to be used throughout the year where points are awarded for improvement, effort, or work in a particular skill or area. Award certificates or small prizes for students at the end of the school year. Longer-term goals can help keep students motivated throughout the year.

Be aware of different learning styles

Different students have different ways of learning. Ensure that each student is catered to: vary approaches and activities to include a combination of visual (pictures, presentations, writing), auditory (listening, pair and group conversation activities), and kinesthetic (moving, computer work) activities.

Be sensitive

Some students may not want their problems shared with the class. Use your discretion when discussing any personal topics in class and be prepared to have an alternative task ready if students are not willing to join the discussion.

Teaching vocabulary and grammar

The following tips give you some ideas for teaching vocabulary and grammar as well as some reminders about commonly confused words and forms.

Remembering words

Encourage students to practice vocabulary by saying words in English when they go to various places. Recommend to students that they spend 10–15 minutes every day writing lists of vocabulary and saying these words aloud. The more they repeat this procedure, the more they will familiarize themselves with the words. Students can surround themselves with English by labeling their home with stickers or sticky notes. Ask students to think of their own method for remembering vocabulary and to try it for a month. At the end of the month, ask them to give feedback to the class on whether their method was successful.

Words in context

In ***Move Beyond***, students always meet new language within a context first so that they can see how the target language is used and in what situations. Encourage students to learn in this way outside the classroom too by choosing three students each month to be "Culture reporter," "Music reporter," and "News reporter." Ask them to spend one hour researching their area on the internet and to report anything interesting they find back to the class.

Test before you teach

Starting a grammar lesson with a *test-before-you-teach* type activity helps you find out how much students already know. If students have problems with form and use in the initial stage, you may need to provide more guidance during the lesson. However, if students are familiar with form and use, you can move more quickly through the lesson.

Make students grammar experts

Each Student's Book contains a Grammar Database with a reference to all grammar points from that level. As a review activity, when you are coming to the end of the level, put students in groups of three or four and assign each group a grammar point from the database that they have studied. Tell them that they have 10 minutes to become "experts" on this grammar and that they should prepare a short presentation of this point with a couple of examples to demonstrate it. Give the groups 10–15 minutes to prepare their presentations. Then put students into new groups, with each of the different grammar points represented. Then have students peer-teach their grammar points to their groups.

Recall, recycle, review

The ***Move Beyond*** course is structured so that students have the opportunity to recall previously learned vocabulary, recycle new language throughout the unit, and review what they have learned.

Look for other ways to incorporate these three stages, for example, by using games to review language or having short conversations at the beginning of the lesson to recycle language in a different context.

B1 Adjectives ending in *-ed* and *-ing*

In Unit 4, students study extreme adjectives. Point out to students that adjectives ending in *-ed* describe how you feel. Adjectives ending in *-ing* usually describe the effect that something has on your ideas and feelings.

Like all adjectives, *-ing* and *-ed* adjectives can be used in front of a noun and can be modified by adverbs such as *very* and *really*. They can also be used in the comparative and superlative forms (e.g., *... are always more exciting than other games*).

B1 *See, look,* or *watch* and *hear, listen,* or *sound*

The verbs *see, look,* and *watch* are all connected to sight, but they have important differences in meaning. *See* means to use your eyes and notice things; for example, *There's so much to see in the city. Watch* means to look at something for a period of time; for example, *I like watching the ocean. It's so blue under the sky. Look* means to have a particular appearance; for example, *Wow, that looks fantastic.*

Hear, listen, and *sound* are connected to the act of hearing – when we *hear* something, the sound comes into our ears without any effort on our part; for example, *I could hear a loud banging noise outside. Listen* means to try to hear a sound; for example, *I like to listen to music when I'm doing my homework. Sound* is similar to *look* above and means to have a particular sound or characteristic; for example, *Their new album sounds amazing.*

B1 *When* and *while*

When students are reviewing past tenses in Unit 1, remind them of how *when* and *while* are used. We use *when* to talk about something that interrupts a longer action or event: *John was cooking when the phone rang.*

We usually use *while* to indicate that during the time that an action was in progress, another event occurred. However, *when* can also be used in this case: *While John was cooking, the phone rang. / When John was cooking, the phone rang.*

B1 *Lend* or *borrow*?

The difference between *lend* and *borrow* can be difficult for some students, as one word covers both transactions in many languages. A short role-play can help make the words more memorable. Put students in small groups, with one person being a bank manager and the others being customers. Ask them to write a short conversation where the customers ask to borrow an amount of money for something and the bank manager declines and makes another offer. For example:

Customer 1: *Can I borrow 50,000 dollars for a Porsche?*

Bank manager: *I'm sorry, we can only lend you 20,000 dollars for that.*

Give students five minutes to write their conversations and then ask each group to perform their scene for the class. If possible, bring in some paper money for the "bank manager" to use so that the lending part is acted out.

B1 Stative verbs

All verbs in English are classified as either stative verbs or action verbs. Stative verbs refer to the way things are, whereas action verbs refer to things we do. The most important difference between stative and action verbs is that action verbs can be used in progressive tenses and stative verbs are rarely used in progressive tenses. Generally, stative verbs fall into four groups: verbs describing thought or opinions (e.g., *know*, *understand*), verbs showing emotions (e.g., *love*, *hate*, *want*, *need*), verbs showing possession (e.g., *have*, *belong*), and verbs showing senses (e.g., *hear*, *smell*).

B1 Present progressive tense

When studying future tenses in Unit 2, remind students that the present progressive is especially common with the expressions *tonight*, *tomorrow*, *this weekend*, etc., and with these verbs: *go*, *come*, *meet*, *see*, *leave*, and *arrive*. Point out that the tense is commonly used with these verbs because it is used to refer to fixed, scheduled plans and appointments in the near future; for example, *On October 23rd I'm seeing my doctor.* Try to incorporate this use into informal classroom conversation, asking students: *What are you doing this Saturday? Where are you going this evening?*

B1 Countable and uncountable nouns

Countable nouns can be used in both the singular and the plural form (e.g., *one egg*, *four eggs*). Uncountable nouns, on the other hand, generally do not divide into separate units and cannot be easily counted. Make sure your students understand that nouns such as *luggage/baggage* are uncountable. Other commonly confused words that are uncountable include *advice*, *news*, *information*, *furniture*, and *travel*. Many nouns can be both, depending on whether they are being used as units or as a mass; for example, *glass* (the material used for windows) is uncountable, but *a glass* (something you drink from) is countable.

Like many other grammar points, you can review countable and uncountable nouns in the reading texts during the course. When students have finished reading, you can ask them to find as many examples as they can of both types of nouns in the text.

B1 Articles

Choosing the correct article (*a*, *an*, *the*, or zero article) can be difficult for learners of English at any stage. Remember always to teach new nouns with *a* or *an* so that the use becomes natural for students. The following activity can help students learn one of the differences between *a* and *the*. Place some real objects (e.g., books) around the room. Drill two simple sentences: *Could you pass me the book, please?* and *Could you pass me a book, please?* Whenever they say *the*, they must point at the specific object they want. When they use *a*, they lift both hands in a general "asking" gesture. The listener now gives them what they asked for (i.e., either a specific book or any book). This student then makes a new request.

B1 Adjective phrases

Students often want to know why certain prepositions are used with certain adjectives or verbs. Unfortunately, there is no simple formula, so memorizing the dependent prepositions is often the only answer.

Some ideas that can help students memorize adjective + preposition combinations are:

- to use them in sentences that mean something personal to students (e.g., *My grandmother's scared of spiders*).
- to group adjectives according to the prepositions that go with them (e.g., *of* with *tired*, *scared*, and *full*).

Teaching skills

Writing

Make it a group activity

Try to incorporate group work into writing lessons so that it is not always a solitary activity. Put students into small groups to work on the processes of writing: brainstorming, planning, structuring, drafting, and reviewing.

Ask students to write to or email you

Set a task once a month where students email or write to you with a response to a set question. This could be anything from *What is your favorite lesson from the unit so far? Why?* to *What are your goals in English?* Remember to indicate to them whether you expect a formal or informal email/letter. This is a very effective way to get feedback from your students and to get them into the routine of regular writing.

Dictation activities

Dictation activities are very useful for practicing listening and writing accuracy. Try to avoid just reading long chunks of text aloud and instead work on using shorter but more engaging dictation activities. The following activity can work well and can incorporate recently studied vocabulary sets:

- Read a numbered list of descriptions of words aloud (e.g., *Number 1, a kind of music; Number 2, an extreme adjective*).
- Students should write down their own answers.
- When they've finished their lists, dictate a short story that you've written, but with blanks where students will write their own chosen words. For example, *Last night I went to a [Number 1] concert. It was [Number 2].*
- Ask one or two students to read their versions aloud at the end.

Speaking

Keep topics interesting and relevant

The topics in ***Move Beyond*** are all designed to be relevant and engaging to teenagers. When you are doing any speaking task, make sure it will be something your class will want to talk about so that students will make an effort to try to communicate on the topic.

Be patient

Don't interrupt or to start talking when students hesitate. Remember to give some time after asking students a question, as they need to assimilate the language and prepare their response. Avoid repeating the question in different ways, as this will disrupt their train of thought.

Manage class discussions

In class discussions, it is common for the more confident students to dominate, but it is important for you to act as a facilitator and encourage everyone to speak. The following technique can be used to ensure that everyone speaks, and physical movement helps maintain interest.

- Put students in pairs and label them A or B. The As stand in a circle facing outward. The Bs stand in a bigger circle around them facing inward, each facing his or her partner.
- Read the first discussion question aloud and give students two minutes to discuss with their partners.
- Clap your hands as a signal for the B students to move one place to their right and either discuss the same question or the next one.
- After four or five turns, ask students to sit down again, and you can then choose one or two students to give their opinions.

Disappearing conversation

Write a short, six-line conversation on the board and ask students to read it aloud and then to practice it in pairs. Start erasing one or two words at a time and ask students to read it aloud again. Soon they will be able to remember the whole conversation with nothing written on the board.

Listening

Encourage prediction

Predicting content is something that we all do in our first language before and while we are listening.

- **Predict the topic.** Where possible, draw students' attention to any images on the Student's Book page and ask them what they think the topic will be.
- **Predict the speakers.** Hand out printouts of the audio script for a chosen conversation in the Student's Book. Ask students to cover the speakers' names with a piece of paper, and then ask them to read the conversation and guess the age, gender, and relationship between the speakers. Write their ideas on the board, and after you have listened to the audio, check whether any of their guesses were correct.
- **Predict the word.** While playing the audio track, press the pause button midsentence and ask students if they can predict the next word. Repeat this process throughout the track. At the end of the exercise, ask students if any of their guesses were correct and, if so, why they chose that word. Remember not to comment on the accuracy of their guesses during the exercise – the goal isn't to get everything right, but to concentrate on the language and topic in order to make guessing possible.

Loop dictation

Loop dictation is a technique that you can use in reading lessons. It gives students the chance to listen more intensively and can be used to introduce a reading text.

- Select the first paragraph (or small section) of the reading text from the lesson. Make sure students have their books closed.
- Start reading aloud at a natural, but steady, speed and ask them to write down what they hear.
- When you get to the end, go straight back to the start and read again so you are repeating the text in a continuous "loop."
- When a student thinks he or she has a perfect version of the text, he or she calls out *Stop!* Put students into groups of three or four to allow them to compare what they have. Then allow them to open their books and check against the original.

Make students active listeners

In most listening exercises, students take a passive "eavesdropping" role that doesn't really prepare them for all situations where they will be expected to both listen and react. To give them some practice at reading and then responding, choose a conversation from the Student's Book or Workbook and read the first line aloud. Ask students to take on the other role (without looking at the audio script). Once they have heard your line, they should respond. Continue the process (either by using the next line of the conversation or by responding to what students have said). At the end, hand out copies of the audio script.

Reading

Jigsaw reading

For longer pieces of reading, put students in pairs and give them a section each to read. When they have finished reading, encourage students to tell each other what they have read and to ask each other questions. Then allow time for them to read the full piece.

Encourage prediction

As with listening, being able to predict what's coming can help understanding. Tell students they are going to read a particular type of text (e.g., a recipe, a letter of complaint, or some instructions on how to drive a car). Have these texts ready on handouts, but don't give them to students yet. Put students in pairs and give them five minutes to write down five words or phrases they think they will read in the text. Then hand out the texts and ask them to circle the words and phrases if they find them.

What's the context?

Knowing the context of a text can help students with the content and goal. Put students in pairs and give each pair a set of decontextualized words and sentences to read. Give them five minutes to answer the following questions:

- Where does the word/sentence/text come from?
- Who might be reading it and when?
- What does it mean?

Some ideas to use are:

- *Danger! This animal can bite!*
- *Click Start and Run.*
- *No smoking in the waiting room.*
- *Turn left at the first traffic light and turn right at the second corner.*

Teaching pronunciation

Be aware of how sounds are made

Pronunciation can often be overlooked in the classroom, but it is a key part of students' ability to communicate effectively, and in a more passive sense to listen and understand language. When approaching pronunciation tasks, make sure that students are aware of all the factors involved in making sounds (the position of the tongue, lips, etc.) and that you can explain how to make them. Remember that the primary goal is not for students to sound like native speakers but for them to produce the sounds in a way that allows students to communicate effectively.

Vary drilling techniques

Drilling can be a useful technique if employed in the right way. Make sure you vary the kind of drilling you do with your class, so that it does not become monotonous and meaningless repetition. Choral drilling (the whole class repeating a word or phrase together after you) works well when students are saying new language for the first time, and you can then move to individuals. Back-chaining (starting at the end of the phrase or word and building up a syllable or chunk at a time) works particularly well with longer sentences. You can alter your delivery (e.g., to a "whisper drill") if your class is becoming a bit noisy.

Stressed and unstressed articles

Articles and prepositions are often unstressed when we speak. This means they are produced more rapidly and with a glide. Drill the stressed (strong) and unstressed (weak) forms:

of /əv/ (weak), /ɒv/ (strong)

a /ə/ (weak), /eɪ/ (strong)

an /ən/ (weak), /æn/ (strong)

Content words are the important words that carry the meaning or sense in a phrase and are therefore usually stressed (these are usually nouns, main verbs, and adjectives).

Sentence stress

Function words are not usually stressed in English. When these words are unstressed, a weak form of the word is used:

you /jə/ (weak), /juː/ (strong)

the /ðə/ (weak), /ðiː/ (strong)

will /wəl/ (weak), /wɪl/ (strong)

Raising awareness of sentence stress will not only help improve students' pronunciation but will also help their listening skills, as they will become used to listening for the content words and to hearing the weak forms of function words.

Stressed and unstressed form of *was*

Counting the number of words in a sentence and sentence dictations are useful activities that can help raise awareness of weak forms. Point out to students that the pronunciation of *was* changes according to its position in the sentence. At the beginning or end of a sentence, it is stressed. In the middle of a sentence, it is often unstressed:

Was the bird carrying something? Yes, it was. /wɒz/

It was flying. /wəz/

B1 Consonant clusters

Consonant sounds that occur together are known as consonant clusters. These can be difficult for students, particularly if the consonants are not normally pronounced together in their own language(s). If your students are having particular difficulty with any of the clusters, try isolating the cluster and asking them to repeat the two sounds a number of times without a pause (e.g., /brbrbrbr/ or /stststst/). You could also try back-chaining (i.e., building up the sounds in the word from the end to the beginning, e.g., *bridge*: /dʒ/, /ɪdʒ/, /rɪdʒ/, /brɪdʒ/).

B1 Past forms

In the simple past and past participle forms, the regular verb ending *-ed* is pronounced /d/ after all voiced consonant sounds and /t/ after all voiceless consonant sounds. Remind students that we do not pronounce the preceding *e* in either of these cases – the extra syllable is only pronounced on verbs that end in a *t* or *d*.

Point out to students that the difference between the /d/ and /t/ is very small, and it is much more important to remember to pronounce /ɪd/ after verbs that end in *t* and *d*. In fact, many teachers do not insist on the distinction between the /t/ and /d/ endings on past tense regular verbs (e.g., *opened* vs. *walked*), preferring to focus simply on whether or not there is an extra syllable (e.g., *started*, *ended*, *visited*).

The important thing is to make sure that students differentiate between the simple present and the past forms by clearly pronouncing the /t/, /d/, or /ɪd/ ending.

B1 Adjectives ending in *-ed*

Remind students that they follow the same pronunciation rules as the *-ed* endings in the simple past:

/d/ after a voiced sound (e.g., *surprised*)

/t/ after an unvoiced sound (e.g., *relaxed*)

/ɪd/ after *t* or *d* (e.g., *excited*)

Drill the *-ed* adjectives in Unit 4, page 42, chorally to practice the pronunciation.

B1 Spelling *g* sounds → /g/, /dʒ/

In the travel vocabulary in Unit 2, two sounds for the letter *g* are represented.

- In *passenger,* the letter *g* is pronounced as /dʒ/.
- In *gate, g* is pronounced as /g/.

A general rule is:

- when *g* is followed by *e*, *i*, or *y*, it is pronounced /dʒ/.
- when it is followed by *a*, *o*, *u*, *l*, or *r*, it is pronounced /g/.

However, there are many exceptions to this rule, such as *get*, *give*, etc.

B1 /ʧ/ sound

The /ʧ/ sound is made by raising the middle of the tongue to the hard palate behind the teeth and blowing air through forcefully to create a small explosion. The most common spelling for the /ʧ/ sound is *ch*. However, as you will see in the example of *departure* in Exercise 6 on page 20 of the Student's Book, the combination of /t/ + /j/ can also result in /ʧ/. Other examples are *picture* or *furniture*. You may want to contrast the /ʧ/ sound with the /ʃ/ sound, as in *share*. If your students are having difficulty with /ʧ/, ask them to repeat the minimal pairs *share/chair* or *wash/watch*. Tell them that /ʧ/ is an abrupt sound, whereas /ʃ/ can continue as long as they have enough breath!

GAMES

Used judiciously, games can be a very useful tool in the classroom. Not only can they inject energy and a change of tempo, but they can also be used to practice and consolidate target language. The games below can be adapted for use with different target language.

The Book Quiz

The Book Quiz is a good way of starting the course and familiarizing students with the Student's Book, but it can also be used as a way of reviewing topics later in the school year. Have 10 questions about the book ready (e.g., *How many units are there? What's the topic of Unit 5? On what page can you find a list of irregular verbs?*). Read the questions aloud, and the student who is quickest at finding the answer wins.

Hot Seat

Divide the class into three or four teams. Place three or four chairs separately, each facing the class with the board or a screen behind them. Each team elects one person to sit in the hot seat. Each team has two minutes to describe as much vocabulary as they can for their team member in the hot seat to guess the word. Explain that teams can't say the word, act out the word, draw the word, spell the word, or point to the word.

Write the first word on the board or screen. If the first person in the hot seat guesses, another student comes to the front, and so on. If the word is too difficult for the person in the hot seat, he or she can "pass" to the next person.

Example: *riding a bicycle*. Possible clues: *It's an activity. You do it in your free time. There are two wheels. You use your legs.*

Broken Telephone

Divide the class into groups of about 10 students, from the front to the back of the classroom.

Give one student in each group a sentence to memorize; for example, *Dave's cousin is coming to stay at 10 o'clock on Friday morning.*

Each student whispers the sentence to the next student, and so on, until it reaches the last person in the group.

The last person in the group then says the sentence out loud. The first person says whether the original sentence has changed, and if so, how.

Kim's Game

- Show students about 10 everyday objects or objects related to the lesson vocabulary one by one (e.g., *backpack, hairbrush, passport, scissors, shampoo, toothbrush, toothpaste, wallet, ticket*). Check that they know the name of each one.
- Place the items on the table and cover them with a cloth.
- Encourage students to work in pairs to remember what's there and where the objects are (e.g., *the hairbrush is next to the shampoo).*
- To make sure students speak in English, write the sentence prompt: *There's a ______ and a ______* .

Snowman

To elicit a word or phrase or to give extra practice at spelling, write blanks for each letter of the word or phrase on the board and invite students to guess letters. For each incorrect guess, draw a part of a snowman: one circle for the head, one for the body, then two arms, three buttons, a hat, two eyes, and a smile.

Mystery Word

This game can be used to introduce students to some of the techniques they will be using in Unit 3, where they look at the subskill of understanding new words when reading.

- On the board, write a nonsense word like *flib.*
- Tell students that *flib* is a mystery word and that to guess the word they will need some more information.
- Now write *a flib* and ask students what they now know about the word (i.e., *that it is a noun*). Prompt them by underlining the article.
- Next add: *We use a flib to eat ...* Elicit ideas for the meaning of *flib.* Prompt students by asking: *What do we use to eat?* and miming someone eating with cutlery. Write students' suggestions on the board.
- Finally write: *We use a flib to eat soup.* Ideally, students will come up with *spoon,* or possibly *bowl.* Either could be correct.
- Remind students how important it is to think about the meaning of the words that come before and after the mystery word, as well as to recognize what type of word the mystery word is.

If you have time, play the Mystery Word game again with *flib* as a verb (e.g., *flib / I flib / I flib English ... / I flib English because it is a useful language in the world today).*

Three in a Row

This can be used to review vocabulary or grammar.

- Divide the class into two teams and draw a 3 x 3 grid on the board.
- In each cell, write words from a vocabulary set or verbs in the base form.
- One team chooses a cell and has to form a correct sentence using that word. If the word is a verb, the sentence must also use the target tense(s) (e.g., simple past or past progressive).
- If their sentence is correct, they "take" the cell and it's the other team's turn.
- The goal is to get three cells in a row. The game can be adapted for use with many of the language items, and a larger grid can be used to make it last longer and improve the opportunities for tactical game play.

Twenty Questions

This is a good game to practice question formation as well as vocabulary.

- Ask one student to think of an object, a person, or a place.
- The rest of the class can ask 20 questions, but the student can answer only *yes* or *no*.
- After 20 questions, the class has to make a guess at what the object, person, or place is.

Categories

Group students in teams of four or five and ask them to write the names of three or four recently studied vocabulary sets, each at the top of a separate column (e.g., travel, music, shopping). Choose a letter of the alphabet and give students two minutes to come up with as many words beginning with that letter as they can that are connected to the categories and write them in the correct column. After two minutes, choose another letter. When students have tried with three letters, count up the number of correctly spelled words, and whichever team has the most wins.

USING THE *MOVE BEYOND* TEACHER'S EDITION

This Teacher's Edition is a valuable and practical resource. With its clear and comprehensive teaching notes, audio scripts and answer keys, background notes, and extra features, it will help you plan and deliver impactful, well-paced, and memorable lessons.

The unit topic, content, and lesson objectives of each unit are clearly presented.

The target language, functions, and stages of each lesson are outlined, with suggested timings for each stage shown visually to help you pace your lesson. The darker gray shading shows the part of the lesson already completed, and the lighter gray shows the amount of time allocated for each stage.

The Get Started feature provides an activity to start the lesson and is an opportunity to recycle language and prepare students for the lesson. These warm-ups don't require any additional preparation or materials.

Activities that recycle language are labeled with the recycle icon.

Clear and concise procedural notes maximize the Student's Book material.

1 LIFE STAGES

IN THE PICTURE Special days

Talk about special days in your life

Pages 4–5

STAGE	TIME	FOCUS
GET STARTED		Introduce yourself and the topic of the lesson. Talk about students' special days.
WORK WITH WORDS		Recycle vocabulary to describe the stages of life and learn new words. Take a quiz and compare ages you need to be to take part in different life events in different countries. Pronounce words with /e/ and /eɪ/ sounds. Watch a video and describe the people and what they are doing.
SPEAK		Do a survey to talk about the age you need to be or experience you need to have to take part in different life events in your own country.

Get started

Introduce yourself to students as a lead-in to the topic of the lesson and to provide them with extra listening practice. Explain that you are going to talk about yourself and that they should think of questions to ask you afterward.

MODEL LIVE LISTENING

My name's Joe Thompson, and I'm 36 years old. I have two children; they are both boys. They both love sports. I love being with them, and it's great having a family. The two days when my children were born were the most special days of my life. Another special day was the day I got married. My wife's name is …

Invite questions from students and answer them; for example, *What are the names of your children? How old are they? Where did you get married?*

Write the title of the lesson, *Special days*, on the board and encourage students to work in pairs or small groups to ask each other *What was a special day in your life?* Elicit interesting examples from the class.

WORK WITH WORDS

1a and 1b RECALL

- Divide the class into pairs to do the tasks. Draw students' attention to the instructions to both Exercises 1a and 1b and the photos on pages 4–5. Ask students to do both tasks, matching the stages of life to the photos and then completing the sentences. Point out that some photos may match more than one word or phrase. Set a time limit of three minutes.
- Encourage students to check their answers in pairs and then choose one pair to say their answers aloud.
- Ask students to do the **Work with Words** task on page 130.

SUGGESTED ANSWERS

Exercise 1a

baby – 7 child – 1 teenager – 2, 3, 4, 6, 9 college student – 9 young adult – 8, 9 adult – 5, 7, 10 parent – 7, 8

Exercise 1b

1 senior – photo 10 2 middle-aged person – photo 8

Fast finishers

Ask fast finishers to write down what ages (approximately) go with each stage of life (e.g., *baby 0–3, child 4–12, teenager 13–19, college student 18–22, young adult 20–30, adult/parent 25+ years*). Encourage students to compare their ideas in pairs.

32

USING THE *MOVE BEYOND* TEACHER'S EDITION

Activity suggestions for fast finishers are provided throughout the lessons.

Answer keys and audio scripts are embedded within the teaching notes.

LIFE STAGES 1

2

- Focus students on photo 4 and ask them what they think is happening. Point out the example answer.
- Divide the class into pairs to match photos (1–10) to the actions in the box. Don't check answers at this point.

3 01

- Play the track for students to listen and check their answers to Exercise 2.

ANSWERS / AUDIO SCRIPT 01

get a driver's license - 6 get a job - 2 get married - 5
go on a first date - 4 go to college - 9 have children - 7
leave home - 8 retire - 10 start school - 1 vote - 3

1 Today I start school. Um ... that's all I can think of to say.
2 Check out the uniform. Well, you can't really see it in the picture. I got this job through a friend and I started today. I don't really like fast food, but that's OK. It's a job!
3 This is a special day for me because it's the first time I can vote in an election. I think it's important for young people to vote.
4 Hi, I'm Johnny.
And I'm Kirsten. And today's special because we're going on our first date.
5 My best friend got married today. I made a video and took some pictures of the wedding
6 What do you think? Isn't this the worst picture you've ever seen on a driver's license? I got it today. Finally. And this is me in Dad's car!
7 Um ... this is my wife, Rosa, and this is little Marc. It's a very special day. Now that we have a baby, I suppose we're a family.
8 Well, as you can see, I'm leaving home. That's Dad in the blue shirt. It's kind of scary but exciting at the same time.
9 These are some of the other students. It's our first day of college, so we're all very serious and a little nervous.
10 This is the first day of the rest of my life. Now that I'm retired, I can relax, take it easy, and spend time with my friends.

4a 02 PRONOUNCE

- Point to the words *get* and *stage* and to the phonemes. Play the track for students to listen and repeat the sounds.

AUDIO SCRIPT 02

See Student's Book, page 4, for audio script.

4b 03

- Before you play the track, ask students to say the words aloud in pairs in order to distinguish between the two sounds.
- Play the track for students to listen and confirm their answers.
- Play the track again for students to listen and repeat.

ANSWERS / AUDIO SCRIPT 03

/eɪ/ age, baby, date /e/ friend, Net

Extra activity

Dictate words from the list below in a different order and ask students to write them next to the correct sound, /e/ or /eɪ/.

/e/ *bread, breakfast, red, head*

/eɪ/ *day, wait, play, same*

5a

- Refer students to the quiz and ask them to complete the sentences and then check their answers in pairs.
- Encourage students to guess the correct words to complete the sentences.

5b 04

- Play the track for students to listen and check their answers. Ask students if they think any of the facts are surprising or interesting.

ANSWERS / AUDIO SCRIPT 04

1 The average age to get married in the USA is 26 to 28.
2 Children in Finland don't start school until they're 7.
3 In Brazil and Austria, you can vote in an election when you're 16.
4 In Venezuela, you can't get a driver's license until you're 18.
5 In Latin America, young people often go on a date with groups of friends.
6 The average family in Colombia has 3.9 people.

Extra activity

Ask students to recycle nationalities and languages for each country; for example, American (English), Brazilian (Portuguese), Austrian (German), Venezuelan (Spanish), Colombian (Spanish), Saudi Arabia (Arabic), Australian (English).

6 THE MOVING PICTURE

- Tell students they are going to watch a video about special days for some people. Play the video.
- Divide the class into pairs to describe the people and say what they are doing.
- Elicit answers from different students around the class.

ANSWERS

1 children getting on school bus (first day of school)
2 couple walking in park after getting married (wedding day)
3 students in class taking notes (going to college)
4 young woman voting (turning 18)
5 couple talking to new baby (having a baby)
6 two senior men playing chess (retirem

The optional extra activities provide ideas for extending the lesson and offering additional practice.

SPEAK

7

- Ask students to work in the sam the questions in the survey. Befo attention to the expressions in t
- Monitor and note good use of language and errors over in a feedback session.
- Discuss answers as a class and find out whether there is general agreement about the ages.

Extra activity

Ask students if they remember questions to ask for meaning, pronunciation, spelling, repetition, or clarification; for example, *What does X mean? How do you pronounce/say this word? How do you spell X? Could you say that again, please? Could you speak more slowly, please?*

You could ask students to make posters of these questions and display them in the classroom for the first month of the course.

MOVE BEYOND

Ask students to do the **Move Beyond** tasks on page 69.

Homework

Ask students to write a short report of about 200 words on what teenagers can and can't do in their country, using the questions in the survey and the expressions in the PHRASE BYTES box to help structure their texts.

Task-based homework is provided at the end of every lesson and is related to the topic or skill of the lesson.

Complete scripts for the Moving Picture videos are embedded in the lesson notes.

Other features

The Teacher's Edition also contains:

Procedural notes for the Unit Reviews and Progress Checks
Full and detailed notes are given for the Unit Reviews and Progress Checks in the Student's Book.

Workbook answer keys and audio scripts
At the back of the Teacher's Edition, answer keys and audio scripts are given for the corresponding Workbook.

Teaching Tips
Pages 24–29 of the Teacher's Edition provide useful tips on classroom management; teaching vocabulary, grammar, skills, and pronunciation; and using games in the classroom.

Alternative procedures
Alternative procedure suggestions are provided for selected exercises, offering a different approach to teaching the Student's Book content. These alternatives appeal to different learning styles and abilities.

Background information
Useful and interesting background information on specific lesson topics is provided in the Move Beyond for Teachers feature to help with the presentation of the content.

1 UNIT LIFE STAGES

IN THE PICTURE Special days

Talk about special days in your life

Pages 4–5

STAGE	TIME	FOCUS
GET STARTED		Introduce yourself and the topic of the lesson. Talk about students' special days.
WORK WITH WORDS		Recycle vocabulary to describe the stages of life and learn new words. Take a quiz and compare ages you need to be to take part in different life events in different countries. Pronounce words with /e/ and /eɪ/ sounds. Watch a video and describe the people and what they are doing.
SPEAK		Do a survey to talk about the age you need to be or experience you need to have to take part in different life events in your own country.

Get started

Introduce yourself to students as a lead-in to the topic of the lesson and to provide them with extra listening practice. Explain that you are going to talk about yourself and that they should think of questions to ask you afterward.

MODEL LIVE LISTENING

My name's Joe Thompson, and I'm 36 years old. I have two children; they are both boys. They both love sports. I love being with them, and it's great having a family. The two days when my children were born were the most special days of my life. Another special day was the day I got married. My wife's name is Julie.

Invite questions from students and answer them; for example, *What are the names of your children? How old are they? Where did you get married?*

Write the title of the lesson, *Special days*, on the board and encourage students to work in pairs or small groups to ask each other *What was a special day in your life*? Elicit interesting examples from the class.

WORK WITH WORDS

1a and 1b RECALL

- Divide the class into pairs to do the tasks. Draw students' attention to the instructions to both Exercises 1a and 1b and the photos on pages 4–5. Ask students to do both tasks, matching the stages of life to the photos and then completing the sentences. Point out that some photos may match more than one word or phrase. Set a time limit of three minutes.
- Encourage students to check their answers in pairs and then choose one pair to say their answers aloud.
- Ask students to do the **Work with Words** task on page 130.

SUGGESTED ANSWERS

Exercise 1a

baby – 7 child – 1 teenager – 2, 3, 4, 6, 9 college student – 9 young adult – 8, 9 adult – 5, 7, 10 parent – 7, 8

Exercise 1b

1 senior – photo 10 2 middle-aged person – photo 8

Fast finishers

Ask fast finishers to write down what ages (approximately) go with each stage of life (e.g., *baby 0–3, child 4–12, teenager 13–19, college student 18–22, young adult 20–30, adult/parent 25+ years*). Encourage students to compare their ideas in pairs.

2

- Focus students on photo 4 and ask them what they think is happening. Point out the example answer.
- Divide the class into pairs to match photos (1–10) to the actions in the box. Don't check answers at this point.

3 ▶01

- Play the track for students to listen and check their answers to Exercise 2.

ANSWERS / AUDIO SCRIPT ▶01

get a driver's license - 6 get a job - 2 get married - 5
go on a first date - 4 go to college - 9 have children - 7
leave home - 8 retire - 10 start school - 1 vote - 3

1 Today I start school. Um ... that's all I can think of to say.
2 Check out the uniform. Well, you can't really see it in the picture. I got this job through a friend and I started today. I don't really like fast food, but that's OK. It's a job!
3 This is a special day for me because it's the first time I can vote in an election. I think it's important for young people to vote.
4 Hi, I'm Johnny.
And I'm Kirsten. And today's special because we're going on our first date.
5 My best friend got married today. I made a video and took some pictures of the wedding
6 What do you think? Isn't this the worst picture you've ever seen on a driver's license? I got it today. Finally. And this is me in Dad's car!
7 Um ... this is my wife, Rosa, and this is little Marc. It's a very special day. Now that we have a baby, I suppose we're a family.
8 Well, as you can see, I'm leaving home. That's Dad in the blue shirt. It's kind of scary but exciting at the same time.
9 These are some of the other students. It's our first day of college, so we're all very serious and a little nervous.
10 This is the first day of the rest of my life. Now that I'm retired, I can relax, take it easy, and spend time with my friends.

4a ▶02 PRONOUNCE

- Point to the words *get* and *stage* and to the phonemes. Play the track for students to listen and repeat the sounds.

AUDIO SCRIPT ▶02

See Student's Book, page 4, for audio script.

4b ▶03

- Before you play the track, ask students to say the words aloud in pairs in order to distinguish between the two sounds.
- Play the track for students to listen and confirm their answers.
- Play the track again for students to listen and repeat.

ANSWERS / AUDIO SCRIPT ▶03

/eɪ/ age, baby, date /e/ friend, Net

Extra activity

Dictate words from the list below in a different order and ask students to write them next to the correct sound, /e/ or /eɪ/.

/e/ *bread, breakfast, red, head*

/eɪ/ *day, wait, play, same*

5a

- Refer students to the quiz and ask them to complete the sentences and then check their answers in pairs.
- Encourage students to guess the correct words to complete the sentences.

5b ▶04

- Play the track for students to listen and check their answers. Ask students if they think any of the facts are surprising or interesting.

ANSWERS / AUDIO SCRIPT ▶04

1 The average age to get married in the USA is 26 to 28.
2 Children in Finland don't start school until they're 7.
3 In Brazil and Austria, you can vote in an election when you're 16.
4 In Venezuela, you can't get a driver's license until you're 18.
5 In Latin America, young people often go on a date with groups of friends.
6 The average family in Colombia has 3.9 people.

Extra activity

Ask students to recycle nationalities and languages for each country; for example, American (English), Brazilian (Portuguese), Austrian (German), Venezuelan (Spanish), Colombian (Spanish), Saudi Arabia (Arabic), Australian (English).

6 THE MOVING PICTURE ▶

- Tell students they are going to watch a video about special days for some people. Play the video.
- Divide the class into pairs to describe the people and say what they are doing.
- Elicit answers from different students around the class.

ANSWERS

1 children getting on school bus (first day of school)
2 couple walking in park after getting married (wedding day)
3 students in class taking notes (going to college)
4 young woman voting (turning 18)
5 couple talking to new baby (having a baby)
6 two senior men playing chess (retirement / no longer working)

SPEAK

7

- Ask students to work in the same pairs to ask and answer the questions in the survey. Before they start, draw their attention to the expressions in the PHRASE BYTES box.
- Monitor and note good use of language and errors to go over in a feedback session.
- Discuss answers as a class and find out whether there is general agreement about the ages.

Extra activity

Ask students if they remember questions to ask for meaning, pronunciation, spelling, repetition, or clarification; for example, *What does X mean? How do you pronounce/say this word? How do you spell X? Could you say that again, please? Could you speak more slowly, please?*

You could ask students to make posters of these questions and display them in the classroom for the first month of the course.

MOVE BEYOND

Ask students to do the **Move Beyond** tasks on page 69.

Homework

Ask students to write a short report of about 200 words on what teenagers can and can't do in their country, using the questions in the survey and the expressions in the PHRASE BYTES box to help structure their texts.

READING Coming of age

Find specific information

Page 6

STAGE	TIME	FOCUS
GET STARTED		Recycle vocabulary to describe stages of life and discuss celebrations related to the stages.
SPEAK AND READ		Compare coming-of-age ceremonies where you live to those in other countries. Read an article about coming-of-age traditions and rituals around the world. Discuss tips on how to find specific information in a text (reading subskill).
REACT		Give your opinions about celebrations and rituals in different countries.

Get started

Recycle vocabulary from the previous lesson by writing the words to describe stages of life in a random order on the board: *middle-aged person, baby, teenager, child, senior, young adult, college student.* Ask students to work in pairs to put the stages in a logical order.

Invite different students to number the stages from 1–7 on the board.

Ask students if there are any important ages or celebrations within any of the life stages on the board.

SPEAK AND READ

1

- Elicit the meaning of *coming of age* (*the age when a person becomes an adult*). Divide the class into pairs to ask and answer the questions. Set a time limit of three minutes.
- Invite different pairs to report their answers.

MOVE BEYOND FOR TEACHERS

Coming of age

Coming of age in the USA, the UK, Ireland, Australia, and New Zealand is celebrated at either 18 or 21. The age of legal adulthood is 18, which means you can vote, get married without parental consent, and sign contracts. In comparison, turning 21 has few legal effects.

Alternative procedure

For this speaking activity, do question 1 as a pair work activity. For question 2 and question 3, divide the class into small groups.

2 05

- Tell students they are going to read the results of research about traditions in different countries. Ask students to read the texts quickly in order to answer the questions. Don't play the audio at this point. It is an extra feature, and a suggestion for using it in class is included at the end of the lesson.
- Encourage students to compare their answers in pairs before you check them as a class.

ANSWERS

1 Students in class 3B at a school
2 Students' own answers

3a

- Divide the class into pairs to discuss what skills they use to find specific information in a text. Prompt their discussion by asking them: *What are the different parts of a text?* (headings, photos, etc.); *How do you find information quickly?* (look for specific words related to the information).
- Refer students to the tips in the HOW TO box, inviting some more confident students to read the tips aloud.
- Ask students if their strategies are the same as or different from the ones in the HOW TO box.

3b

- Ask students to scan the texts quickly to find the information they need to complete the table. Point out that if a text doesn't include the information, they should write *Doesn't say*.
- Walk around and monitor, helping students if necessary.
- Write the table on the board and choose different students to come up and write their answers.

ANSWERS

Name	Type Party? Ritual?	Boys/ Girls	When	Age	Clothes	Activities
Seijin no Hi	*Ceremony*	Both	*Second Monday in January*	20	A special kimono for girls; a suit for boys	A ceremony at the local city offices called Seijin-Shiki, then a party with friends and family
Satere-Mawé	Ritual	Boys	Doesn't say	12 or older	Gloves with ants inside them	Boys have to wear gloves with hundreds of ants in them for 10 minutes, and they mustn't scream.
Quinceañera	Party	Girls	On their 15th birthday	15	Usually a beautiful dress and a crown	A church ceremony, then a big party

- Ask some comprehension questions to check full understanding of the texts:
  - Seijin no Hi: *What is a kimono*? (a traditional form of dress for women in Japan, like a long dress with sleeves).
  - Satere-Mawé: *What's special about the bullet ant*? (its bite hurts more than any other insect bite in the world); *What mustn't boys do when they are wearing the gloves?* (they mustn't scream); *How many times do they have to do this ritual*? (20 times).
  - Quinceañera: *What present does the birthday girl get*? (a doll called *la última muñeca* – "the last doll"); *What does she do with it*? (she dances with it and then gives it to a younger girl).

4

- Elicit from students which tips in the HOW TO box they used to help them in Exercise 3b and ask them to check them.

Extra activity

Write these definitions on the board: *a party or special event* (celebration, /ˌseləˈbreɪʃ(ə)n/); *something you do regularly and always in the same way* (ritual, /ˈrɪtʃuəl/); *a formal, public event with special traditions* (ceremony /ˈserəˌmoʊni/).

Ask students to match the definitions to the words in the text. Chorally drill the pronunciation.

REACT

5

- Divide the class into pairs to discuss the questions.
- Choose different students to share their point of view with the class and say why. Try to develop a class discussion about the different traditions. Start by asking some questions such as: *Do you think that the Satere-Mawé ritual is dangerous? Do you think that coming-of-age celebrations should be fun or serious events? Should they be different for girls and boys?*

Extra activity

Have students close their books. Write these sentence prompts on the board and ask students to complete them from memory:

1 In Japan, you can't vote until you're …
2 The bite of the bullet ant …
3 During the Satere-Mawé ritual, the boys …
4 At a quinceañera, the birthday girl dances with …
5 Now that she's 15, the girl can …

Ask students to look at the texts again if necessary to check their answers.

ANSWERS

1 20.
2 hurts more than any other insect bite in the world.
3 have to wear gloves with hundreds of ants inside them.
4 a doll.
5 go on her first date.

MOVE BEYOND

Have students close their books and ask them to each choose one of the rituals and write down whatever they remember about it.

Encourage them to read their notes aloud to a partner to see if their partner can remember any further details. Finally, ask students to check their notes by reading the texts again.

Recorded reading text 05

The reading text is recorded as an extra audio track that can be exploited for various purposes.

In this lesson, you can use the audio as part of the checking process in Exercise 3b. Ask students to raise their hands when they hear the specific information they used for the table.

Homework

Ask students to write about how coming of age is celebrated in their own country or in another one of their choice. Encourage students to make notes and present their information in the next class in groups of five or six.

GRAMMAR Present tenses review

Talk about present actions *Page 7*

STAGE	TIME	FOCUS
GET STARTED		Brainstorm ideas for having a low-cost or an expensive party.
READ AND LISTEN		Read and listen to a conversation about a coming-of-age party.
STUDY		Use the conversation to review the use of the simple present and the present progressive.
PRACTICE		Complete exercises with the correct form of the simple present or the present progressive.
SPEAK		Ask and answer questions about habits and routines and what is happening now.

Get started

As a class, brainstorm things that are important for a party. Write students' ideas on the board (e.g., *music*, *food*, *decorations*, *clothes*, *activities*, *entertainment*, *theme*, *drinks*, *invitations*).

Divide the class into pairs to think of ideas for a low-cost party and an expensive party. Draw two columns on the board with the headings *Low-cost party* and *Expensive party*. Invite students to come up and write their ideas in the columns. Discuss which party students think they would enjoy most and why. Use the opportunity in this discussion to pre-teach *to afford* (*to have enough money for*), as this comes up in Exercise 1.

READ AND LISTEN Grammar in context

1 06

- Refer students to the photo and ask them what they think the conversation is going to be about.
- Play the track for students to read and listen to the conversation. Ask students where the girls are and what they are doing.
- Ask a few comprehension questions to check full understanding of the text: *What is the name of the typical coming-of-age party in the USA?* (a Sweet 16); *Why is Tina unhappy about her sister's coming-of-age party?* (her sister wants a big party, but Tina thinks it is too expensive).

ANSWERS / AUDIO SCRIPT 06

They're at the home of one of the girls. They're celebrating her 16th birthday.
See Student's Book, page 9, for audio script.

STUDY

2a

- Refer students back to the conversation in Exercise 1 and ask them to underline nine examples of the simple present and circle four examples of the present progressive. (See Teaching Tips, *Present progressive tense*, page 26.)
- Choose students to read the examples.

ANSWERS

Simple present: They're, It's, do people (usually) do, They do, the party is, My sister wants, she talks, The problem is, I don't think
Present progressive: are these girls doing, This girl is celebrating, They aren't wearing, She's preparing

2b

- Ask students to read the grammar explanations and complete the examples with time expressions.
- Choose students to read the grammar explanations and examples aloud.

ANSWERS

usually right now

Extra activity

Students may not remember the spelling rules for the *-ing* form. Write these verbs and the spelling rules on the board and ask students to make present progressive sentences using the following verbs:

lie (Change the *-ie* to a *-y* and add *-ing*, i.e., *lying*.)

get, run, swim, sit (For verbs with one syllable, ending in one vowel and one consonant, double the final consonant and add *-ing*; for example, *getting*.)

have, give, take, celebrate (For verbs ending in *-e*, remove the *-e* and add *-ing*; for example, *having*.)

PRACTICE

3 07

- Refer students to the photo and the conversation. Ask them to circle the correct options to complete the conversation.
- Play the track for students to listen and check their answers.
- Ask students extra questions to check their understanding of the grammar; for example, *Why is the answer to 2 in the simple present?* (because it is a stative verb); *Why is the answer to 3 in the present progressive?* (because she is describing an action that is taking place now); *Why are the answers to 4, 5, and 6 in the simple present?* (because they are describing a tradition that is repeated every year).

ANSWERS / AUDIO SCRIPT 07

2 don't know 3 's preparing 4 do the girls dance
5 lasts 6 dance
See Student's Book, page 9, for audio script.

Extra activity

Divide the class into pairs to practice reading the conversation aloud.

4

- Ask students to complete the questions with the simple present or present progressive form of the verbs in parentheses. Before they start, draw students' attention to the example and elicit why the present progressive is used.
- Walk around and monitor, helping students if necessary.
- Encourage students to compare their answers in pairs before you check answers as a class.

ANSWERS

2 Do you think 3 are most teenagers wearing
4 Do adults usually wear 5 does a person really become
6 are they doing

Fast finishers

Encourage fast finishers to look at the texts on page 8 and find an example of the present progressive tense (*the girls are wearing traditional kimonos*).

SPEAK

5

- Divide the class into pairs to ask and answer the questions in Exercise 4. Remind students to ask each other follow-up questions to request examples, details, and reasons.
- Ask a more confident pair of students to demonstrate this activity before students continue in pairs.

Homework

Ask students to find a photo of a celebration or a ceremony and write notes to prepare a presentation for the next class. Encourage students to describe the photo using the simple present and the present progressive. For less confident students, write a short plan on the board: *Describe where the photo is taken*; *Describe what is happening*; *Describe what the people are doing*; *Describe this ritual or celebration (time of the year, traditions)*; *Say what you think about it.*

LISTENING AND VOCABULARY Leaving home

Recognize informal speech

Page 8

STAGE	TIME	FOCUS
GET STARTED		Play a game to recycle the simple present and present progressive tenses.
SPEAK AND LISTEN		Describe objects from your childhood. Listen to a conversation about a person leaving home and sorting out objects he has stopped using. Learn how to recognize informal speech (listening subskill).
REACT		Discuss what is going to happen when the person leaves home.
WORK WITH WORDS		Order adjectives to describe objects.
SPEAK		Talk about an interesting present you gave and one you received.

Get started

Play a game of *Three in a Row* (see Games, page 29). To win a square, teams take turns choosing a square and making a question with the simple present (SP) or the present progressive (PP) using the verb given in the square.

SP: study	PP: wear	SP: think
PP: prepare	SP: think	PP: dance
SP: know	PP: do	SP: celebrate

SPEAK AND LISTEN

1

- Refer students to the photos. Divide the class into pairs to discuss the questions. Encourage students to use adjectives and to add as much extra detail as possible for the descriptions in question 1.

2 08

- Explain to students that they are going to listen to a conversation between Aidan and his sister, Katie, about him leaving home. Play the track for students to listen and put photos a–d in the order they hear them mentioned.

ANSWERS / AUDIO SCRIPT 08

1 d 2 b 3 c 4 a

Katie: What's in this box?
Aidan: Nothing. Just stuff I'm throwing out. Take anything you want.
Katie: Look at this. It's enormous.
Aidan: Hey, don't laugh. That was my first cell phone. Mom gave it to me when I started school.
Katie: Does it still work?
Aidan: I dunno.
Katie: So it's not very useful. Who does this tiny blue shirt belong to?
Aidan: That's my Chelsea soccer jersey.
Katie: I don't think it fits you anymore. Why do you still have it?
Aidan: It's ... kinda ... you know ...
Katie: Colorful?
Aidan: No.
Katie: Unusual?
Aidan: Special.
Katie: Why?
Aidan: It was a present from Uncle Harry. He gave it to me on my eighth birthday when he took me to see a game – my first.
Katie: So if it's special, why are you throwing it away?
Aidan: I dunno. I have too much stuff. I can't keep everything. You take it.
Katie: No, thanks. I don't want your old cotton soccer jersey. Aha! Here's something really embarrassing. Big brother's plastic doll.
Aidan: It's not a doll. It's an action figure. It's an antique.
Katie: Old-fashioned, you mean.
Aidan: It's probably valuable.
Katie: Hello? It's broken. Anyway, they're only worth money if they're in the original packaging. Can I keep these?
Aidan: What? I can't see.
Katie: Here's a clue. They're round plastic things you keep in a kind of square case?
Aidan: Are you talking about my CDs? I thought you didn't like my music.
Katie: I don't. But I can play them when I miss you.
Aidan: Hey, that's a really nice thing to say.
Katie: Not really. When I hear your terrible music, I'm gonna remember how lucky I am that you're not here.
Aidan: Very funny.
Dad: Aidan?! Are you ready to go?
Aidan: Coming, Dad!
Katie: Got everything?
Aidan: Think so.
Katie: So ... see ya.
Aidan: Yeah. See ya.

3 08

- Focus students on the sentences. Play the conversation again for students to decide if each sentence is correct (*C*) or incorrect (*I*).
- Encourage students to compare their answers in pairs and ask them to correct the incorrect sentences. Check answers as a class.

ANSWERS

1 I (His mother gave him the phone.) 2 I (The shirt is tiny.) 3 C
4 I (Aidan thinks it's probably valuable.) 5 C
6 I (She says she doesn't like his music.)

4a

- Encourage students to think of how they can recognize informal speech when they listen.
- Ask students to read the tips in the HOW TO box and compare them with the ideas they thought of.

4b (▶09)

- Play the extracts from the conversation and ask students to complete them with words from the HOW TO box.
- Ask students to find five contractions in the excerpt.
- Give students extra practice with the new informal words and phrases to help them sound natural. Chorally drill them and then ask students to practice the excerpts in pairs.

ANSWERS / AUDIO SCRIPT (▶09)

1 Hey 2 kinda 3 you know 4 dunno 5 stuff 6 So 7 ya 8 Yeah

Contractions: It's, don't, It's, it's, can't

See Student's Book, page 8, for audio script.

REACT

5

- Divide the class into pairs to discuss the questions.

WORK WITH WORDS

6 (▶10)

- Point out to students that when they see more than one adjective before a noun, the adjectives follow the order in the table. Give and elicit some more examples (e.g., *a beautiful old wooden chair*).
- Ask students to complete the table with the adjectives in the box.
- Play the track for students to listen and check their answers.
- Play the track again for students to listen and repeat.

ANSWERS / AUDIO SCRIPT (▶10)

Opinion: useful, old-fashioned, unusual, valuable, special
Size: enormous, tiny
Age: old, antique
Shape: square, round
Color: red, colorful
Material: cotton, plastic

Fast finishers

Ask students to write another adjective in each column.

SPEAK

7a

- Ask students to work individually to write a few sentences about an interesting present they gave and one they received, using more than one adjective. Before they start, invite a volunteer to read the model sentences aloud.

7b

- Divide the class into pairs to talk about their presents. Encourage them to use and respond with informal language, looking back at the excerpts in Exercise 4b if necessary.

Alternative procedure: less confident classes

Disappearing conversation: create the conversation together on the board; for example:

A: Hey! What interesting present did you receive?
B: I got a kind of interesting present for my last birthday.
A: What was it?
B: It was an enormous lion for my bedroom.
A: Yeah, kind of interesting.
B: What interesting present did you give?
A: I gave my brother a pet frog. He loves frogs, you know.
B: Yeah, that's definitely different!

Erase the middle part of the conversation. Ask students to try to reconstruct the conversation in pairs, each one saying his or her part. Then erase almost all of the conversation and ask students to switch roles and try to remember as much as they can. Walk around and monitor. Invite a pair who can remember it all to say the conversation to end the activity.

MOVE BEYOND

Ask students to do the **Move Beyond** task on page 69.

Homework

Ask students to cut out pictures from magazines or newspapers and write sentences with more than one adjective to describe them (e.g., *an interesting old Spanish politician*; *a fast red sports car*; *a small round black box*).

GRAMMAR Past tenses review

Talk about past actions *Page 9*

STAGE	TIME	FOCUS
GET STARTED		Play a game to recycle irregular past tense forms.
READ AND LISTEN		Read and listen to a conversation about a mystery object and guess what kind of object it is.
STUDY		Read grammar explanations about past tenses and complete examples.
PRACTICE		Practice the simple past and past progressive in written exercises.
SPEAK		Talk about things you've lost.

Get started

Play a game of *A–Z List*. Divide the class into small teams to write an A-to-Z list of irregular past tense verbs. Point out that there are no irregular verbs that begin with *j*, *n*, *q*, *v*, *x*, *y*, or *z*. Set a time limit of three minutes. Invite students to write the verbs on the board. Then encourage students, in the same groups, to ask each other and answer three questions starting with a question word (e.g., *When did you … ? What did you … ?*) and choosing from the irregular verbs on the board. Remind them of the question order if necessary (question word – auxiliary – subject – verb [infinitive form]), and ask them to answer with complete sentences.

READ AND LISTEN Grammar in context

1 11

- Refer students to the photo and ask them: *How do you think the girl is feeling? Can you describe her?* (She looks excited. She is a teenager with long brown wavy hair. She is carrying shopping bags.)
- Play the track for students to read and listen to the conversation and guess what kind of object they are talking about.
- Invite different students to share their ideas with the class.

ANSWER / AUDIO SCRIPT 11

They're talking about a musical instrument.
See Student's Book, page 9, for audio script.

STUDY

2

- Ask students to read the grammar explanations and then to complete the example sentences from the conversation.
- Check answers as a class.

ANSWERS

played; sounded   bought   were going   were walking; saw

PRACTICE

3

- Refer students to the text and ask them to choose the correct options. (See Teaching Tips, *Stative verbs*, page 26.)
- Encourage students to compare their answers in pairs before you check them as a class.

ANSWERS

1 met   2 was visiting   3 became   4 occasionally went
5 were sitting   6 saw

4 12

- Ask students to complete the conversation with the simple past or past progressive form of the verbs in parentheses.
- Play the track for students to listen and check their answers.

ANSWERS / AUDIO SCRIPT 12

1 did you see   2 saw   3 was visiting   4 were talking
5 noticed   6 put   7 were helping   8 saw   9 was doing
10 put
See Student's Book, page 9, for audio script.

Extra activity

Ask students to practice saying the conversation in pairs. First, ask them to prepare the conversation by underlining all the stressed words. You can play the track again if necessary.

When they read the conversation, ask them to "glide" over the unstressed words. Encourage them to put more emphasis and volume on the stressed words to reproduce the rhythm in English speech.

5

- Ask students to write questions with the simple past, past progressive, or both, if necessary. Focus students on the prompts and the example question.
- Ask students to compare their answers in pairs before you check them as a class.

ANSWERS

2 When and where did you lose it?
3 What were you doing when you lost it?
4 How long did you look for it?
5 While you were looking for it, did other people help you?
6 Did you ever find it?

6

- Ask students to think of something they lost in the past and write answers to the questions in Exercise 5.
- Walk around and monitor, helping students if necessary.

SPEAK

7

- Divide the class into pairs to talk about the things they lost. Encourage them to ask follow-up questions, as well as the questions they wrote in Exercise 5, in order to have a more natural conversation and get more information from their partner. Refer students to the model conversation for some examples of follow-up questions.
- Ask them to make notes about their partner's lost item and invite them to share their information with the class.

Extra activity

Ask students to change partners and repeat the activity without using their notes.

Homework

Ask students to write a short text of 150 words about a dream they had. Tell students a dream you had or make one up and ask them to listen to the key points of the dream while taking notes. Ask students to include at least one sentence with *while* and another with *when*. In the next class, have students read their dreams aloud in pairs or small groups.

LANGUAGE &BEYOND GET ORGANIZED

Collaborate to organize a group activity *Page 10*

STAGE	TIME	FOCUS
GET STARTED		Introduce the topic of working in a group and talk about personal strengths.
SPEAK AND READ		Discuss the last time you organized an activity and complete a survey about organizing activities. Make a list of tips for organizing activities to discuss in a group.
DO		Work in groups to plan a sale of secondhand things.
REFLECT		Reflect on which tips were useful and how you performed in the group activity.
EXTEND		Plan a school trip in groups.

LIFE SKILLS

COLLABORATE TO ORGANIZE A GROUP ACTIVITY
Group work can motivate students and help them develop problem-solving and decision-making skills. It also helps students identify their own strengths and weaknesses and discover if they are good negotiators, leaders, or motivators. Acknowledging the strengths and talents of others helps students develop the social skills they need for life, such as cooperation and respect. The skills students learn by taking part in group tasks make them highly valued in the workplace. Employers want to hire people who can work well with others to analyze arguments and complete tasks on time.

Get started

Play a game of *Talent Party*. Explain to students that they have all been invited to a party, but instead of bringing food to share, they are going to bring the strengths they think they contribute to this group. Brainstorm a few ideas (e.g., *a creative thinker*, *a good note taker*, *can motivate others*, *a good listener*, *very organized*).

Ask students to write down two strengths or talents that they're going to bring to the party. Encourage students to compare with a partner what they are going to bring to the party. Then ask them to join up with another pair to see what strengths they now have as a group of four. Invite students to write their strengths on the board and to read what other people have written. Explain to students that today they are going to look at ways of working together. Elicit whether they think the party would be better if they organized it alone or as a group. Do not erase the strengths. Review them at the end of the lesson to see if students have discovered new talents.

SPEAK AND READ

1
- Divide the class into pairs to answer the questions.
- Invite different students to tell the class about their discussion.

2
- Refer students to the photo at the top of the page and ask when they work in groups in class (*projects*, *discussions*, *presentations*, *problem-solving activities*, etc.).
- Ask students to take the survey about group work individually.

3
- Divide the class into groups to compare their answers before you elicit them from different students around the class.
- For each question, invite students to raise their hands for either the A or B options to see which option most people chose. For each answer, read the following comments aloud and discuss the different options as a class.

  1 *A – You prefer a fair division of work where everyone is responsible.*
  B – You are interested in completing the task and think the result is more important than the organization.

  2 *A – You think control and organization are the most important things.*
  B – You think it's a good idea to explore ideas and take turns listening to the views of others.

  3 *A – You like to appoint a leader in a group.*
  B – You prefer everybody's opinion to be equal.

  4 *A – You prefer to take on a role.*
  B – You prefer things to be open and unstructured.

4
- Encourage students to write a list of tips for organizing a group activity.
- Ask them to compare their lists with the tips on page 75 and to discuss the differences in pairs or small groups.

DO

5
- Explain to students that they're going to organize a sale of secondhand things to make money for a school trip. Divide the class into groups and ask a student to read the tasks aloud to make sure they understand the instructions. Explain to them that they're going to give a short presentation to the class on what they have discussed. Before they start, draw students' attention to the PHRASE BYTES box and encourage them to use these expressions to structure their answers.
- Monitor and help students with any language difficulties.

6
- Invite each group to present its decisions to the class.
- Then ask students to pool their ideas and, as a class, decide how they are going to organize the sale.
- You could ask students to vote by raising their hands for the best decision for each category (day, place, etc.).

REFLECT

7
- Focus students on the REFLECTION POINT and ask them whether they agree or not. Invite students to discuss the questions as a class.

MOVE BEYOND FOR TEACHERS

Collaboration

Emphasize the importance of exploring ideas together and agreeing on a set of "talk rules" to make sure everyone takes turns speaking, taking on a role, and collaborating to complete the task.

You could read aloud this case study of a group of teenagers who didn't enjoy a group work activity and ask students to recommend ways for them to work better in the future:

We argued a lot in our group, and we didn't get anywhere. We all had different ideas, and we couldn't agree on anything at all. Some people in the group didn't say anything, and one person talked all the time. When I said something, someone laughed at me.

Suggestions:

- All group members should feel a sense of personal responsibility for the success of their teammates and realize that their individual success depends on the group's success.
- Assign different roles to the group members so that they are all involved in the process (e.g., recorder, spokesperson, timekeeper).
- Specify clear objectives.
- Don't make fun of each other, and accept everyone's ideas.

EXTEND

8

- Divide the class into groups to plan their school trip.
- Give them a few minutes to write down where they're going, what needs to be done, and who's going to do what.
- Point out to students that they are going to write up their plan for the school trip for homework. They should take careful notes at this stage to help them complete the homework task.
- Ask students to present their ideas to the class. Discuss which idea is the best as a class.

Extra activity

Ask students to review the strengths they talked about at the beginning of the lesson and add any more important qualities for working together successfully in groups.

Homework

Ask students to write up their plan for a school trip. In the next class, collect their plans for grading as a writing assignment.

SPEAKING Invitations

Make and react to invitations

Page 11

STAGE	TIME	FOCUS
GET STARTED		Introduce the topic of the lesson, what to put in an invitation, and collocations with the word *invitation*.
SPEAK		Discuss the last time you went to a party and recycle talking about events in the past.
LISTEN		Listen to teenagers talking about who can come to a birthday party. Work with phrases to accept and refuse an invitation and ways of saying "thank you" (speaking subskill).
ACT		Role-play inviting someone to a party and accepting or refusing the invitation.

Get started

Recycle vocabulary for celebrations and talk about a party you went to, using different collocations with the word *invitation*; for example, *Last year, I got a wedding invitation from my best friend in the USA. He wanted me to be the best man and make a speech. I didn't want to refuse the invitation, but it was on a Friday, so I had to take the day off work. I accepted the invitation, and it was a great wedding.*

Ask students to say the verbs that go with *invitation*. Ask: *Can you think of any others?* (*send*, *decline*, *turn down*, *say no to*, etc.). Elicit the kinds of events they would receive an invitation for and what information is usually included in an invitation. Refer students to the invitation on page 11 to see if it has the same information they thought of.

SPEAK

1

- Divide the class into pairs and ask them to look at the invitation and answer the questions.
- Elicit answers from different students and encourage them to explain their answers.

LISTEN

2 13

- Refer students to the picture and ask them to predict what the conversations are going to be about.
- Play the conversations for students to listen and find out who can't come to the party and why not.
- Ask students to read the conversations to check their answers before you confirm as a class.

ANSWERS / AUDIO SCRIPT 13

Leo, because he's visiting his grandparents that day.

Ethan: Hi, Alice. Can you come to my birthday party?
Alice: When is it?
Ethan: It's next Saturday, the 6th. I'm having a barbecue.
Alice: Sure. That sounds great. Thanks for inviting me.
Ethan: Great. See you there!

Ethan: Hey, Leo. I'm having a birthday party next Saturday. Are you free?
Leo: I'd love to come, but I can't. I'm visiting my grandparents that day.
Ethan: That's too bad.
Leo: Yeah, but thanks for the invitation!

Ethan:	Max, <u>would you</u> like to come to my birthday party?
Max:	Yes, I'd love to. When is it?
Ethan:	It's next Saturday.
Max:	I'm sorry, but I can't. I'm going to a barbecue in Wilson Park.
Ethan:	A barbecue in Wilson Park?
Max:	Yeah. Alice is going, and she invited me.
Ethan:	Max, that's my party!
Max:	Really? Well, I guess I'll see you there!

3 ▶13

- Ask students to complete the questions in the conversation.
- Play the conversation again for students to listen and check their answers.

ANSWERS

1 Can you 2 Are you 3 would you

4 ▶14

- Play the track for students to listen and repeat the invitations. Drill the questions chorally.

AUDIO SCRIPT ▶14

1 Can you come to my birthday party?
2 I'm having a birthday party next Saturday. Are you free?
3 Would you like to come to my birthday party?

Extra activity

Ask students to read the conversations aloud in pairs. Remind them to pay special attention to the rising intonation in the invitations.

5a

- Ask students to underline the sentences for accepting and refusing an invitation and for saying "thank you." Do not check answers at this point.

5b ▶15

- Play the track for students to listen and check.
- Play the track again for students to listen and repeat.

ANSWERS / AUDIO SCRIPT ▶15

1 Sure. That sounds great. 2 Yes, I'd love to.
3 I'd love to come, but I can't. 4 I'm sorry, but I can't.
5 Thanks for inviting me. 6 Thanks for the invitation!

Extra activity

Recycle the present progressive for future use. Refer students back to the conversation and ask them to use a different color to underline all the sentences they can find with the present progressive for future use. Ask them to also underline a time expression. Ask students to discuss in pairs what their plans are for next Saturday. Choose several students to answer.

ACT

6 ▶16

- Ask each student to write an invitation to a party, using Ethan's invitation to help them.
- Divide the class into A/B pairs. Student A should invite Student B to his or her party. Student B should accept or refuse the invitation, giving a reason as necessary. Before they start, play the track of the expressions in the PHRASEBOOK box and encourage students to use them in their conversation.
- Ask students to switch roles and act out the situation again with Student B's invitation.

7

- Encourage students to work in the same pairs and write out one of their conversations from Exercise 6. Monitor as they work, helping as necessary.
- Then invite pairs to join up with another pair to present their conversations.

Homework

Ask students to imagine that they've been invited to spend a weekend with their English e-pal's family. Ask them to write a short email to say why they can't go and give a reason why not. Remind them that this is quite a formal piece of writing and they should remember to say thank you for the invitation. In the next class, have students work in pairs and read their emails to each other. You may want to collect the emails for grading.

WRITING A special object

Make a writing plan Page 12

STAGE	TIME	FOCUS
GET STARTED		Discuss memory and facts about elephants.
SPEAK AND READ		Describe and compare model elephants. Read a description of a special object. Discuss the difference between *remember* and *remind.* Talk about how to make a writing plan (writing subskill).
PRACTICE		Edit and complete a writing plan for another description.
DISCUSS		Discuss types of special objects and describe a special object.
WRITE		Use a writing plan to write a description of a special object.
SHARE		Read your description aloud for the class to guess your special object.

Get started

Play the game *What's the Question?*. Write this short, famous poem about elephants on the board:

I have a memory like an elephant.
In fact, elephants often consult me.
(Noel Coward, 1899–1973)

Ask students if they think it is true that elephants have long memories.

Write these answers in clouds on the board: *mammoth*; *Asian and African elephant*; *ivory*; *5 kg*; *16 hours a day*.

Ask students to think of five questions to ask that would give them those answers; for example, *What is the prehistoric ancestor of the elephant called? What two species of elephant are left in the world? What is the elephant hunted for?* or *What are its tusks made of? How much does an elephant's brain weigh? How many hours a day does an elephant spend eating?* Set a time limit of three minutes for this.

Choose different students to read their questions aloud for you to write on the board until you have a question for each answer.

Elicit any other facts students know about elephants.

SPEAK AND READ

1

- Refer students to the photos. Divide the class into pairs to describe and compare the elephants.
- Encourage students to tell their partner which elephant they like best and why.
- Choose different students to share their descriptions and opinions with the class. Use the opportunity to recycle comparative and superlative adjectives.

2

- Ask students to read Jessica's description and decide which elephant she is describing and what Lucy's elephant looks like.
- Choose a student to share the answer with the class.

ANSWER

Jessica is describing elephant c. Lucy's elephant looks exactly the same.

3a

- Ask students to read the tips in the HOW TO box. Invite a volunteer to read them aloud.

3b

- Focus students on Jessica's plan and encourage them to find the answers to the questions in Jessica's description.
- Elicit from the class the sentences that answer the questions in each section.
- Ask the class if Jessica followed all the steps and answered all the questions. (There were some questions she didn't answer in the corresponding paragraph, e.g., *Is it old or new?*)

ANSWERS

Description: It's a small black wooden elephant. It's standing on a shelf in my room ...
History: I got the elephant while I was staying with my friend Lucy in Chicago. She said they were best friends like us.
Importance: When I see my elephant, it reminds me of that summer and my friend. It's a nice feeling to know that Lucy has an identical elephant.

PRACTICE

4

- Ask students to number the steps in a writing plan in the correct order and to write one question for each section. You may want to let them do this in pairs.
- Choose a student to say the correct order of the steps (*Description, History, Importance*).
- For each section, ask several students to say what questions they wrote.

SAMPLE QUESTIONS

Description: What or who is in the photo?
History: When and where did you get it or take it?
Importance: Why is this photo important to you?

DISCUSS

5

- Write the title of the lesson on the board: *A special object*.
- Invite students to give you some suggestions of the types of objects that might be special to people (e.g., *a toy*, *a piece of jewelry*, *a poster*, *a book*, *a photo*, *an ornament*, *a piece of clothing*, *a plant*).
- If they are finding it difficult to think of ideas, you could draw some of these things on the board and elicit the vocabulary items.
- Divide the class into pairs and ask students to discuss some objects that are special to them.
- Encourage them to describe the object and talk about its history and importance. Refer them to the questions under these topics in the writing plan. Set a time limit of five minutes for the discussion.

WRITE

6

- Explain that students are going to write a description of the special object they have discussed.
- Refer students to Jessica's writing plan and suggest that they structure their writing plans in a similar way. Tell them to use Jessica's questions as a guide to what they should include in their description.
- Remind students to use the present tense to describe the object. Give an example from Jessica's text; for example, *It's a small black wooden elephant.* Contrast this with the use of the past tense when talking about the history of the object and select another example; for example, *They weren't expensive, so we bought both of them.*
- Set a time limit of 10 minutes for students to write their descriptions.

SHARE

7

- Tell students they are going to read their descriptions aloud, but they should not mention the name of the object itself. Whenever the object is mentioned, they should say *BEEP*. For example, *My special object is a small black wooden BEEP.*
- Explain that they should listen carefully to other students' descriptions in order to try to guess what the object is. Tell them not to interrupt if they think they know, but to write down their ideas. At the end of each student's description, ask the class or group what they think the object is. If you have a large class, you may prefer to do this activity in groups.

Homework

Ask students to write another description of a special day or a special object. Have them read their descriptions aloud in pairs or groups in the next class.

Introduction

Unit Reviews bring together all the grammar and vocabulary seen in the unit. Students can refer to the Grammar Database and Words & Beyond pages first and then try to do the exercises. Alternatively, they can try the exercises first and then study the reference material if necessary. Unit Reviews can be used in the classroom or for self-study at home. Procedural notes are provided here for their use in the classroom.

As in a test, in the Unit Reviews, students can clearly see how many points they can score for each exercise. When they have finished, encourage students to exchange books with a partner and mark each other's work, totaling up the score.

VOCABULARY Special days

1

- Focus on the title of the text and ask students what things could be included in a life plan (e.g., *going to college*, *getting married*).
- Ask students to read Tony's life plan and complete it with the words and phrases in the box.
- Check answers as a class.

ANSWERS
1 school 2 driver's license 3 first date
4 high school 5 college 6 job 7 married
8 children 9 vote 10 Retire

Adjectives for describing objects

2

- Explain to students that they are going to read a list of things for sale. Ask students to read the introductory text and say why these things are for sale. (*Tony needs money to buy a car.*) Elicit the three items for sale (*watch, carpet, MP3 player*).
- Set a time limit of three minutes for students to complete the adjectives in the descriptions. Point out that the first and the last letter of each adjective are given.
- Encourage students to compare answers in pairs before you check them as a class.

ANSWERS
1 antique 2 useful 3 fashioned 4 valuable
5 enormous 6 colored 7 cotton 8 square
9 tiny 10 unusual

GRAMMAR Present tenses review

3

- Explain to students that they are going to read a conversation between two men who haven't seen each other for a long time. Focus on the options and ask students to say what the two tenses are (*simple present and present progressive*) and when we use them.
- Ask them to complete the conversation by choosing the correct options.
- Circulate and monitor as they do the task. If you feel they are having difficulty, stop them midtask and do a quick review of the use of the simple present and present progressive, as well as stative and action verbs.
- Check answers as a class.

ANSWERS
1 are you doing 2 'm not working 3 usually spend
4 'm looking 5 Do you ever see 6 don't know
7 'm making

Past tenses review

4

- Explain to students that they are going to read an email from Tony to an old school friend.
- Ask students to complete the email with the simple past or past progressive form of the verbs in parentheses.
- Ask fast finishers to think of two more ways to start and sign off an email; for example, *Hi! Hi, there! Hello! Take care, Speak to you soon.*
- Check answers as a class. If students have the wrong answers, guide them toward the correct answers by asking questions such as: *Did the action happen once or over a period of time? Was Stan in the middle of an action?*

ANSWERS
1 was looking 2 found 3 spoke 4 called
5 were doing 6 saw 7 was shopping 8 got

Extra Resources

Go to the Teacher's Resource Center at mee2.macmillaneducation.com for:

- downloadable audio and audio scripts for the Student's Book and Workbook;
- videos and video scripts;
- extra vocabulary at two levels of difficulty;
- extra grammar at two levels of difficulty;
- CLIL lessons, with full teacher's notes;
- a life skills lesson, with full teacher's notes;
- Speaking Database materials;
- the *Move Beyond Level 5* wordlist;
- tips for using the Grammar Database;
- and more!

Go to Workbook pages 80–91 for further practice material.

2 UNIT PACK YOUR BAGS

IN THE PICTURE Travel

Talk about travel items *Pages 14–15*

STAGE	TIME	FOCUS
GET STARTED		Introduce the topic of the lesson and think about words related to travel.
WORK WITH WORDS		Recycle methods of transportation and associated prepositions and verbs. Describe and categorize travel items. Pronounce words with /p/ and /b/ sounds. Watch a video of an airport scanner and list the items you see.
SPEAK		Plan what to pack for a school camping trip in your area.

Get started

Write the unit title, *Pack your bags*, on the board and elicit what it means (*to put your possessions into a bag, case, or box so that you can take or send them somewhere*).

Ask the class what they think the unit is going to be about (*travel*) and write synonyms or partial synonyms for the topic of travel in a random order for students to figure out; for example, *pirt* (trip), *yegova* (voyage), *yonurej* (journey). Ask students to work in pairs to say what the difference is between these words and the word *travel*.

ANSWERS

travel: a verb to say you go from one place to another
trip: a noun meaning to go somewhere and come back again (the word we most often use in this context)
voyage: long-distance travel by sea
journey: a longer or more adventurous trip, or the time you spend traveling (more common in British English)

WORK WITH WORDS

1 a, b, and c RECALL

- Refer students to the instructions for each of the three exercises. Divide the class into pairs to do the three tasks. Set a time limit of two minutes.
- Copy the table onto the board and invite different students to add methods of transportation under the headings. Then check the answers to the other tasks as a class.
- Ask students to do the **Work with Words** task on page 131.

ANSWERS

Exercise 1a
See table on page 70 of Student's Book.
Exercise 1b
to by by
Exercise 1c
drive a *bus*, car, train, streetcar, taxi, boat, ferry
fly a helicopter, plane
ride a bike, horse, motorcycle, scooter; ride a bus (as a passenger)
sail a ship

Fast finishers

Ask fast finishers to think of unusual forms of transportation to add to their lists (e.g., *hot-air balloon*, *racecar*, *canoe*, *yacht*, *rowboat*, *horse*).

Extra activity

Ask students to underline the stressed syllables in the multisyllable words in the table.

Extra activity

Recycle the structure of the simple present with adverbs of frequency. Divide the class into pairs and ask students to find out what kind of transportation their partner often uses and one kind of transportation their partner never uses. If necessary, elicit questions and write them on the board. Choose different students to report their partner's answers.

2 ▶17

- Refer students to the pictures of items a–l. Focus them on the categories, *luggage/baggage*, *personal items*, and *money and documents*, and point out the example. Divide the class into pairs to put the items in the correct categories.
- Play the track for students to listen and check.

ANSWERS / AUDIO SCRIPT 17

Luggage/baggage: suitcase, backpack, sleeping bag
Personal items: toothbrush, toothpaste, shampoo, hairbrush, scissors
Money and documents: passport, visa, boarding pass, wallet

3a 18 PRONOUNCE

- Play the track for students to listen to the words and repeat. Ask them to pay particular attention to the /p/ and /b/ sounds. Point out that there should be a little puff of air after *p*. Drill any sounds they have problems with.

AUDIO SCRIPT 18

See Student's Book, page 16, for audio script.

3b 19

- Play the track for students to listen to the words and circle the one they hear.
- Play the track again for students to listen and repeat both words.

ANSWERS / AUDIO SCRIPT 19

1 back	2 peach	3 pen	4 bear	5 bill
back, pack	beach, peach	Ben, pen	bear, pear	bill, pill

4

- Divide the class into pairs and ask students to take turns describing and guessing the objects in Exercise 2. Before they start, draw students' attention to the model conversation.

Alternative procedure: less confident classes

In less confident classes, give students time to prepare their descriptions. Recycle ways of describing objects and write model sentences on the board to help students structure their own sentences:

It's something that/which you use to keep your hair neat.
People use it to keep their hair neat.
It's used for keeping your hair neat.

5

- Refer students to the pictures and ask them to work in the same pairs to make a list of the other objects in the backpack and suitcase.

ANSWERS

suitcase: some batteries, a hat, a pair of shoes, some sunglasses
backpack: a cell phone, a phone charger, a book, a pen, a bottle of water, an MP3 player with headphones/earbuds, a plug

Extra activity

Point out to students that *backpacking* is a noun to describe a way of traveling that is very popular, especially with young people. Ask students to think of the advantages and disadvantages of backpacking versus traveling with a suitcase, for example:

Backpacking: *It is easier to get on and off a train or a bus with a backpack; it's lighter; you wear it on your back, so it's easy to move around*, etc.

Traveling with a suitcase: *You can fit more things in; it's safer if you lock it with a key; your things are more protected because they are in a harder case*, etc.

Point out to students that the verb *to backpack* (e.g., *We backpacked around India*) is as common as *We went backpacking around India.*

6 THE MOVING PICTURE

- Explain to students that they are going to watch a video of an airport scanner. Discuss what they think this is.
- Ask students if they have ever had a problem going through airport security (e.g., carrying too much liquid or sharp objects) or any other type of security.
- Play the video and ask students to write the names of the items they see.

ANSWERS / VIDEO SCRIPT

1 suitcase, wallet, hairbrush, toothpaste, shampoo, toothbrush, tennis shoes, sunglasses, hat, batteries
2 backpack, boarding pass, passport, scissors, visa, sleeping bag, cell phone, phone charger, a plug, book, water bottle, pen, MP3 player, earphones
3 suitcase, magazine, shoes, pants, shampoo, toothpaste, toothbrush, shirt
4 bag, MP3 player, earphones, brush, cell phone, phone charger, a plug, notebook, boarding pass, pen
5 backpack, wallet, money, sunglasses, passport, book, bottle of water, pocket knife, sandwich

This is a special announcement.
For security reasons, please keep your luggage and all packages with you at all times, until they are checked. Unattended baggage will be removed immediately for inspection and may be damaged or destroyed.

Extra activity

Recycle *There's/There are* ... , *a/an*, and *some*. In pairs, ask students to try to remember all the items that were in the video. Set a time limit of two minutes for this. The pair with the most items on their list wins the game.

SPEAK

7

- Explain to students that they are going on a school camping trip in their area. Divide the class into pairs to decide the five most important things to pack.
- Invite them to look at the pictures for ideas and to think of other items (e.g., *a camera*, *a first-aid kit*, *a flashlight*, *a box of matches*, *a compass*). Draw students' attention to the expressions in the PHRASE BYTES box and encourage them to practice using these in their conversation.
- Monitor and note good use of language and errors to go over in a feedback session.
- Ask each pair to compare their ideas with another pair.

Extra activity

Ask the same groups to eliminate some of their items so that they have only five items to pack. Then ask groups to come up to the board and write their items.

Encourage students to discuss similarities and differences among the groups' lists.

Finally, tell the class that they can take only five of these items, as a class. Lead a class discussion to decide which ones they are going to eliminate from the board.

MOVE BEYOND

Ask students to do the **Move Beyond** task on page 70.

Homework

Ask students to write a short story of 150 words about the school camping trip and to include all the objects in their list in their story. They should say why they were important or what they used them for. In the next class, choose a few students to read their stories aloud.

READING Be a vacation volunteer

Identify the purpose of a text *Page 16*

STAGE	TIME	FOCUS
GET STARTED		Recycle vocabulary to describe methods of transportation and find the odd one out.
SPEAK AND READ		Talk about your best vacation. Read a text from a website about voluntourism. Discuss tips on how to identify the purpose of a text (reading subskill).
REACT		Give your opinion on voluntourism and talk about communities in need.

Get started

Write these words to describe methods of transportation on the board in groups of four: *bike*, *motorcycle*, *car*, *horse*; *plane*, *helicopter*, *balloon*, *canoe*; *car*, *bus*, *subway*, *taxi*; *boat*, *ferry*, *ship*, *kayak*.

Explain that three words in each group have something in common and one is the "odd one out." Ask students to work in pairs to say which word is the odd one out and why.

Ask students to come up to the board and circle the odd one out in each group. Have students say why they chose each odd item and ask each other why they have chosen different options. Note that different answers are possible.

SPEAK AND READ

1

- Divide the class into pairs to answer the questions and talk about their best vacation. Set a time limit of three minutes.
- Choose different students around the class to report on what their partner said.

Alternative procedure: less confident classes

In a less confident class, model this activity first yourself. Tell students about your best vacation and then ask them to answer questions 1–3. This will give students a clearer idea of what is expected of them in this activity and help familiarize them with the questions. Give students time to write down their answers to the questions before they do this as a speaking activity.

2a

- Ask the same pairs to discuss how they can identify the text type, who the text is written for and by, and the writer's goal. Prompt their discussion by asking them: *How do you know what a text is going to be about before you read it? Is it important to know who is writing a text? How do you know if a text is going to be interesting before you read it?*
- Refer students to the tips in the HOW TO box, asking some more confident students to read the tips aloud.
- Elicit whether the ideas they had are the same as or different from the ones in the HOW TO box.

2b 20

- Ask students to scan the first part of the text and identify the text type, the reader, and the writer's goal. Set a 30-second time limit for this to encourage students to skim over vocabulary they do not know. Don't play the audio at this point. It is an extra feature, and a suggestion for using it in class is included at the end of the lesson.

ANSWERS

Text type: website
Reader: students aged 14–18 who would like to be voluntourists
Writer's goal: to persuade readers to do one of the company's voluntourist programs

3

- Ask students which tips in the HOW TO box they used to help them in Exercise 2b and encourage them to check them.

4 20

- Ask students to read the second part of the text more closely and complete the report form for Molly and Alex.
- Circulate and monitor students, helping if necessary.
- Copy two report forms onto the board and choose different students to come up and write their answers.
- Find out from students if they have heard of similar voluntourist programs.
- Ask some comprehension questions to check full understanding of the texts: *How old do you have to be to be a voluntourist?* (14–18); *How long do they usually go for?* (two to four weeks); *What did Molly like best about her time in South Africa and why?* (the people because they were always cheerful and ready to share food or tell stories); *What does she miss most?* (the children in the activity center where she worked); *Why was Alex nervous?* (she had never been overseas); *Why didn't she feel homesick?* (she made lots of new friends).

ANSWERS

Molly
Area: South Africa
Project: Worked in an activity center
Project length: Four weeks
How the program has helped you: I learned that you don't need a lot of money or material things to enjoy life.
Alex
Area: Boston, USA
Project: Helped elderly people with housework and shopping
Project length: Two weeks
How the program has helped you: I made new friends and have become much more confident.

Fast finishers

Ask fast finishers to find words in the text to match these definitions: *in or to a foreign country* (overseas); *people who let you stay in their home* (host family); *someone's feelings about something, shown by their behavior* (attitude); *happy, friendly* (cheerful); *feeling sad and alone because you are far from home* (homesick).

REACT

5

- Divide the class into pairs to discuss the questions.
- Lead a class discussion by inviting students to share their point of view and explain their reasons.

MOVE BEYOND

Ask students to underline the names of the six continents in the text and say which continent is missing.

ANSWERS

North America, South America, Africa, Asia, Europe, and Australia
The missing continent is Antarctica.

MOVE BEYOND FOR TEACHERS

Continents

Depending on the convention used, there are six or seven continents. In some countries, students are taught to consider North and South America to be a single continent. Australia is sometimes referred to as Oceania, but not by its inhabitants.

Recorded reading text 20

The reading text is recorded as an extra audio track that can be exploited for various purposes.

In this lesson, you could use the audio to support less confident students the first time they read the text. Encourage them to read at the same speed as the audio; then, if necessary, allow them to read again at their own pace.

Homework

Ask students to research a voluntourist program they would like to go on and write about why it is interesting for them. In the next class, put students in small groups to share their ideas.

GRAMMAR Present perfect

Talk about how long something has happened *Page 17*

STAGE	TIME	FOCUS
GET STARTED		Talk about natural disasters to introduce the topic of the lesson.
READ		Read an article about a family on a voluntourist vacation.
STUDY		Use the article to study and recycle knowledge about the present perfect with *ever/never*, *just/yet/already*, and *for/since*.
PRACTICE		Use adverbs and the correct present perfect forms of verbs in written exercises.
WRITE AND SPEAK		Ask and answer questions about activities you do regularly and say how long you have done these activities.

Get started

Write these questions on the board and ask students to discuss them in pairs. Set a time limit of two minutes and give regular updates (*one minute to go*, etc.):

What are some different kinds of disasters?
Do some natural disasters occur repeatedly in the same area?
What's the difference between a hurricane and a typhoon?
What's the difference between a hurricane and a tornado?
Can you think of any famous natural disasters?

Ask students to discuss the questions in pairs.

Choose different students to say their answers.

SUGGESTED ANSWERS

Avalanche, famine, tsunami, drought, earthquake, hurricane, tornado, typhoon
Natural disasters often occur repeatedly in the same area.
If a storm forms in the Atlantic (i.e., the USA) or eastern North Pacific Ocean, it's called a hurricane. A typhoon is generally any storm that begins in the western North Pacific.
A hurricane is a large storm system, and a tornado is a column of rotating air.
The earthquake near Fukushima, Japan, in 2011; Hurricane Katrina in 2005 in New Orleans, USA; Cyclone Yasi in Australia in 2011; Hurricane Wilma in Mexico and the USA in 2005; tornadoes in the central USA in 2013, etc.

READ Grammar in context

1

- Refer students to the photo and elicit what has happened. (*The photo shows hurricane damage.*)
- Ask students to read the article and say what volunteer activities the Rawlins family is doing and why.
- Ask a few comprehension questions to check full understanding of the text: *How many homes were destroyed?* (300,000); *How many hours a day are they working?* (eight hours a day); *Are they enjoying their vacation?* (they are having a fantastic time).

ANSWER

They're rebuilding places in New Orleans that were destroyed by Hurricane Katrina.

STUDY

2

- Focus students on the explanations for the present perfect and ask them to underline examples of the three different uses of the present perfect in Exercise 1.
- Choose students to read the sentences aloud.
- Read the explanation of the form of the tense aloud, referring students to the past participles in the list of irregular verbs on page 74 of the Student's Book.

ANSWERS

For past actions when we don't know the exact time: Since we arrived ... I've had a fantastic time.
With *ever/never* for experiences in your life: I've never been on a trip like this before. Have you ever worked on vacation?
With *just/yet/already* for recent events: ... the city hasn't completed rebuilding work yet. We've already finished a playground, and we've just started on a park project.

Extra activity

Students often get confused with the meanings of these common time adverbs. This is often because in the L1 a different structure from the present perfect is usually used to express these ideas.

Ask students to think about their schedule for the day and write sentences using *just/yet/already*; for example, *I've just had math. I haven't had science yet. I've already had English twice this week.*

3

- Ask students to underline *for* and *since* in Exercise 1.
- Ask them to complete the explanations with *for* and *since*. Then choose a student to read the completed grammar explanations aloud.

ANSWERS

since for

Extra activity

To give students more practice understanding the difference between *for* and *since*, ask them to write two columns in their notebook with the headings *for* and *since*. Read this list of time expressions aloud and ask students to write them in the correct column:

20 minutes, three days, 9 a.m., four years, January, I left school, two centuries, 1600, Monday, a long time

Point out that *for* can be used with all tenses, whereas *since* can be used only with the perfect tenses.

Ask students to think of two more examples for each column and compare them in pairs before they write their examples in the correct columns.

ANSWERS

For: 20 minutes, three days, four years, two centuries, a long time
Since: 9 a.m., January, I left school, 1600, Monday

PRACTICE

4a

- Ask students to complete Ben's interview with the present perfect form of the verbs and the adverbs in parentheses.
- Invite two students to read the completed conversation aloud for the rest of the class to listen and check their answers.

ANSWERS

1 Have you ever been 2 've already visited
3 Have you ever stayed 4 've never been
5 've slept 6 Have you ever worked
7 haven't done that yet 8 've just changed

Extra activity

Divide the class into pairs to practice the conversation.

4b

- Ask students to write their own answers to the three questions in Exercise 4a using *already*, *not yet*, and *never*.
- Circulate and monitor, helping students if necessary.
- Encourage students to compare their answers in pairs before you ask for volunteers to read their answers aloud.

Fast finishers

Ask fast finishers to look at the text on page 16 and find seven sentences with the present perfect tense.

Ask students to identify the different uses of the present perfect for each sentence and explain why they are used.

ANSWERS

You've probably heard of volunteers. Since 2001, *Vacation Volunteers* has offered voluntourist programs ... . I've learned that you don't need a lot of money or material things to enjoy life. Since the trip, I've felt much more confident. (past actions, don't know exact time)
I've just spent four weeks in South Africa. I've been home for a week now, and I haven't gotten used to it yet. (recent events)
I've never been overseas. (experience in life)

5

- Ask students to complete the visitor's form by writing the questions and completing the answers with *for* or *since*.
- Go over the first one as a class to check that they understand and point out the example answer.
- Encourage students to compare their ideas in pairs before you check them as a class.

ANSWERS

1 have you spent your vacations in Orlando?; *since*
2 have you stayed at the Beach Campsite?; for
3 have you been here?; since
4 have you had good weather?; since
5 have you looked forward to this vacation?; for

WRITE AND SPEAK

6a

- Ask students to work individually to write five activities they do regularly. Before they start, draw students' attention to the example sentences. Then divide the class into pairs to exchange lists with their partner.

6b

- Encourage students to ask each other how long their partner has done the activities on the list and take turns answering each other's questions. Before they start, invite one pair to read the model conversation aloud.

6c

- Invite students to tell the class one interesting thing about their partner.

Homework

Ask students to write six sentences about themselves with *already*, *just*, and *yet*. Ask them to write one false sentence. At the beginning of the next class, have students read their six sentences aloud to their partners for them to decide which sentence is false.

LISTENING AND VOCABULARY Around the world

Listen for the information you need Page 18

STAGE	TIME	FOCUS
GET STARTED		Play a game to recycle the present perfect with *already*, *yet*, *just*, *since*, *for*, *ever*, and *never*.
SPEAK AND LISTEN		Talk about favorite ways to travel and the positive and negative aspects of traveling by boat. Listen to a video blog about a boy who is sailing around the world with his parents. Practice understanding main ideas and extracting specific information when listening (listening subskill).
REACT		Discuss the good and bad things about living on a boat and homeschooling.
WORK WITH WORDS		Complete a map and an online ticket with travel words. Create your own online ticket and ask questions to find out the details of your partner's trip.

Get started

Play a game of *Three in a Row* (see Games, page 29) with the grid below. To win a square, teams take turns choosing a square and making either an affirmative sentence (✓), a negative sentence (✗), or a question (?) with the adverb given in the square and the correct form of the present perfect.

already ✓	yet ?	just ✓
never ✗	ever ?	since ✓
for ✗	not yet ✗	for ✓

SPEAK AND LISTEN

1

- Divide the class into pairs to take turns asking and answering the questions. Set a time limit of three minutes.
- Invite different students to report their partner's answers.

2 Refer students to the photo and the beginning of Oscar's blog. Ask them to read it quickly to find out why he's writing it.

ANSWER

His family is sailing around the world on a boat for two years.

3a

- Elicit ideas from students about how they can understand main ideas and specific information when they do a listening activity in class.
- Ask students to read the tips in the HOW TO box. Invite a volunteer to read them aloud.

3b ▶21

- Explain to students that they are going to listen to Oscar's video blog.
- Before you play the track, ask students to read the questions. Remind them that in the first listening, they should listen for the main ideas only and write down answers to the questions in their notebooks. In the second listening, they should then add details to their answers.
- Play the track twice for students to listen and answer the questions as indicated.

ANSWERS / AUDIO SCRIPT ▶21

1 They're getting ready for their departure to Australia. They're buying food and getting fuel for the boat and the stove.
2 He's looking forward to it. He thinks it's amazing to see water everywhere, but he thinks a boat can be kind of small when you can't get away from the other people.
3 He does homeschooling with his dad; he reads something and writes about it.
4 He fishes and then he helps with dinner. He likes cooking, but he hates washing dishes.
5 He's meeting his friend Callum. He and his family are going to be on vacation there.
6 They're going to take the train to Sydney with Callum's parents, and they're going to spend a few days there.

"Hi, everyone. We're in a harbor in Tahiti now, but our next destination is Australia. Tomorrow we leave for Brisbane, so we're getting ready for our departure. Today we're going to buy food and get fuel for the boat and the stove.

I'm looking forward to being on the ocean again. It's always amazing to just see water everywhere you look. Especially when you sit outside on deck at night and there's a full moon ... that's so cool. But it's also great to just go on land when you want. A boat can be kind of small when you spend all your time ... you know, 24/7 ... with your family and you can't get away. Sometimes I just need a little more personal space!

We'll probably be at sea for two weeks this time. We've had good weather for weeks, but unfortunately hurricane season starts soon, so we're likely to have storms. That might mean a change in the route that we take and a delay in our arrival date. I'll keep you posted. Bye!"

"Hi, everyone. Now that I'm at sea, I'm homeschooled by my dad every morning as usual. Basically he just gives me some books, tells me to read something, and then I write about it. In the afternoon, I usually fish and then help with dinner. I like cooking, but I hate washing the dishes. People forget that when you're on a boat, you still have to do stuff like that. And we don't have a dishwasher!

We'll be in Brisbane in five days. We're meeting my friend Callum and his parents, who are going to be on vacation there. I've known Callum for years, so it'll be great to see him. Sometimes I really miss my old friends. Callum, his parents, and I are going to take the train down to Sydney and spend a few days there ... it'll be cool to be a train passenger for a change!

OK, time to go! Check back soon!"

4

- Ask students which tips in the HOW TO box they used to help them in Exercise 3b and encourage them to check them.

REACT

5

- Divide the class into pairs to ask and answer the questions. Encourage students to explain their reasons.
- Invite students to share their ideas with the class. Start a class discussion by asking other students if they agree or have anything to add to the answers.

WORK WITH WORDS

6 ▶22

- Encourage students to complete the labels on the map and the online ticket with words from the box.
- Play the track for students to listen and check their answers.
- Play the track again for students to listen and repeat.

ANSWERS / AUDIO SCRIPT ▶22

b destination c departure d arrival e connection f delay g passenger h reservation i seat j fare

7a

- Ask students to work individually to make an online ticket like the one in Exercise 6, changing the trip details. They can add as much artistic detail as they like! They shouldn't show their partners at this point.

7b

- Divide the class into pairs to ask and answer questions about the details of their partner's trip and make notes.
- Ask students to join up with another pair to tell them about their partner's trip and say whether they think it's interesting, expensive, or complicated.

Alternative procedure: less confident classes

In a less confident class, brainstorm all the questions that students will need to ask and write them on the board: *What is the destination? What is the route to get there? What is the departure time? What time do you arrive? Do you have to make a connection? Are any delays expected? How many passengers are there? What are your seat numbers? How much does the trip cost?*

Ask students to do the activity first with the partner they are sitting next to and then repeat the activity with a different partner. The second time, erase the questions from the board.

Extra activity

Ask students to make a mind map with the key word *travel*. Encourage them to include the travel words from the unit so far with these different headings: *verbs*, *kinds of trips*, *travel items*, *methods of travel*, and *words associated with traveling*.

MOVE BEYOND

Ask students to do the **Move Beyond** task on page 70.

Homework

Ask students to imagine they have been on the trip they planned in Exercise 7. Ask them to write a short text of about 100 words to describe the travel details and what happened on their trip. In the next class, have students read their descriptions aloud in pairs or small groups.

GRAMMAR The future

Talk about events in the future *Page 19*

STAGE	TIME	FOCUS
GET STARTED		Play a game to recycle travel words from the unit so far.
READ		Read a chat message and define an InterRail trip.
STUDY		Read explanations about future forms and find examples in a text. Learn how to use the adverbs *definitely* and *probably*.
PRACTICE		Practice the target language in written exercises and distinguish between the different future forms.
WRITE AND SPEAK		Talk about your plans and dreams for the future.

Get started

Play a game of *Hot Seat* (see Games, page 29). Use 10 words from the unit so far (e.g., *backpack*, *trip*, *crew*, *luggage*, *fare*, *route*, *vacation*, *sleeping bag*, *voluntourism*, *delay*).

READ Grammar in context

1

- Ask students to describe what they see in the photo.
- Ask them to read the chat message quickly to find out what an InterRail trip is. Elicit the answer from the class.
- Ask some comprehension questions: *Who is going on an InterRail trip?* (Dan's big sister); *What is her first destination?* (Paris); *What time does she leave?* (twelve o'clock); *How long is she traveling for?* (a month).

ANSWER

A trip by train around Europe, using a ticket that allows you to travel in 30 countries for one month

STUDY

2

- Ask students to read the explanations about future forms and underline examples in the text in Exercise 1.
- Check answers as a class. As you do so, point out that in affirmative sentences with *will*, the adverb (e.g., *probably*, *definitely*) comes AFTER *will*. In a negative sentence, the adverb comes BEFORE *won't*.
- Ask students to use adverbs to complete the examples from the chat.

ANSWERS

Present progressive: My big sister's starting her InterRail trip; she isn't traveling alone.

Simple present: Her train to Paris leaves at twelve o'clock

be + *going to* + base verb: She's going to travel around Europe; What countries are they going to visit?

will/won't + base verb: that'll be amazing; Will she be OK?; my parents will definitely call her; They probably won't remember.

be + *likely to* + base verb: She isn't likely to have any problems; it's likely to be a lot.

Extra activity

Ask students to write complete affirmative and negative sentences with *will*, the verb *rain*, and the given word.

It / probably ✓ ✗ *It / definitely* ✓ ✗

It / likely to ✓ ✗ *It / possibly* ✓

Then ask students to complete the table matching the approximate meaning of these future phrases.

ANSWERS

It'll definitely rain.	100% chance of rain
It'll probably rain. It's likely to rain.	80%–95%
It'll possibly rain.	50%–80%
It probably won't rain. It isn't likely to rain.	5%–20%
It definitely won't rain.	0% chance of rain

PRACTICE

3 23

- Explain to students that they are going to hear Felipe telling a friend about the vacation he's going on. Elicit anything students may already know about Ecuador.
- Ask them to choose the correct options to complete the conversation.
- Play the track for students to listen and check their answers.

ANSWERS / AUDIO SCRIPT 23

1 're going 2 does your train leave 3 arrives
4 're traveling 5 likely to be 6 Are you going to sleep
7 're staying

See Student's Book, page 21, for audio script.

4

- Ask students to read the quotes by students about their plans and dreams and write the correct future forms.
- Encourage them to compare their answers in pairs before you check them as a class. Elicit why each form was used for each question to help consolidate the rules.

ANSWERS

2 starts 3 'm going to learn 4 'll/will definitely be
5 isn't likely to come 6 'll/will probably get

WRITE AND SPEAK

5a

- Divide the class into pairs. Ask students to write three sentences about their plans and dreams using the time phrases given, without showing their partner.
- Remind them that if something is a definite, scheduled arrangement (e.g., a trip), they can use the present progressive. If it is a plan, they can use *going to*. If it is a prediction, they should use *will* with *definitely* or *probably*.
- Circulate and monitor students, helping them if necessary.

5b

- Ask students to write three sentences predicting their partner's future, using their own ideas.

5c

- Draw students' attention to the model conversation. Ask them to take turns telling their partner their ideas.
- Ask students to exchange sentences from Exercise 5a to see if any of their predictions were correct.
- Elicit some examples of correct predictions from the class.

Homework

Ask students to write sentences with different future forms including these words or phrases: *polar bears / become extinct*; *school / Friday*; *get married*; *fish for dinner / tonight*; *pass / English test*; *use cell phone / tomorrow*; *dark sky / rain*; *party / this weekend*; *watch TV / internet*. At the beginning of the next class, have students compare their sentences with a partner.

LANGUAGE & BEYOND RESPECT OTHERS

Respect other people's personal space Page 20

STAGE	TIME	FOCUS
GET STARTED		Introduce the topic of personal space and differences among cultures.
READ		Read an article about personal space and compare feelings about being in closed spaces.
DO		Do a task to test your awareness of personal space.
REFLECT		Reflect on your own ideas about personal space and how you protect it.
EXTEND		Talk about your own behavior and whether personal space is important to you.

LIFE SKILLS

RESPECT OTHER PEOPLE'S PERSONAL SPACE

Speaking good English does not always guarantee effective communication because nonverbal factors such as an awareness of personal space also affect communication. Among different cultures, ideas about personal space can vary. What's polite and acceptable in one culture can be considered rude, unacceptable, or confusing in another.

In this lesson, students are made aware of their own behavior, and they reflect on how different people have different ideas about personal space. This is important when establishing good relationships at both a social and professional level. By interpreting body language correctly, students can increase their comprehension and expression, hold their listener's attention, and be more successful in the communication process.

Get started

Write the words *personal space* on the board and ask students to think of situations where there is a small amount of personal space (*on a crowded bus*, *in a line*, *in an elevator*, *in crowds at concerts*, etc.). Ask students how they feel in these situations.

Write these statements on the board: *Two boys usually get closer together when they talk than two girls. People in China and India need a lot of personal space. People in South America or southern Europe need less personal space than people in North America and northern Europe.*

Divide the class into pairs to discuss whether they think these statements are correct or incorrect and say why. Set a time limit of two minutes. Put some expressions on the board to help students; for example, *I think that the first statement is correct/incorrect because … ; I agree/don't agree with you; I'm not sure.*

Invite students to share their ideas with the class.

READ

1

- Ask students to look at the picture and say what they think it shows. Refer them to the introduction to the article to check their answer.
- Then ask them to read the rest of the article to check their answers to the **Get started** activity.

2

- Ask students to read and choose the correct options for themselves. Review the meaning of *I don't mind* (*I don't feel upset or unhappy about something*).
- Invite students to raise their hands for their chosen option to compare their answers with the rest of the class.
- Encourage students to think of recent examples when they have been in these situations and describe how they felt.

DO

3

- Divide the class into groups of three to read and follow the instructions in order to measure their own personal space.
- Invite groups to share their findings with the class in order to compare them.

MOVE BEYOND FOR TEACHERS

Social distances

Social distances vary from person to person, but there is a good general rule that Hall (1966) identified for Americans:

Public Zone: 3 m – When we are walking behind someone in town, we try to keep a 3 m distance from them.

Social Zone: 1.5 m–3 m – When someone moves into the social zone, we start to feel a connection with them.

Personal Zone: 0.5 m–1.5 m – In the personal zone, the conversation gets more direct.

Intimate Zone: 0.5 m or less – When a person is within arm's reach or closer, we can look them in their eyes. This can be either romantic or threatening!

REFLECT

4

- Focus students on the REFLECTION POINT and have a class vote on whether they agree or not. Draw students' attention to the expressions in the PHRASE BYTES box and encourage them to use these to help structure their discussions.
- Lead a class discussion of the questions one by one, choosing different students to share their answers.

MOVE BEYOND FOR TEACHERS

Personal space

By respecting personal space, students can create a positive impression. Remind students that within the first 60 seconds of meeting somebody, you have formed an impression about what type of person that person is, and 55 percent of this will be based solely on body language. This is important when students go to a job interview; the interviewer is judging what kind of employee someone would make from the minute he or she walks in the door.

In the classroom, as teachers, we also need to be aware of personal space. Bend down to the student's level as much as possible and always try to speak to students eye to eye. In a student-centered classroom, we should be moving around the classroom listening, making sure students are on task, and clarifying any questions or concerns.

Extra activity

Write these quotes on the board. Divide the class into pairs to discuss what advice they would give.

1 *My friend gets too close when she talks to me. I don't know what to do.*
2 *Every morning I get on a crowded bus. My hands sweat, and I feel nervous.*
3 *I have a Japanese friend who doesn't like me standing close to her.*
4 *At an interview, I shake hands with the person who's interviewing me, but then I'm too close.*

EXTEND

5a 24

- Explain to students that they are going to listen to sentences about areas of personal space and that they should write *agree*, *disagree*, or *not sure* for each sentence.
- Play the track, pausing after each sentence for students to write their response.
- Play the track again if necessary.

AUDIO SCRIPT 24

1 My bedroom is my space. My family should only come in when I allow them.
2 My diary or journal is for my eyes only. Nobody else should read it.
3 My phone messages are private. Nobody should read them.
4 My social media page is for me and my friends – not for my parents.
5 My parents don't need to know where I go or what I do with my friends.

Alternative procedure: less confident classes 24

Less confident students will probably feel uncomfortable discussing these sentences if they don't see them written down. Ask students to write down any words they hear the first time they listen. Encourage them to compare their answers in pairs to try to reconstruct whole sentences. Play the track again for students to try to complete their sentences. Ask five students to come up and write the sentences on the board to check.

5b

- Divide the class into pairs to compare their answers and explain any differences to each other.
- Ask students to present their opinions to the class and hold a class discussion to close the lesson. You could ask some opening questions to start the discussion; for example, *Do you keep a diary? Do you feel that your bedroom is your own private space? Is it right for parents to look at their children's emails and messages? Do you tell your parents where you are going when you are going out?*

Homework

Ask students to write a short text of about 150 words on personal space, based on their answers in Exercise 5b. In the next class, ask them to compare their texts with a partner.

SPEAKING At the airport

Check in at the airport

Page 21

STAGE	TIME	FOCUS
GET STARTED		Recycle vocabulary and present new words for talking about traveling by plane.
SPEAK		Discuss the best way to get to the airport near your home and talk about your experiences at an airport. Learn words to describe places in an airport.
LISTEN		Listen to a conversation at an airport. Work on important phrases when you check in at the airport and recycle ways to check that you understand (speaking subskill).
ACT		Role-play a conversation at a check-in desk.

Get started

Write the following sentences on the board. Point out that they are all associated with traveling by plane and ask students to complete them with the correct verb.

1 *The plane ______ at your destination.*
2 *You ______ your luggage if you haven't done this electronically.*
3 *The plane goes down the runway and ______ .*
4 *You ______ your seat belt and turn off your cell phone.*
5 *You ______ at the airport at least two hours before your flight.*
6 *You ______ passport control and ______ your passport.*
7 *You ______ the correct gate and then you ______ your flight.*

Choose different students to come up to the board and complete the sentences.

Divide the class into pairs to put the sentences in a logical order. Check answers as a class and encourage students to think of other words associated with flying and being at an airport.

ANSWERS
1 arrives/lands 2 check in 3 takes off 4 fasten
5 arrive 6 go through/pass through; show
7 go to/walk to; get on/board
Correct order: 5, 2, 6, 7, 4, 3, 1

SPEAK

1

- Divide the class into pairs to discuss the questions.
- Choose different students to explain how to get to the nearest airport from their homes and to say how many times they have been to the airport.

2

- Refer students to the airport signs and ask them to match the signs to the correct activities 1–6.
- Encourage them to compare their answers in pairs before you check them as a class.

ANSWERS
2 c 3 a 4 f 5 d 6 b

LISTEN

3 25

- Play the conversation for students to listen and decide where Bella is and what other places in an airport are mentioned. You may want to do this with books closed.
- Play the conversation again for students to check their answers. Choose a student to say the answers.
- Ask some comprehension questions to check full understanding of the conversation: *Where is Bella flying to?* (Rome); *How many bags is she checking in?* (one suitcase); *Does she have any sharp objects in her carry-on bags?* (yes, she has a pair of scissors); *What does she do with them?* (she puts them in her suitcase).

ANSWERS / AUDIO SCRIPT 25

Bella is at the check-in desk.
Departures and Gate 30 are also mentioned.
See Student's Book, page 21, for audio script.

4 ▶26

- Refer students back to the conversation in Exercise 3 and ask them to underline the sentences and phrases for situations 1–4.
- Play the track for students to listen and check.
- Play the track again for students to listen and repeat. Ask students to underline the stressed words in each sentence.

ANSWERS / AUDIO SCRIPT ▶26

1 I'd like to check in for the flight to ...
2 Here you go.
3 I have a backpack.
4 Which gate number is it?

Extra activity ▶25

Ask students to read the conversation aloud in pairs. Play the conversation again for students to listen and pay special attention to the intonation and to stressed and unstressed words (see underlined words in box above).

5a

- Ask students to read the tips in the HOW TO box. Invite a volunteer to read them aloud.

5b ▶27

- Ask students to cover the conversation and try to complete phrases 1–4 from the conversation.
- Encourage students to compare their answers in pairs before you play the track for them to listen and check.
- Play the track again for students to listen and repeat.

ANSWERS / AUDIO SCRIPT ▶27

1 Sorry, I don't understand.
2 Sorry, I didn't hear that.
3 Could you repeat that, please?
4 Can you say that again, please?

ACT

6 ▶28

- Divide the class into pairs to role-play a scene as described in the instructions: Student A is at the check-in desk (Agent) and Student B wants to check in (Traveler).
- Ask the "travelers" to first decide where they are flying to, how much luggage they have, and if they have any sharp objects in their carry-on bags.
- Play the track with the phrases from the PHRASEBOOK box and encourage students to use these phrases when acting out their scenes.
- Suggest to the travelers that they check their understanding at different points in the scene by using the PHRASEBOOK expressions.
- Invite students to join up with another pair to present their scenes.

Alternative procedure: less confident classes

In less confident classes, students may need to practice the conversation in a more structured way. Copy this structure onto the board and elicit key sentences for each stage, writing them on the board. Ask students to act out the conversation in pairs. Then ask them to form different pairs and try to perform the conversation without looking at the board.

Traveler	Agent
Greet / Say destination	Passport?
Give passport	Check in luggage?
Describe luggage to check in	Carry-on bags?
Describe carry-on bags	Sharp objects?
Say yes/no	Yes – in suitcase
	Give boarding pass
Gate number?	Say gate number
Check you understand	Repeat gate number

Homework

Ask students to investigate different ways to get to the airport(s) in their town or area and write a short text about the different methods of transportation and how much each one costs. Take a class vote on the best method in the next class.

WRITING Wish you were here

Use correct verb tenses Page 22

STAGE	TIME	FOCUS
GET STARTED		Brainstorm words connected to vacations and vacation activities and play a game to introduce the topic of the lesson.
SPEAK AND READ		Talk about when you send postcards and who you receive them from. Read a postcard and match pictures to the text. Discuss how to use correct verb tenses (writing subskill).
PRACTICE		Write sentences in another postcard in the correct tense.
DISCUSS		Talk about an imaginary vacation.
WRITE		Write a postcard to a friend describing your imaginary vacation.
SHARE		Read your postcard to the class. Take a class vote to decide whose vacation sounds most interesting.

Get started

Play a game of *A–Z List*. Divide the class into small teams to write an A-to-Z list of words or phrases connected to vacations, vacation activities, and transportation (except *u* and *z*). To make this game more challenging, tell students that in order to get a point, they must both say a word with the correct letter and identify the part of speech (noun, verb, or adjective). Set a time limit of five minutes. Use this opportunity to recycle vocabulary students will need in the lesson. Invite the teams to say their words beginning with the successive letters in the alphabet. Teams win an additional point if they say a word that no other group has written.

SUGGESTED ANSWERS

airport, boat, car, departure, eat, fly, gate, hotel, InterRail, journey, kilo, luggage, mountains, no sharp objects, on time, plane, quarter to (hour), reservation, subway, train, visa, weather, yet (Has the bus left yet?)

SPEAK AND READ

1

- Divide the class into groups to answer the questions.
- Choose different students to share their answers.

2

- Ask students to read Vicky's postcard and check the correct picture for each category.
- Encourage students to compare their answers in pairs before you check them as a class.

ANSWERS

Trip: c Campsite: a Weather: b Food: a

3a

- Encourage students to read the tips in the HOW TO box. Invite a volunteer to read them aloud.

3b

- Ask students to look at Vicky's postcard and underline examples of seven different tenses. Encourage them to identify the tenses.
- Encourage them to compare their answers in pairs before you check them as a class.
- Ask different students around the class to read their sentences aloud to check the answers. Point out that there are several different sentences for most of the tenses.

SUGGESTED ANSWERS

We've been in Spain for three days now, (present perfect)
I'm having a fantastic time! (present progressive)
The trip was terrible. (simple past)
I was getting really tired of waiting (past progressive)
But our campsite is fantastic! (simple present)
... we're going to do some sightseeing. (*going to* future)
I think it'll be exciting. (*will* future)

PRACTICE

4

- Ask students to write the sentences in the correct tenses, using the tips in the HOW TO box to help them.
- Circulate and monitor students.
- Check answers as a class.

ANSWERS

1 got 2 play 3 haven't played 4 are going to watch / are watching 5 is raining 6 will stop

DISCUSS

5

- Tell students you would like them to imagine that they are on vacation. Read a series of questions to get them thinking about their imaginary vacation, but tell them not to write anything at this stage. Suggested questions: *Where are you? What was your trip like? Where are you staying? Who is with you? What activities have you already done? What did you do yesterday? What are you going to do in the next few days? What is the weather like? When are you going home?*
- Ask students to work in pairs and to talk about their imaginary vacations, saying what they've already done and what they plan to do. Remind them that you want them to imagine that they are on vacation as they speak. It might help to give them an example; for example, *I'm at the beach with my family. The weather is fantastic. We've been to the beach every day, gone swimming, and played volleyball. Tomorrow we're going to visit a lighthouse. It will be interesting.*
- Encourage them to ask each other questions to find out more information.

Alternative procedure

In order to help students imagine that they are on vacation as they speak, you could set up the discussion as a role-play telephone conversation. Ask them to sit back-to-back and imagine that they are talking on the telephone from their imaginary vacation destinations.

WRITE

6

- Tell students you would like them to write a postcard to a friend from their imaginary vacation destination.
- Refer them to the objective of the lesson, which is to use correct verb tenses, and remind them to use the tips in the HOW TO box as they are writing.
- Read through the three steps in the box and ask students to give you some examples from Vicky's postcard.
- Set a time limit of 10 minutes for writing.

SHARE

7

- Invite students to read their postcards aloud to their classmates.
- Finish the activity by asking students to say whose vacation sounded the most interesting and why.

Alternative procedure: more confident classes

Ask students to write their postcards on separate sheets of paper. Then ask them to draw a picture that represents the description of their ideal vacation. Collect the postcards and pictures and redistribute them in groups of six. Ask students to read the postcards and match the descriptions to the pictures.

Homework

Draw students' attention to the first part of Vicky's postcard and elicit what went wrong at the beginning of the vacation. Ask students to write a postcard about the worst vacation they can imagine. Ask them to describe what went wrong on the trip, at the campsite or hotel, and with the weather and food. In the next class, ask students to work in pairs, read each other's postcards, and decide whose trip sounds worse.

VOCABULARY Travel items

1

- Refer students to the picture and ask them to describe where the boy is and what his problem is. (*He is picking up his luggage from baggage claim and his suitcases are very heavy*.) Ask students if they know what the maximum weight is for luggage on most flights (*about 23 kg*) and elicit which items can be very heavy (*books*, *toiletries*, *shoes*, etc). Explain to students that the conversation is between the boy and the teacher, and they're going on a school trip.
- Ask them to complete the conversation with the correct words, pointing out that the first letter of each word is given.
- Check answers as a class.

ANSWERS
1 suitcases 2 backpack 3 sleeping bag
4 toothpaste/toothbrush 5 toothbrush/toothpaste
6 hairbrush 7 shampoo 8 boarding pass(es)
9 visa 10 scissors 11 passport 12 wallet

Travel

2

- Explain to students that the travel plan gives details about a trip to Peru. Ask students what they know about Peru and what they can visit there (e.g., *museums*, *historic buildings*, *Machu Picchu*, etc.).
- Ask students to choose the correct options to complete the travel plan. Allow three minutes.
- Encourage students to compare their answers in pairs as they finish. Then choose different students to read their answers aloud.
- Encourage fast finishers to underline the stressed syllables in the nouns.

ANSWERS
1 delays 2 reservation 3 seat 4 departure
5 passengers 6 arrival 7 connection
8 destination 9 route 10 fare

GRAMMAR Present perfect

3

- Ask students where Luke and his classmates are. (*They're in a museum.*)
- Write the words *for* and *since* on the board and elicit when we use each one (for = *period of time,* since = *a specific point in the past*).
- Ask students to complete the conversation by writing the verbs in parentheses in the present perfect and choosing *for* or *since*.
- Check answers as a class.

ANSWERS
1 's/has been 2 since 3 've/have worked 4 for
5 For 6 has wanted 7 've/have just decided
8 hasn't taken

The future

4

- Ask students to read the initial sentences and choose the teacher's next sentence (A or B) in each case.
- Choose different students to read their answers aloud, inviting the rest of the class to help you correct any errors.

ANSWERS
1 A 2 A 3 B 4 B 5 A 6 B

Extra Resources

Go to the Teacher's Resource Center at mee2.macmillaneducation.com for:

- the Speaking section of the Progress Check 1&2;
- a downloadable project linked to Units 1–2;
- downloadable audio and audio scripts for the Student's Book and Workbook;
- videos and video scripts;
- extra vocabulary at two levels of difficulty;
- extra grammar at two levels of difficulty;
- culture lessons, with full teacher's notes;
- a life skills lesson, with full teacher's notes;
- Speaking Database materials;
- the *Move Beyond Level 5* wordlist;
- tips for using the Grammar Database;
- and more!

Go to the Workbook pages 92–103 for further practice material.

PROGRESS CHECK 1&2

Preparing for the Progress Check

The Progress Check can be done either as a review of the two preceding units or as a formal test. For the first Progress Check, it is a good idea to get students to prepare as thoroughly as they can so that they get into the habit of regularly reviewing what they have learned. Reassure the class that the Progress Check contains material that they have covered in Units 1 and 2.

Vocabulary review

- Write the following on the board and ask students which words are needed to complete the phrases for life experiences:
  get .... (married; a job; a driver's license; a degree)
  start .... (school; college)
  go on .... (a first date)
  leave .... (school; college; home)
  go to .... (school; college)
  have .... (children)
  .... *from your job* (retire)
- After a few suggestions, ask students who can find the rest of the words in the **Words & Beyond** section on page 69 (suggested answers are given in parentheses above).
- To review adjectives for describing objects, ask the class to turn to Exercise 6 on page 8. Remind them of the work they did on word order there. Explain to students that they are going to play a quick memory game and they have to try to remember what was said before.
  - Begin by asking Student A: *What do you have?* Student A should then answer with a noun described by two adjectives; for example, *I have a valuable old watch.*
  - Encourage Student A to ask Student B the same question. Student B then repeats the item and adds one more; for example, *I have a valuable old watch and a new red bag*. Student B then asks Student C, who repeats the previous two items before adding a third.
  - Keep going around the class until someone makes a mistake or fails to think of a new item. If the chain is broken, start again with the next student and continue until all students have had a turn.
- Divide the class into pairs to review travel items. Give them exactly one minute to look at the vocabulary on pages 14 and 15. Next, pairs should see how many items they can remember with their books closed. Students then look in the book to see if they forgot any words. Ask several pairs to tell you if they forgot anything important.
- Working individually, students call out other words related to travel that they can remember from the book. Write these on the board as you hear them. When suggestions begin to slow down, or if they seem to be coming from the same students each time, ask the class to look at Unit 2 and the Unit Review on page 23. This time, try to get suggestions from students who have contributed the least so far.

Grammar review

- To remind the class of the grammar they have studied in the previous two units, start a "race," where students check the book and tell you the main grammar points from each unit. The grammar for this Progress Check is:
  - Unit 1: Present tenses review; Past tenses review
  - Unit 2: Present perfect; The future
- Write these on the board, asking for example sentences as students call out the grammar points out. Deal with any problems by correcting mistakes and referring students to the grammar explanations on pages 7, 9, 17, and 19.

Optional warm-up activities

These activities are suitable when you are not using the Progress Check as part of a formal test.

READ Exercise 1

- Tell students that they are going to practice skimming a text. Explain that skimming will give them a good idea of what the text is about, what the main points are, and how the text is organized. Give them one minute to skim the text for gist. Remind students that they are not expected to read it in detail.
- After a minute, ask them to close their books and tell you what they remember. Elicit the main points about the text, correcting anything students have misunderstood.
- Point out how useful it can be to skim a reading text. Explain that they will have to read more closely when they do the exercise but that this will be easier because they will now be able to find the relevant sections of the text quickly.

LISTEN Exercise 2

- Refer students back to the listening activities and the HOW TO boxes they covered on pages 8 and 18. Ask several students to tell you which tips they thought were the most useful.
- Remind them of the importance of reading ahead before they listen. Point out that listening activities, especially in tests, are not an opportunity to sit back and rest. They need to use all the time available to predict what they will hear. If they do this, what they hear will make more sense to them.
- Divide the class into pairs and ask them to look at the blanks in the form in Exercise 2 and say which one requires the following (answers are given in parentheses): a number (*3*), a period of time (*1*), a place (*5*), a noun (*4*).
- If students are worried about the listening section, you could ask them to suggest what the answers might be. Do not, however, give any indication of the actual answers. Instead, respond by saying *It could be that* or by pointing out why a suggestion is unlikely (e.g., because the student suggests an adjective and that wouldn't fit syntactically).
- Finally, point out to students how much useful information they have gathered *without* listening. They will now be much more focused when they do listen.

WRITE Exercise 3

- Students following the *Move Beyond* course have done transformation exercises before. However, some students might not be familiar with them, so make sure they understand that they cannot use more than three words and that the second sentence must have the same meaning as the first.
- You should also remind students that the blanks usually depend on the grammar that they have studied in the two previous units (see the grammar review above).
- Write the following sentences on the board:
  I have been here since 9 o'clock.
  I was a student in 2010.
  Do you want a drink?
  I'm still waiting for my test grade.

- Ask the class how they could write these sentences differently but with the same meaning. Accept suggestions, dealing with any problems that might occur. You can then write some of the following on the board and explain that they say the same thing but in a different way:
  - *I have been here for (three) hours. I came here at 9 o'clock. I came here (three) hours ago.*
  - *I have been a student since 2010. I started studying in 2010.*
  - *Would you like a drink? Can I get you something to drink?*
  - *I haven't gotten my test grade (yet). My test grade hasn't come out (yet). My teacher hasn't given me my test grade (yet).*
- Point out that there is sometimes more than one way to transform a sentence. Remind students that the meaning has to be the same after the transformation.

WRITE Exercise 4

- Refer students back to the HOW TO box on page 22 and remind them that they have been reviewing tenses in these two units.
- Ask students to look at the bullet points in Exercise 4 and ask them which tenses they will use for each bullet point. Elicit the following:
  - First bullet point: present progressive
  - Second bullet point: present perfect
  - Third bullet point: *going to*

  In addition, students could use:
  - simple present to say what day it is today or tomorrow
  - simple past to say what happened yesterday, on Monday, etc., or to add details after a present perfect
  - present progressive for future arrangements
- Divide the class into pairs and ask them to make notes on some of the things they could write for each bullet point. They do not have to write complete sentences.

Doing the Progress Check

READ

1

- Ask students to look at the HOW TO boxes that they have studied (on pages 6 and 16). Make sure they remember that they have several different strategies to choose from in order to do this kind of task.
- Go through the first tip for how to do a true/false activity in the **Test-Taking Tips**. Then give students a minute or two to read sentences 1–10. Prompt them with some very basic questions; for example:
  - *Where in the world are we talking about?* (Liverpool)
  - *Who do you think Paul McCartney and John Lennon are?* (members of a group)
  - *Who were The Beatles?* (a music group)
  - *What do you think Mendips and Forthlin Road are?* (places where the musicians lived)
- If you have decided not to do the full warm-up, tell students that a good thing to do next would be to read the text quickly to understand how it is organized (and where they might find the answers).
- Go through the remaining tips for how to do a true/false activity. Ask if the headings or the picture help them with more information. Then ask them to read the text carefully, checking details and answering the questions. Allow 15 minutes for this section.

ANSWERS

1 I 2 I 3 I 4 I 5 C 6 C 7 I 8 C 9 C
10 C

LISTEN

2 29

- If you have decided not to do the full warm-up, encourage students to spend a minute or two looking at the blanks and predicting what they might hear. Make sure that they understand that they have to write a word, number, or short phrase in each blank.
- Go through the **Test-Taking Tips** for the listening task, briefly referring students back to the work they did on pages 8 and 18.
- Point out that they will hear everything twice. Students should try to fill in each blank the first time, but they must be careful not to lose their place and miss the answer to one of the questions. The second listening should be for checking and filling in any blanks they have left.

ANSWERS / AUDIO SCRIPT 29

1 12 years 2 working together 3 $30 4 boarding pass
5 (the) station

Organizer: Hi, everyone. Can I just say a few words before you get ready to leave? First of all, I'd like to say how much we've enjoyed our time with you over the last week. We've been organizing our Adventure Weeks for 12 years, and you've been one of our best groups. On a personal level, I hope you'll keep in touch with your new friends. I also hope you remember what you've learned here. Working together to organize things is one of the most important skills you'll ever need. It'll help you at school and when you leave home and get a job.
I'd just like to tell you about a few practical things next. For those of you who are traveling back home by plane, the bus to the airport leaves at 10. Please don't be late. We can't delay your plane's departure! If you miss the bus, you'll have to pay for a taxi to the airport, and the fare is $30.
Remember to put your passport in your carry-on bag, not in your suitcase. And have you all printed your boarding passes? No? OK, if you *haven't* printed your boarding pass, could you please go to reception when I finish talking and they'll do that for you. It'll save you time at the airport, and you can also reserve the seat you want. And when you've printed it, remember to keep your boarding pass with your passport.
If you're traveling by train, a different bus is going to take you to the station. It leaves at 11, so you have a little more time to fold up your sleeping bags and get all your belongings into your backpacks.
That's it. It's nine o'clock now, so I'll see some of you down here in an hour.

WRITE

3

- Read through the **Test-Taking Tips** for this task. Make sure students understand that they can write one, two, or three words in the blanks, but no more.
- Remind students that this kind of task is often grammar based. They should expect past, present, and future tenses to be included.
- Explain that spelling is important in this kind of task because in a real test they will lose credit for spelling mistakes, so checking is very important.

ANSWERS

1 were studying 2 you like 3 for two weeks
4 hasn't answered

4

- Spend a few minutes going through the task with students and eliciting who they have to write to and what their message must include (the three bullet points).
- Remind them that even if their writing is excellent, they won't get full credit if they do not include all the points in the task.
- Refer students back to the work they did and the postcard they wrote on page 22. Point out that this message is similar to a postcard, only here they have to write fewer words.
- Explain that they shouldn't spend too long on their beginnings and endings. Suggest that they begin with *Hi, Neil,* and end with *Write soon, [name].*
- Stress that the correct tenses are important. Briefly remind them of the work they did on tenses on page 22 and the optional writing warm-up activity above.
- Finally, remind students of the word limit and the importance of checking their spelling, grammar, etc.

MODEL ANSWER

Hi, Neil.
How are things? It's Friday after school, and I'm reading my messages. It's been a hard week. I've had tests every day since Monday. But tomorrow's Saturday. We'll probably go to a theme park, but it's likely to rain.
Write soon,
Jim

After the Progress Check

Optional game

This game follows up on the past, present, and future tenses, as well as the travel vocabulary that students have been reviewing, and will help lighten the atmosphere after the test.

- Ask students to open their books to Unit 2.
- Divide the class into pairs. Explain that they are going to write conversations together. On a clean sheet of paper, each pair writes the first two lines of a conversation about two people getting ready for a trip. Ask students to include at least one example of the present perfect in their conversations.
- Pairs then pass their piece of paper to the pair on their right, who read the beginning and add two more lines of conversation. They continue in this way, adding two lines each time until they have finished. Remind students to refer to Unit 2 if they need help with any grammar or vocabulary. Then ask pairs to act out the conversation they started.
- Ask the class to listen carefully while the conversations are read aloud. When all the conversations have been heard, ask students to vote for the best one.

Feedback and extension

After the Progress Check has been graded, provide feedback to the class as a whole and individually as far as possible. Ask students which parts they found the most difficult and how they think they could improve their grades next time.

READ

- Review sentences 1–10 one at a time, reminding students that all of the details in each question must be found in the text for it to be marked as *correct*. For example, in sentence 1, you could point out that paragraph 1 clearly states that Woolton is now a part of Liverpool, but in 1957 it was a separate village.
- Ask students where they found the answers each time. If they made mistakes, make sure they understand why.
- Emphasize to students the importance of reading English, either online or in magazines, etc. The more they can read, the better it will be for them. Ask students what kinds of things they read in their own language and suggest suitable English equivalents (e.g., pop or sports magazines, websites about hobbies, or more general interest magazines and sites such as *National Geographic Kids* or *Focus* [www.sciencefocus.com]). If students have a hobby or interest, they might be motivated to read about it in English.

LISTEN

- Handing out photocopies of the audio script is a good way to provide feedback. Deal with any mistakes in this way. You could make one photocopy per pair and ask students to discuss where they went wrong. Seeing the conversations written down will help students recognize if they have misheard something.
- As with reading, every opportunity students have to listen to English is valuable because most tests have a listening component. Through the internet, students can readily get access to lyrics, for instance, if they enjoy listening to songs in English. Radio and television are also excellent sources of spoken English. If you know of any stations, channels, or programs that are suitable for their age group, encourage students to listen, even if for only five minutes. This could become an ongoing project, with students reporting back on what they have heard or seen.

WRITE

- Students who had difficulty with Exercise 3 need to focus on the grammar points from the unit. Write one or two example sentences that use the target grammar point on the board and then put students in groups of four to come up with more examples of their own. If necessary, ask students to write more sentences for homework.
- For students who had difficulty with Exercise 4, do a similar task, building up a model on the board. Write the following, asking different students for ways to fill in the blanks:
  Hi, Ben.
  I'm having a good/bad week because ....
  This week, I have .... *and* ....
  On the weekend, I ....
- When the model is complete, ask other students to suggest alternatives. You could then erase the previous suggestions and fill in the blanks with new ones.

MOVE BEYOND FOR TEACHERS

The Beatles

The reading text in this Progress Check is about The Beatles. If students enjoyed reading about them, you could ask them to search online for more information about the group. For example, divide the class into two groups and give them the names of the other two Beatles. Half of the class could then look online for information about George Harrison, while the other half looks up Ringo Starr. If you think your students would be more interested in contemporary bands or musicians, ask them to choose one and find out more by searching for the name online. Remind them that they will find difficult words, but they should try to understand the general meaning. They should aim to find between six and ten main points and report back in the form of a mini presentation in the next class.

3 MY MUSIC

IN THE PICTURE Live music

Talk about music and music events

Pages 26–27

STAGE	TIME	FOCUS
GET STARTED		Introduce the topic of the lesson and talk about music.
WORK WITH WORDS		Recycle different genres of music and kinds of groups, musicians, and instruments. Learn new music vocabulary and listen to and complete sentences with the new words. Pronounce words with /ɔ/ and /ɑ/ sounds. Watch a video of musical performances and describe what you see.
SPEAK		Ask and answer questions in a music survey.

Get started

Ask students to work individually to write three personal statements about music – two true statements and one false one. Divide the class into pairs to read their statements aloud to their partner and take turns asking questions to find out which statement is false. Model this activity first with students so that they have a clear idea of what types of things to say; for example, *I have seen Rihanna in concert. I play the guitar. Music was my favorite subject in school.*

Refer students to the title of the lesson (*Live music*) and ask them to say what it means (*live music can be watched or listened to at the same time as it happens*). Practice the pronunciation of *live*. Remind students that the pronunciation is /laɪv/ when it is an adjective and /lɪv/ when it is a verb. If necessary, review the difference in meaning. Read these two sentences with blanks aloud and ask students to call out the correct word: *We found a restaurant that has* ________ *music on Friday nights. Miami is a nice place to* ________ .

WORK WITH WORDS

1a and 1b RECALL

- Divide the class into pairs to do both tasks. Set a time limit of three minutes.
- First, have students refer to the photos and make lists of words under the headings. They can use the photos to help them, but they should write as many words as they can in each category. Then ask them to match the verbs *listen* and *play* to the correct categories.
- After three minutes, choose different students to say their answers. Note that several categories use both *listen* and *play*.
- Ask students to do the **Work with Words** task on page 71.

SUGGESTED ANSWERS

Kinds of music	Instruments	People	Kinds of groups	Places & events
rock	*guitar*	*singer*	*band*	*concert*
folk	flute	guitar player	brass band	performance
jazz	trumpet	audience	orchestra	venue
opera	drums	conductor		concert hall
classical	violin	drummer		auditorium
	tuba			stage

listen: singer, guitar player, etc. / (brass) band, orchestra, etc. / concert, performance
listen or play: rock, folk, jazz, etc. / guitar, flute, trumpet, etc.

2

- Ask students to match two words from the box to each of the photos a–f and add them to the table, if they do not already have them there.

ANSWERS

b audience, opera c jazz, trumpet d folk, performance
e conductor, orchestra f brass band, flute

Extra activity

Ask the class to call out the names of musicians or groups that they associate with each genre that they listed in the table in Exercise 1 (e.g., *jazz – Louis Armstrong*; *opera – Plácido Domingo*; *rock – Muse*; *classical – Beethoven*; *heavy metal – Led Zeppelin*; *reggae – Bob Marley*; *pop – One Direction*; *folk – Ed Sheeran*; *hip-hop – Jay Z*; *R&B – Alicia Keys*).

3 ▶30

- Play the track for students to listen and match the speakers to the photos.
- Encourage students to compare their answers in pairs before you check them as a class. Ask students which key words helped them decide on their answers.

ANSWERS / AUDIO SCRIPT ▶30

1 f 2 e 3 c 4 b 5 d 6 a

1 We started playing together a year ago, but I've played the flute since I was 12. I also play the trumpet in the school brass band.
2 The sound of the orchestra in the concert hall is fantastic. I've seen the conductor before, but I've never seen him conduct Beethoven.
3 Thank you for coming to the Newton Jazz Festival. Now please welcome one of the greatest trumpet players of all time. Ladies and gentlemen, put your hands together for …
4 I don't like opera very much, but a friend gave me tickets, and I'm really enjoying it. I think the rest of the audience is having a good time too. People are shouting "Bravo!" all the time.
5 I usually perform folk songs … a mix of old traditional songs and more modern stuff. If I give a good performance, then people give money.
6 The venue is amazing. I've never been to a concert in a place like this with all these hills and rocks. And the band is performing really well.

4a ▶31

- Ask students to use the words from Exercise 2 to complete the sentences.
- Play the track for students to listen and check.

ANSWERS / AUDIO SCRIPT ▶31

1 venue; band 2 Jazz; trumpet 3 folk; performance
4 flute; brass band 5 opera; audience 6 orchestra; conductor
See Student's Book, page 28, for audio script.

4b ▶32

- Ask students to cover the box in Exercise 2. Play the track for them to listen and repeat the words.

AUDIO SCRIPT ▶32

See Student's Book, page 28, for audio script.

5a ▶33 PRONOUNCE

- Play the track for students to listen to the target sounds in the words.
- Play the track again for students to listen and repeat.

AUDIO SCRIPT ▶33

See Student's Book, page 28, for audio script.

5b ▶34

- Play the track for students to listen and focus on the bold letters in the words and repeat the words.
- Elicit which words have the /ɔ/ sound and which have the /ɑ/ sound.

ANSWERS / AUDIO SCRIPT ▶34

/ɔ/ audience song lost
/ɑ/ stop concert modern
See Student's Book, page 27, for audio script.

6 THE MOVING PICTURE ▶

- Play the video and ask students to describe what they see.
- Ask students what type of performances these are.

ANSWERS

Scene 1: an orchestra with a conductor; classical music
Scene 2: a guitar player performing outside
Scene 3: the audience at a rock concert
Scene 4: a jazz band playing brass instruments
Scene 5: a woman singing opera
They are all *live* performances.

7

- Explain to students that they are going to answer questions in the music survey. Divide the class into pairs. Refer Student A to the questions on page 141 and Student B to the ones on page 29. Encourage students to answer the questions about themselves and make notes.

SPEAK

8

- In the same pairs, have Student A ask Student B the questions on page 141 and Student B ask Student A the questions on page 29, making note of each other's answers.
- Encourage students to compare and discuss their answers with their partners.
- Circulate and monitor, noting good use of language and errors to go over in a feedback session.
- Choose different students to tell the class one interesting thing about their partner.

MOVE BEYOND

Ask students to do the **Move Beyond** task on page 132.

Homework

Ask students to write about a group or a singer who sings in English. Encourage students to use words from the lesson to describe how, where, what, and when the person performs; when he or she first discovered this music; and what it means to him or her. In the next class, have students read their descriptions aloud in pairs or small groups.

READING A dream concert

Understand new words *Page 28*

STAGE	TIME	FOCUS
GET STARTED		Recycle vocabulary used to describe music, instruments, and performers.
SPEAK AND READ		Read a concert program and talk about José Ángel Salazar, a 14-year-old conductor of the Symphony Orchestra of Nueva Esparta, Venezuela. Discuss tips on how to understand new words when you read (reading subskill).
REACT		Discuss the characteristics a conductor needs and whether you possess these qualities.

Get started

Play a game of *Twenty Questions* (see Games, page 29). Divide the class into two teams and explain that they have 20 questions to guess the name of a famous musician.

Write this list of words on the board: *singer*, *conductor*, *concert*, *venue*, *guitar*, *keyboard*, *alive*, *dead*, *drums*, *piano*, *rock*, *hip-hop*, *reggae*, *classical*, *jazz*, *trumpet*, *pop*, *star*, *performance*, *band*, *group*. Point out to students that if they use vocabulary from the previous lesson, they can "win" an extra question (e.g., *Is she a singer?* wins an extra question).

Keep a tally on the board of the number of questions students have asked.

SPEAK AND READ

1

- Refer students to the poster and the photo below. Elicit the answer to the question (*a classical concert*).

2 35

- Ask students to read the concert program and guess the answers to the questions. Don't play the audio at this point. It is an extra feature, and a suggestion for using it in class is included at the end of the lesson.
- Encourage students to compare their answers in pairs before you check them as a class.

ANSWERS

1 because he was the youngest conductor in the world
2 the conductor 3 He wants to study languages.

3a

- Divide the class into pairs to talk about how they can understand new words when they read. Prompt their discussion by asking them: *What do you do when you read a word you don't understand in a text? What happens if you use a dictionary all the time to look up new words? What can you do to figure out the meaning of new words without a dictionary?*
- Refer students to the tips in the HOW TO box. Invite a couple of volunteers to read the tips aloud.
- Ask students if the ideas they had are the same as or different from the ones in the HOW TO box.

3b

- Ask students to read the text again and try to understand the underlined words by following the tips in the HOW TO box. Ask students to work in pairs if you think they need additional support.

ANSWERS

auditioned
Type of word: verb in the simple past, infinitive *audition*
Roots/cognate: *audience*, *audio* (i.e., related to the verbs *to hear*, *to listen to*)
Context: ... to join the Symphony Orchestra
gestures
Type of word: plural noun
Roots/cognate: *gestura*, Latin root meaning "manner of carrying the body"
Context: movements ... and expressions to communicate
tell off
Type of word: phrasal verb (informal)
Roots/cognate: *tellen*, Dutch/German for "to reckon" or "to count"
Context: hard because I have to find the way to ... kids who are much older than me
convey
Type of word: verb
Roots/cognate: *conveyer*, Anglo-French; *conviare*, Latin
Context: ... confidence to the musicians in order to get a confident performance back from them
aware
Type of word: adjective
Roots/cognate: *gewær*, Old English
Context: ... of the importance of words for a conductor
grasp
Type of word: noun
Roots/cognate: *graepsen*, Old English for "to touch or feel"
Context: I'd have a better ... of if I spoke German.

4

- Ask students to match the dictionary definitions to the underlined words in the text. Students can write the words at the ends of the definitions in the Student's Book, or they can write the words in their notebooks and copy the correct definition after each word.

ANSWERS

1 aware 2 convey 3 tell off 4 grasp 5 auditioned
6 gestures

5

- Ask students to say which tips in the HOW TO box they used to help them in Exercises 3b and 4 and encourage them to check them.

MOVE BEYOND FOR TEACHERS

José Ángel Salazar and El Sistema

José Ángel Salazar is one of the success stories of the Venezuelan symphony orchestra program known as El Sistema (the system). There are more than 285 youth orchestras serving 350,000 young people across the country, and the program has especially benefitted children from disadvantaged backgrounds. El Sistema was conceived 37 years ago by José Antonio Abreu, a retired economist and politician who was also a conductor and pianist. His objective was to make music accessible to all.

Abreu was surprised by Salazar's talents, and he made sure that Salazar received instruction from Gustavo Dudamel (the world-famous conductor of the Los Angeles Philharmonic Orchestra).

REACT

6

- Divide the class into pairs to discuss the questions. Before they start, draw their attention to the expressions in the PHRASE BYTES box.
- Invite different students to explain their point(s) of view to the class. Try to develop a class discussion of the different points. You could start the discussion by asking a few general questions; for example, *Do you know any other unusual stories about musicians? Why did they become famous? What characteristics does a pop star need?*

MOVE BEYOND

Ask students to write different questions about the text on José Ángel Salazar.

Divide the class into pairs to ask and answer each other's questions.

Recorded reading text 35

The reading text is recorded as an extra audio track that can be exploited for various purposes.

For more confident students, you could use the audio track for a loop dictation (see page 27).

Homework

Ask students to write five quiz questions about music to test a partner in the next class. At the beginning of the next class, take a few minutes to check students' questions before they test their partners in a speaking activity.

GRAMMAR Verbs followed by gerunds or infinitives

Talk about things you enjoy doing

Page 29

STAGE	TIME	FOCUS
GET STARTED		Recycle words related to music and famous musicians.
READ		Read an advertisement and discuss whether you would like to attend The Rock School and say why or why not.
STUDY		Use the advertisement to study verbs followed by gerunds or infinitives.
PRACTICE		Complete an interview and a text and write questions with verbs followed by gerunds or infinitives.
SPEAK		Ask and answer questions about music, free-time activities, and hopes for the future.

Get started

Play a game of *Three in a Row* (see Games, page 29) with the grid below. Divide the class into two teams. To win a square, teams take turns choosing a square and answering the question that you ask them. They should answer with one of the options given in the square.

1 baton / stick	4 Herbert von Karajan / Luciano Pavarotti	7 guitar / cello
2 saxophone / tuba	5 Mahler / Beethoven	8 88 / 76
3 six / four	6 conductor / violinist	9 guitar / flute

Questions

1. *What does a conductor use to keep time?* (a baton)
2. *Which instrument is often used in jazz?* (a saxophone)
3. *How many strings does a violin have?* (four)
4. *Who was a famous conductor?* (Herbert von Karajan)
5. *What's the name of a famous music composer from the 19th century?* (Mahler)
6. *What does Vanessa-Mae do?* (She is a famous violinist.)
7. *Which instrument has four strings?* (cello)
8. *How many keys does a normal piano have?* (88)
9. *Which instrument can be acoustic or electric?* (a guitar)

READ Grammar in context

1

- Refer students to the photo and the first question in the text. Ask them what type of text they think they are going to read (*a brochure advertising The Rock School*).
- Ask students to read the advertisement. Elicit whether they would like to go to The Rock School and why or why not.
- Ask a few comprehension questions to check full understanding of the text: *What types of instruments can you study at The Rock School?* (guitar, drums, keyboard, and bass); *What is the main objective of The Rock School?* (to help young musicians achieve their ambitions); *What is their motto?* ("to inspire kids to rock on stage and in life"); *What are the conditions for joining The Rock School?* (you have to live in the USA or Mexico and be between eight and eighteen).

STUDY

2

- Focus students on the grammar explanations and ask them to complete the examples with verbs from the advertisement in Exercise 1.
- Choose students to read the explanations and completed examples to the class.

ANSWERS

singing to become

PRACTICE

3

- Ask students to read Marta's interview and choose the correct option (or options) for each sentence.
- Check answers as a class.

ANSWERS

1 coming / to come 2 being 3 to play 4 to be
5 singing 6 playing / to play 7 doing
8 swimming / to swim

Extra activity

Divide the class into pairs to practice reading the conversation.

4

- Focus students on the text and ask them to complete it with the correct form of the verbs in the box.
- Encourage students to compare their answers in pairs before you choose different students to read aloud a section each.

ANSWERS

2 to learn 3 to give 4 making 5 to perform
6 to become

5

- Ask students to write questions using the prompts and the correct form of the verbs in blue.
- Encourage students to compare their questions in pairs before you check them as a class.

ANSWERS

1 Which instruments are you learning to play right now?
2 Which other instruments would you like to learn?
3 Do you enjoy singing?
4 Do you like performing / to perform in front of people?
5 What do you hope to do in the future?
6 What other things do you like doing / to do in your free time?

SPEAK

6

- Divide the class into pairs to take turns asking and answering the questions in Exercise 5.
- When they have finished, invite students to tell the class one interesting thing about their partner.

Homework

Dictate these sentence prompts to students and ask them to complete the sentences about themselves for homework using verbs followed by gerunds or infinitives: *I love*; *I'd like*; *I don't mind*; *I imagine myself … in 10 years' time*; *I prefer*; *Last year I decided*; *I hope*; *I plan.*

At the beginning of the next class, have students take turns reading their sentences aloud in pairs. Encourage them to ask follow-up questions to find out more information about their partner.

LISTENING AND VOCABULARY Talking music

Transfer spoken information to a table *Page 30*

STAGE	TIME	FOCUS
GET STARTED		Recycle words to describe different types of music.
SPEAK AND LISTEN		Talk about the music you listen to when you are doing different activities. Read about and practice tips on how to transfer spoken information to a table (listening subskill). Listen to different people talking about how music affects them.
REACT		Discuss when you listen to music and whether listening to music can help you study.
WORK WITH WORDS		Look at adverbs of degree and word formation of adverbs with *-ly*. Listen to people being interviewed and complete sentences with adverbs.
WRITE AND SPEAK		Write and talk about whether music helps you do things better.

Get started

Divide the class into pairs or small groups to brainstorm adjectives that describe different types of music (e.g., *happy*, *upbeat*, *energetic*, *cheerful*, *sad*, *bluesy*, *melancholy*, *instrumental*, *easy listening*, *wild*, *danceable*, *background*, *jazzy*). Set a time limit of three minutes. When eliciting the words, introduce two key words for the lesson into the discussion – *rhythm* and *beat*.

SPEAK AND LISTEN

1

- Divide the class into pairs to discuss their answers to the questions.
- Choose different students to report on what their partner has said.

2a

- Elicit ideas from students about how they can transfer spoken information to a table.
- Ask students to read the tips in the HOW TO box. Invite a volunteer to read them aloud.

2b 36

- Explain to students that they will hear different people talking about the music they listen to. Ask them to complete the missing information in the table for each person. Remind them that in the first listening, they should listen for the main ideas only and write down brief notes in the table. In the second listening, they should check their answers and add details to their notes if necessary.
- Play the track twice for students to listen and complete the table.
- Encourage students to compare their answers in pairs before you check them as a class.

ANSWERS / AUDIO SCRIPT 36

1 doing homework 2 running
3 helps her run farther 4 rap 5 working
6 doesn't help her work better because it distracts her

Presenter: So, today's question is about music and how much music can help us do things better. Does music help you do things better?
Marty: Hi. My name's Marty. Does music help me do things better? Sure it does. I always listen to rock music while I'm doing homework. It helps me think much more creatively.
Presenter: Did you know that music has a positive effect on memory? It's extremely good for your brain.
Marty: Really? Seriously? No, I didn't know that.
Presenter: It depends on the music, of course. Apparently, baroque classical music works the best.
Marty: Broke music?
Presenter: Baroque. It's a type of classical music. It has a very steady rhythm of 60 beats a minute.
Marty: That sounds terribly boring.
Jeannine: My name's Jeannine, and music doesn't help me run faster, but it helps me run farther. As you can probably hear, I'm listening to music now. It's pretty extreme.
Presenter: What is it?
Jeannine: Don't laugh. It's heavy metal. There's something about the beat. It helps me get into the rhythm really quickly, and it keeps my energy levels up.
Sergio: Rap songs. They're incredibly good to listen to before a test.
Presenter: Can you tell us your name?
Sergio: Oh, OK. Sorry. I'm Sergio. Yeah – rap songs. They help me get totally focused, and when I go in to the test, I'm ready for anything.
Presenter: Do you have any favorite rap artists?
Sergio: Dustin Dredd. He's really powerful.
Sheila: My name's Sheila. I work weekends here at the mall, and sometimes I listen to music while I work, but it doesn't help me work a lot better.
Presenter: Why not?
Sheila: I find it a little distracting. I enjoy listening to pop songs that I can sing along to. But I can't sing and work at the same time.

MOVE BEYOND FOR TEACHERS

Baroque music

Research reveals that baroque music (e.g., classical music composed by Bach, Handel, Vivaldi, or Corelli) has about 60 beats per minute and stabilizes mental, physical, and emotional rhythms. People who study with baroque music in the background say that they concentrate more deeply and learn information better.

3

- Ask students which tips in the HOW TO box they used to help them in Exercise 2b and encourage them to check them.

REACT

4

- Divide the class into pairs to answer the questions.
- Give the pairs five minutes to discuss the questions. Then ask several pairs to share their ideas with the class.

WORK WITH WORDS

5 37

- Focus students on the table and go over the examples with them. Ask students to write the remaining adverbs of degree in the correct columns according to their intensity.
- Play the track for students to listen and check.
- Play the track again for them to listen and repeat.

ANSWERS / AUDIO SCRIPT 37

1 *a little*, pretty, fairly 2 *a lot*, really, very
3 *extremely*, incredibly, terribly, totally

6 38

- Focus students on the interview excerpts in the box. Play the track for students to listen and complete the sentences with the adverbs from Exercise 5.
- Check answers as a class.
- Play the track again for students to listen and repeat.

ANSWERS / AUDIO SCRIPT 38

1 extremely 2 very 3 terribly 4 pretty 5 really
6 incredibly 7 totally 8 really 9 a lot 10 a little
See Student's Book, page 30, for audio script.

Alternative procedure: more confident classes
Ask students to complete the sentences before you play the track. Then play the track for them to listen and check.

WRITE AND SPEAK

7

- Ask students to first work individually to write their answers. Remind them to use the interviews to help give them ideas and to include at least three adverbs of degree.
- Walk around, monitoring and helping students.
- Divide the class into pairs. Ask students to tell their partner their answer. Encourage them to compare their answers and to try to find at least one similarity and one difference.

Fast finishers
Students who finish early could choose one of the photos and write a description of the person's appearance. Then have them read their text aloud to a partner or the class for them to guess who is being described. Encourage students to use adverbs of degree in their descriptions.

MOVE BEYOND

Ask students to do the **Move Beyond** task on page 71.

Homework

Ask students to write a music survey to interview a partner at the beginning of the next class. Ask them to write down these sentence prompts and complete them to make six questions with a variety of tenses:

Do you … (e.g., have a favorite band or singer?)
What are you … (e.g., listening to these days?)
When was the last time you … (e.g., bought a CD?)
How many … (e.g., songs do you have on your playlists?)
Have you ever … (e.g., listened to baroque music?)
Do you ever … (e.g., sing in the shower?)

In less confident classes, brainstorm an example for each sentence prompt.

GRAMMAR Comparison of adverbs

Compare how people do things

Page 31

STAGE	TIME	FOCUS
GET STARTED		Talk about something you are good at and say how you can further improve.
READ AND LISTEN		Read and listen to a music teacher talking about improvement through practice.
STUDY		Use the text to study comparative and superlative adverbs.
PRACTICE		Practice the target language in written exercises and complete sentences with your opinions.
SPEAK		Exchange opinions and compare your ideas.

Get started

Write this quote by jazz saxophonist James Moody on the board and ask students to say the sentence in their own words:

A wise man practices slowly; a wiser man practices even slower. (You don't get good by doing things quickly.)

Ask students to think about something they are good at (e.g., a sport, a musical instrument, a language) and encourage them to mark on a line where they would situate themselves from *beginner* to *very good* level.

Invite students to reflect on what they have to work on to improve, writing down two main things they need to do in order to achieve this goal.

Ask students to compare and discuss their talent lines with several classmates. You could model this activity first yourself and use the opportunity to recycle comparative and superlative adverbs.

MODEL PRESENTATION

I decided last year that I wanted to take up running again. I was the best in the class at school, but I wasn't as fit as I was then. I decided if I was going to get better, I had to run every day. It's difficult sometimes because it can be cold and rainy, but I go running every day. I've changed my diet to eat more nutritious food and not eat as much sugar. The most important thing for me was to learn how to keep up my rhythm and to breathe in the right way.

READ AND LISTEN Grammar in context

1 (▶39)

- Ask students to read and listen to a music teacher talking about his training and then answer the question.
- Choose a student to say the answer. (*Yes, he believes it's positive.*)

AUDIO SCRIPT (▶39)

See Student's Book, page 31, for audio script.

Alternative procedure: more confident classes

With more confident students, you could play the track with books closed for students to answer the question and then ask them to read the text to check.

STUDY

2

- Ask students to read the explanations and complete the examples with comparative and superlative adverbs.
- Check answers as a class.

ANSWERS

longer; more quickly   the hardest; the most successfully
better; the worst

3

- Ask students to look back at Exercise 1 and complete the examples.

ANSWERS

accurately   quickly

Extra activity

To give students further practice using comparative and superlative adverbs, ask them to write two groups of six names of people (famous singers and musicians they know), six verbs, and six adverbs.

Roll a die to choose one item from each list. Ask students to write a sentence comparing the person in the first list with the person in the second list.

Example: You roll the die four times. You get a 1, a 2, a 3, and a 5.

1 = Rihanna, 2 = Beyoncé, 3 = dance, 5 = bad

Rihanna dances worse than Beyoncé.

Repeat the procedure until they have made sentences with all the people. Decide as a class whether all the sentences make sense and make changes as necessary. Then ask students to make sentences using superlative adverbs; for example, *Rihanna dances the worst*.

PRACTICE

4

- Ask students to read the sentences and choose the correct options.
- Encourage students to compare their answers in pairs before you check them as a class.

ANSWERS

1 the fastest   2 better   3 as fast as   4 more carefully
5 the highest   6 as well as

5 (▶40)

- Explain to students that they are going to complete sentences about a talent show. Ask them if they have ever been in a talent show and what happens there (*singers, dancers, etc., compete to show their ability*).
- Ask them to complete the conversation using comparative and superlative adverbs or adverbs that show equality or inequality.
- Play the track for students to listen and check their answers.

ANSWERS / AUDIO SCRIPT 40

2 more loudly 3 as well 4 more beautifully 5 as high
6 the hardest 7 longer 8 the fastest
See Student's Book, page 33, for audio script.

Extra activity
Ask students to practice saying the conversation in pairs. Ask them to put more emphasis on the stressed words to reproduce the rhythm of English speech.

6

- Ask students to work individually and complete sentences 1-4 with names to give their opinions. Tell them to write original sentences for sentence 5 comparing how two people do something.

SPEAK

7

- Divide the class into pairs to take turns reading their opinions aloud and responding, saying whether they agree or not and giving reasons. Before they start, invite two confident students to complete and read the model conversation aloud.
- Circulate and monitor, helping students if necessary.

Homework

Ask students to research a famous sports star or team. Ask them to write a paragraph using comparative and superlative adverbs to compare the star or team to other stars or teams. Remind them to use the sentences in Exercise 4 to help them structure their writing. In the next class, invite students to read their comparisons to the class.

LANGUAGE & BEYOND *GET ORGANIZED*

Stay on task and avoid distractions

Page 32

STAGE	TIME	FOCUS
GET STARTED		Write excuses for not doing homework.
SPEAK AND READ		Read a comic strip and discuss possible reasons for not doing homework.
DO		Look at tips and discuss what the character in the comic strip could do to stay on task.
REFLECT		Discuss whether you agree or disagree with the REFLECTION POINT.
EXTEND		In groups, look at the importance of staying on task in a variety of professions.

LIFE SKILLS

STAY ON TASK AND AVOID DISTRACTIONS
Learning how to stay on task and avoid distractions can have a great positive impact on your life on a personal and professional level. Effective time management, decision-making skills, discipline, and determination are all key skills for the workplace.

Not staying on task can have negative effects on school grades and career prospects. In a project at school or at work, everyone's actions depend on someone else's. If you are not good at staying on task, you can cause a holdup and may be exposed as the bottleneck in the chain.

All of us can be easily distracted, especially when there is something we don't really want to do. There could be negative reasons why students do not stay on task, such as a fear of failure or not understanding the task. Many people feel frustrated that they have not managed to stay on task and can feel anxious and guilty. In this lesson, students discuss whether they find it difficult to stay on task and look at ways to help them modify their habits.

Get started

Tell the class about some of the excuses you have heard students use when they don't do their homework; for example, *My dog ate my homework! I left it at home by accident! My computer crashed!*

Divide the class into pairs to think of a good excuse to say why they didn't do the homework and write it on a piece of paper.

Collect the pieces of paper and read the excuses aloud a few at a time. Invite students to say whether the excuses are believable or not.

SPEAK AND READ

1

- Divide the class into pairs to read the comic strip and say what reasons Dom gives for not finishing his homework.
- Choose a student to say the answer.

ANSWER
He says it was too difficult and he didn't understand what to do.

2

- Ask the same pairs to think of more possible reasons for Dom not finishing his homework. Before they start, draw students' attention to the expressions in the **PHRASE BYTES** box and encourage them to use these to structure their answers.
- Elicit possible reasons as a class.

DO

3

- Divide the class into groups to read and discuss which tips Dom should follow.
- Ask students to talk about each tip and encourage them to say why each tip could help them stay on task.

Alternative procedure: less confident classes

For less confident classes, briefly recycle the form and use of *should* and *shouldn't* for giving advice.

4

- Ask students to brainstorm other things Dom could do to stay on task.
- Invite students to write their ideas on the board.
- Discuss the ideas as a class and ask students which tips they think are the most relevant for them.

REFLECT

5

- Focus students on the **REFLECTION POINT** and elicit whether they agree or not.
- Lead a class discussion of the questions one by one, choosing different students to share their answers.

Extra activity

Write these quotes from interviews with students on the board. Divide the class into pairs to discuss what comments or advice they would give.

1 *I make a list of things I have to do and put stars next to the most important things.*
2 *I never know if it's better to start with the small tasks or the big one(s) first.*
3 *To get started, I open a folder, create subfolders, and add titles.*
4 *I would finish my homework more quickly if I could type faster.*

EXTEND

6

- Divide the class into groups to discuss when it is important for pilots, teachers, surgeons, and electricians to stay on task.
- Encourage students to do the same for some other jobs.
- Invite different groups to share their answers with the class.

Extra activity

Explain to students that there is a way to organize doing homework, called a Homework Flow Chart.

Draw an example of a flow chart on the board and see if students can tell you how they think a flow chart works (a flow chart is a drawing that represents a process by using a series of lines to show the different choices you can make).

Explain to students that all flow charts have a start and an end point, with a series of instructions and decision boxes in between. Draw these on the board as examples:

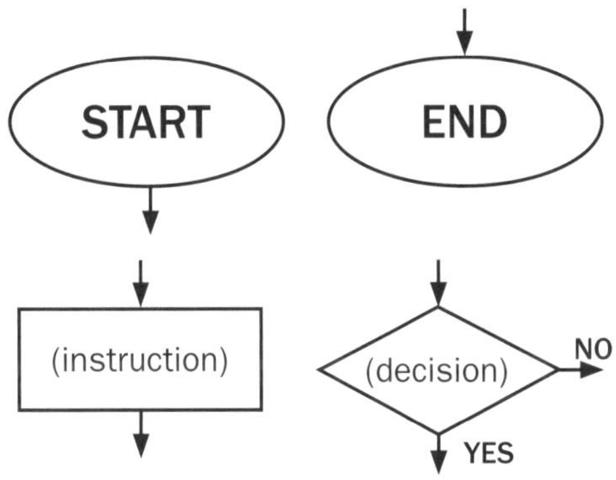

Write the Start sentence on the board: *Do you have homework to do?*

Divide the class into pairs to make a flow chart of the steps they would take to do their homework. Ask them to think about things that can distract them from their task.

Encourage students to compare their ideas with another pair and ask some students to come up and draw their flow charts on the board.

Homework

Ask students to write a short text to describe where they usually work and distractions they have around them. Ask them to choose three of the tips from today's lesson and explain how they are going to implement changes to help them stay on task and avoid distractions. In the next class, have students share their ideas in pairs or small groups.

SPEAKING My sister thinks ...

Present other people's opinions Page 33

STAGE	TIME	FOCUS
GET STARTED		Play a game to recycle adverbs of degree and comparative adverbs.
SPEAK		Discuss your favorite singers or groups.
LISTEN		Listen to a conversation between two people talking about other people's opinions (speaking subskill). Practice sentence stress for emphasizing and contrasting information.
ACT		Prepare and present a scene where you talk about different opinions.

Get started

Play a game of *Three in a Row* (see Games, page 29) with the grid below. To win a square, teams take turns choosing a square and making a grammatically correct sentence with an adverb of degree or a comparative or superlative adverb. The sentence must be related to the topic given; for example, [music] *I think Adele gave a really great performance.* [sports] *Usain Bolt runs faster than any other runner.*

Sports	Countries	Singers/groups
Music	Movies	Jobs
Food and drink	Famous people	Places

SPEAK

1

- Divide the class into pairs to complete the tasks. Set a time limit of five minutes.
- Choose different students to tell the class about the singers and groups on their lists and their partners' lists.

LISTEN

2 ▶41

- Ask students: *What do you think the couple in the photo are doing?* (listening to music); *Do you think they like what they're listening to?*
- Have students close their books. Play the conversation for them to listen and decide what Veena wants to ask Finn's sister.
- Ask students to read the conversation and check their answers.

ANSWER / AUDIO SCRIPT ▶41

Veena wants to ask Finn's sister what Finn thinks about a band because he won't say.

Veena: What do you think?
Finn: My sister thinks they're great. She has all their albums.
Veena: You're lucky. My sister really hates them.
Finn: Why?
Veena: She says they can't sing. She says they're terrible.
Finn: Oh yeah. A lot of people didn't like their last concert.
Veena: People are always saying bad things about them.
Finn: Maybe they're right. My brother says they don't play their instruments.
Veena: I don't care what other people think. I think they're totally amazing.
Finn: Good.
Veena: So what's your opinion?
Finn: What?
Veena: You've told me what everyone else thinks. What about you? What do you think?
Finn: Honestly? I don't have an opinion.
Veena: Liar. I'll have to ask your sister.

3 ▶41

- Focus students on the conversation and encourage them to write in as many of the missing words as they can.
- Play the conversation again for students to listen and check, or complete, their answers.

ANSWERS

See underlining in Exercise 2.

4 ▶42

- Play the track for students to listen and repeat, paying special attention to the words that are stressed. You could drill the sentences chorally and individually.

ANSWERS / AUDIO SCRIPT ▶42

1 My sister thinks they're great.
2 My sister really hates them.
3 She says they can't sing.
4 She says they're terrible.
5 People are always saying ...
6 My brother says ...

Extra activity

Divide the class into pairs to read the conversation aloud. Encourage them to pay special attention to the words that are stressed.

5

- Divide the class into pairs to discuss the questions.
- After a few minutes, invite different students to give their answers. Note that different answers are possible.

ACT

6 ▶43

- Divide the class into groups of three or four to complete the tasks.
- First, ask students to talk about things they like and find something they have different opinions about.
- Then ask students to prepare a scene similar to the conversation in Exercise 2. Remind them to include different opinions and other people's opinions. Before they start, play the track with the expressions in the PHRASEBOOK box and encourage students to use them.
- Invite groups to present their scenes to other groups.

Alternative procedure: less confident classes

In less confident classes, students may need to practice the conversation in a more structured way. Copy this structure onto the board and elicit key sentences for each stage. Ask students to act out the conversation in pairs and then ask them to form different pairs and try to perform the conversation without looking at the board.

Student A	Student B
Ask for an opinion about a band or a singer.	Say what someone else thinks.
Ask why.	Give a reason for the other person's opinion.
Ask what B's opinion is.	Give your opinion.
Agree or disagree and say what other people think.	Agree or disagree with what A says.

Homework

Ask students to research opinions about a singer or group of their choice and write a short report with the results.

Give them these general guidelines: *Summarize what people have said and don't go into too much detail. Say who made each comment. Say what you have discovered and write a sentence or two to sum up your report.*

In the next class, ask students to read and discuss their reports in small groups.

WRITING My music profile

Link contrasting ideas

Page 34

STAGE	TIME	FOCUS
GET STARTED		Discuss music you have listened to or played over the last week and recycle music vocabulary from the unit.
SPEAK AND READ		Read a music profile and talk about a famous musician. Learn how to link contrasting ideas with *but*, *although*, *even though*, and *however* (writing subskill).
PRACTICE		Link sentences together to make them more complex.
DISCUSS		Find out about a partner's favorite musicians or bands.
WRITE		Write a profile about a musician or band member.
SHARE		Share profiles and compare opinions of musicians.

Get started

Ask students to work individually and write five sentences about all the different types of music they have played or listened to over the last week. Encourage them to use at least five words from this unit in their sentences.

Invite students to read their sentences aloud to a partner for the partner to listen and write down all the words connected to music.

Ask students to discuss each other's sentences and find two similarities and two differences.

SPEAK AND READ

1

- Refer students to the young man in the photo. Divide the class into pairs to discuss what kind of music they think he plays. Don't confirm the answer at this point. Before they start, focus students on the expressions in the PHRASE BYTES box and encourage them to use these in their answers.

2

- Ask students to read the music profile to check their answer to Exercise 1.
- Ask them if they are surprised by the answer.

ANSWER

Lang Lang is a classical pianist.

MOVE BEYOND FOR TEACHERS

Lang Lang

At the age of two, Lang Lang fell in love with music when he watched the Tom and Jerry episode "The Cat Concerto," which features Hungarian Rhapsody no. 2 by Franz Liszt. According to Lang, this first contact with Western music was what motivated him to learn piano. When Lang was nine years old, he had some difficulties with his lessons and he was expelled from his piano tutor's studio for "lack of talent." The music teacher at his state school and his family encouraged Lang to keep playing.

Extra activity

Write the following statements on the board and ask students to say whether they are true or false and to correct the false ones.

Lang Lang came from a rich background. (False – He grew up in a poor area of Beijing, and his family didn't have much money.)

His piano teacher helped make Lang Lang famous. (False – His piano teacher told him that he had no talent and should stop playing.)

He practiced a lot to become a star. (True – He practiced night and day.)

Everybody likes Lang Lang. (False – Some people don't like his music.)

3a

- Ask students to read the tips in the HOW TO box. Invite a volunteer to read them aloud.

3b

- Elicit the linking words to contrast ideas that appear in the HOW TO box. Ask students to underline these words in the text and say which word appears twice.

ANSWER

However appears twice.

PRACTICE

4

- Ask students to link the sentences together using the words in parentheses. If necessary, go over the first one as an example with the class.
- Encourage students to compare their sentences in pairs before you check them as a class.

ANSWERS

1 Although Lang Lang's teacher said he had no talent, he managed to become successful.
2 He grew up in China. When he was 15, however, he moved to the United States. / He grew up in China. However, when he was 15 he moved to the United States.
3 He normally records classical music, but he has also recorded music for video games.
4 Even though he lives a rock star's life, he finds time to help young people play music.

DISCUSS

5

- Ask students to work in pairs to find out about their partner's favorite musicians or bands and why their partner likes them.
- To make the activity more challenging, tell students that they will each have only three minutes to find out as much as they can from their partner. Encourage them to ask relevant questions to find out more information.
- Let students decide who will be Student A and who will be Student B.
- Start by asking Student As to interview Student Bs. Remind them of the three-minute time limit and count down from five as the three minutes comes to an end.
- Repeat the process with Student Bs interviewing Students As.
- Invite individual students to tell the class what they learned about their partner's musical tastes.

WRITE

6

- Explain that you would like students to write a profile of a musician or band member that they like.
- Refer students to Steps 1 and 2 in the box and tell them that these steps are a guide to the content they should include in their profile.
- Have them read through Steps 1 and 2 and underline *how* and the *wh-* words, as these introduce key content points. Ask individual students to say what words they underlined and what information the question words refer to (e.g., *when and where the person was born, how the person became interested in music*).
- Remind students that an important part of their profile should be to contrast their opinions with the opinions of other people. Refer them to the HOW TO box and tell them to use the linking words in their texts. Set a time limit of 10 minutes for writing.

Alternative procedure

Students need a lot of practice writing under test conditions. It is a good idea to practice this during the year at different points. You could set up Exercise 6 as a simulation of a writing test. Tell students that they have a time limit of 18 minutes and that they must write at least 80–100 words. Make sure that students have only the things allowed in a real test and that their books are closed. If possible, give them a blank piece of paper to write on.

Collect the texts and grade them in a similar way to how they are graded on a test at this level. Give out the grades in the next class and discuss the different areas students are assessed on in writing, as well as any difficulties they had when writing under test conditions.

SHARE

7

- Ask students to stand up and move around the room sharing their profiles with different classmates by reading aloud and listening.
- When students have spoken to three or four classmates, ask them to take their seats. Find out what kinds of music and which musicians are the class favorites. Encourage students to compare and contrast their opinions in a class discussion.

Homework

Ask students to research another famous person who was told he or she had no talent and would never succeed (e.g., *J. K. Rowling, Walt Disney, Michael Jordan, Steven Spielberg*). Ask them to bring their stories to share with others at the beginning of the next class. Ask them to write notes to help them present their information orally. Tell students that you will collect their written notes and grade them.

VOCABULARY Music words

1

- Divide the class into pairs to look at the words in the box and say what they mean. Encourage them to circle any words they don't remember.
- Ask students to work individually to read and complete the poster with the words in the box. Point out that they can use the pictures to help them.
- Encourage them to compare their answers in pairs and to say if they now remember the meaning of any items they circled earlier. Then check answers as a class.

ANSWERS
1 audience 2 venue 3 performance 4 opera
5 Orchestra 6 conductor 7 jazz 8 trumpet
9 folk 10 flute 11 brass band 12 bands

Adverbs of degree

2

- Invite students to look quickly at the quotes by members of the audience after Justin's concert and to say if most people thought it was good or bad. (*Most people thought it was good.*)
- Ask students to complete the quotes with adverbs of degree. Point out that the first letter of each missing word is given.
- Choose different students to read each of the quotes aloud, asking them to exaggerate the intonation on the adverb of degree.
- Check the spelling of the answers by inviting students to write them on the board.

ANSWERS
1 really 2 fairly 3 little 4 totally 5 pretty
6 extremely 7 very 8 terribly 9 incredibly
10 little

GRAMMAR Verbs followed by gerunds or infinitives

3

- Explain to students that they are going to read an interview with Justin.
- Ask them to complete the interview with either the gerund or the infinitive form of the verbs in parentheses.
- Check answers as a class. Then divide the class into pairs to read the conversation aloud.

ANSWERS
1 coming 2 playing 3 to finish
4 working / to work 5 playing / to play
6 performing / to perform 7 being / to be
8 to spend

Comparison of adverbs

4

- Encourage students to read the news story about Justin's concert quickly and say whether he played well or badly (*badly*).
- Ask them to complete the story with the correct form of the adverbs, reminding them to add *as* where necessary.
- Choose different students to read their answers aloud to the class.

ANSWERS
1 faster 2 the hardest 3 as well 4 as quickly
5 longer 6 harder

Extra Resources

Go to the Teacher's Resource Center at mee2.macmillaneducation.com for:

- downloadable audio and audio scripts for the Student's Book and Workbook;
- videos and video scripts;
- extra vocabulary at two levels of difficulty;
- extra grammar at two levels of difficulty;
- CLIL lessons, with full teacher's notes;
- a life skills lesson, with full teacher's notes;
- Speaking Database materials;
- the *Move Beyond Level 5* wordlist;
- tips for using the Grammar Database;
- and more!

Go to Workbook pages 104–115 for further practice material.

UNIT 4 VERY IMPORTANT PEOPLE

IN THE PICTURE Relationships

Talk about people you know

Pages 36–37

STAGE	TIME	FOCUS
GET STARTED		Introduce the topic of the lesson and talk about relationships.
WORK WITH WORDS		Recycle ways to describe people's appearance and character. Review the difference between *What's she like?* and *What does she look like?* Learn new words related to people and relationships. Describe relationships and personalities. Watch a video of a teenager making a relationship tree and talking about the people on it.
SPEAK		Make your own relationship tree and talk about people you know well, acquaintances, and relatives.

Get started

Write the initials of these famous couples on the board: *Romeo and Juliet*, *Mickey Mouse and Minnie Mouse*, *Brad Pitt and Angelina Jolie*.

Invite students to complete their names. If they are not sure, invite them to ask you some *Yes/No* questions to help them guess.

Divide the class into pairs to think of as many famous couples as they can from history or modern day, real or fictional. Set a time limit of two minutes for this. The pair with the most couples on their list will be the winner. When the time is up, invite students to write their famous couples on the board. Encourage students to say whether they think they are good couples together and to describe them. Prompt them with questions if necessary. Recycle *What's he/she like?* and *What does he/she look like?*

> **Extra activity**
>
> Display a picture of a famous person or couple. Write on the board: *What does he/she look like?* and elicit answers from different students. Recycle hair color, eye color, height, and weight; for example, *He/She has blond hair and blue eyes. He/She's tall, handsome/beautiful ...* . Then repeat the procedure with *What's he/she like?*; for example, *He/She's funny, intelligent, friendly ...* .
>
> Show students a different picture and ask them to work in pairs to ask and answer the two questions.

WORK WITH WORDS

1a and 1b RECALL

- Divide the class into pairs to do both tasks. Refer students to the instructions and set a time limit of three minutes.
- Ask students to complete the sentences with the words in the box.
- Encourage students to make a list of four other ways to complete each answer.
- Elicit and check answers as a class.
- Ask students to do the **Work with Words** task on page 72.

> **ANSWERS**
>
> Exercise 1a
>
> She's bad-tempered / patient / shy.
> She's tall. And she has a small nose / wavy hair.

2

- Divide the class into pairs to take turns describing a person in the photos for their partner to guess.

3 ▶44

- Explain to students that they will hear some definitions of relationships for them to match to the words. Play the track, pausing after the first definition to point out the example.
- Encourage students to compare their answers in pairs. Don't confirm the answers at this point.

> **ANSWERS / AUDIO SCRIPT** ▶44
>
> See Exercise 4 for answers.
>
> 1 A really good friend
> 2 Somebody who lives near you
> 3 A friend who you've known for a long time
> 4 Somebody in your class at school
> 5 Somebody who you communicate with on the internet
> 6 Somebody who comes to your home to visit
> 7 A member of your family who doesn't usually live with you
> 8 Somebody you're having a romantic relationship with
> 9 A friend's friend, not your friend
> 10 Somebody who plays on the same team as you
> 11 Somebody that you know a little, but not a good friend
> 12 The opposite of a friend

Extra activity 44

Play the track again and ask students to write down key words. Then ask students to work in small groups and compare their notes. One person in each group acts as "secretary" to write down the definitions. Encourage them to try to reconstruct the whole definitions. When they have finished, play the track again for students to compare their definitions to the original ones.

4 45

- Play the track for students to listen and check their answers. Ask students which key words helped them decide on their answers.
- Play the track again for students to repeat the words. Point out the silent letters in *friend* and *guest*.

ANSWERS / AUDIO SCRIPT 45

1 *close friend* 2 neighbor 3 old friend 4 classmate
5 online friend 6 guest 7 relative 8 boyfriend/girlfriend
9 friend of a friend 10 teammate 11 acquaintance
12 enemy

5 46

- Explain to students that they are going to listen to Louise talking about people on her relationship tree. Play the track for students to listen and write a relationship from Exercise 2 next to each name. Encourage them to write down the person's personality too, if the information is given.

ANSWERS / AUDIO SCRIPT 46

Mel: old friend Nicola: friend of a friend; shy
Jack: neighbor Matt: close friend; smart
Donna: relative; cheerful, kind, friendly

Mia: Who's that girl with the red hair?
Louise: That's Mel. She's a really old friend. Our moms are friends, so I've known her all my life.
Mia: And that girl? The one who looks really confident. Is she really ambitious?
Louise: That's Nicola. She's one of Marc's friend's. And she's not confident or ambitious at all. She's really very shy.
Mia: And that boy?
Louise: That's Jack. He lives next door to us, so I see him almost every day.
Mia: Is that his real hair color?
Louise: No, he has dark hair, but he dyes it blond.
Mia: Ooh, look. There's your boyfriend!
Louise: Matt is not my boyfriend. We're just really good friends.
Mia: He's very good-looking. And so smart too!
Louise: Well, he was good-looking, but his hair's too short now. He looked better with long hair.
Mia: And that woman with the big smile?
Louise: She's my aunt Donna. She lives in Australia, but we video chat every month.
Mia: She looks cheerful.
Louise: Yeah, she's one of those really kind, friendly people.

6 46

- Play the track again for students to match the people described in Exercise 5 to the corresponding photos.

ANSWERS

Mel – picture 3 Nicola – picture 8 Jack – picture 4
Matt – picture 1 Donna – picture 5

7 THE MOVING PICTURE

- Explain to students that they are going to watch a video of Alexa making a relationship tree.
- Ask students to write down the names of the people and their relationship with her.

ANSWERS / VIDEO SCRIPT

1 Rico – old friend
2 Anna – aunt
3 Tim – neighbor
4 Lucy – online friend
5 Samantha – best friend

This is Rico. He's an old friend. We met at elementary school when we were just six years old. He's cool.

This is my aunt, Anna. She's married to my mom's brother. She's really nice, and she buys me nice presents too. I really like her.

This is my neighbor, Tim. He likes watching movies. He has a big collection of them.

This is Lucy. She's my online friend. We only talk on Fridays. She loves talking, and she lives in Australia.

This is Samantha. She's my best friend. We love playing soccer together at school. I really love this photo.

SPEAK

8a

- Ask students to draw their own relationship tree.

8b

- Divide the class into pairs to talk about the people on their relationship trees. Before they start, draw students' attention to the expressions in the PHRASE BYTES box and encourage them to use these in their conversations.
- Choose different students to tell the class one interesting thing about their partner's relationship tree.

Alternative procedure: less confident classes

In less confident classes, you could draw a relationship tree on the board for yourself and model this activity first with students. Ask them to ask you questions about some of the people, and tell them about the others.

MOVE BEYOND

Ask students to do the **Move Beyond** task on page 72.

Homework

Ask students to write about the people on their relationship tree using the vocabulary and expressions they have learned in this lesson. In the next class, have students talk about the people on their relationship trees in pairs or small groups.

READING Close friends

Recognize examples

Page 38

STAGE	TIME	FOCUS
GET STARTED		Tell a famous short story about two close friends to introduce the topic of the lesson.
SPEAK AND READ		Define what a close friend is and talk about how many close friends people generally have. Read a text about the important qualities of a close friendship. Discuss tips on how to recognize examples when you read and find example sentences in the text (reading subskill).
REACT		Discuss close friends and which qualities are most important in a close friendship.

Get started

Draw these simple stick pictures on the board:

Explain to students that you are going to tell them a short story from India and that they must put the pictures in order.

Two boys, Raju and Vijay, were good friends. They were on vacation together and they went for a walk in the forest. They were enjoying the walk when suddenly they saw a bear coming toward them. They were frightened. Raju knew how to climb up a tree, so he ran to the nearest tree and climbed up quickly. He did not think of Vijay. Vijay didn't know how to climb a tree. He thought for a second. He remembered that animals do not like dead bodies. He fell to the ground and did not move. The bear looked at him and thought he was dead, so he went away.

Raju asked Vijay, "What did the bear say to you?"

Elicit students' ideas about what they think the bear said and then tell students the ending: *Vijay replied, "The bear told me to keep away from friends like you," and he went on his way.*

Write the expression *A friend in need is a friend indeed* on the board. Ask students what it means. (*A true friend is someone who helps you when you need them.*) Elicit whether they have similar expressions in their culture.

SPEAK AND READ

1

- Divide the class into pairs to discuss and answer the questions. Set a time limit of two minutes for this.
- Choose different students to report on what their partner said.

2 47

- Explain to students that they are going to read an article about close friends. Don't play the audio at this point. It is an extra feature, and a suggestion for using it in class is included at the end of the lesson.
- Ask students to read the article and match the friendship qualities in the box to the paragraph headings 1–5.
- Encourage students to compare their answers in pairs before you check them as a class. Elicit the number of close friends we have according to the article.

ANSWERS

1 Respect 2 Honesty 3 Support 4 Good company
5 Trust
The survey says that we generally have just two close friends.

Fast finishers

Ask fast finishers to do a word-building exercise with the word *friend* and think of as many words as they can (*unfriendly*, *friendly*, *friendless*, *friendship*, *friendliness*, *befriend*).

3a

- Ask students why examples are important when they read a text. (*They make things easier to understand and help us follow the logic in arguments.*)
- Refer students to the tips in the HOW TO box. Invite volunteers to read the tips aloud.

3b

- Ask students to read the text again and underline the four expressions that come before examples.

ANSWERS

For instance, if you count everybody ...
... people you don't usually meet, like online friends, ...
... you *don't* want to hear, such as pointing out ...
... things like hobbies and interests ...

3c

- Explain to students that the first sentence in two of the sections is an example. Encourage them to compare their thoughts in pairs before you ask them to identify the two sections as a class.

ANSWERS

3 Support 4 Good company (Both sentences are examples of what a good friend is.)

4

- Ask students which tips in the HOW TO box they used to help them in Exercises 3b and 3c and encourage them to check them.

Extra activity

Have students close their books. Dictate these unfinished sentences and ask students to complete them from memory. Encourage them to read the article again to either complete or check their answers.

1 Some people have thousands of friends if they include …
2 If you respect your close friends, you don't want …
3 Sometimes a close friend needs to tell you things …
4 If other people are giving you problems, a close friend will …
5 To be good friends with someone, it isn't necessary to …
6 Close friends don't talk about you …

ANSWERS

1 online friends 2 them to change
3 you don't want to hear 4 defend you
5 have hobbies and interests in common 6 behind your back

REACT

5

- Divide the class into pairs to discuss the questions.
- Choose different students to share their points of view with the class, giving their reasons. Try to develop a class discussion on the different points. You could ask some general questions to open the discussion; for example, *How many good friends do you have? How do you know you have a good friend? What can change a friendship?*

Extra activity

Write these prompts on the board: *How you met*; *How long ago you met*; *What special qualities he/she has*; *How often you see each other*; *How he/she makes you feel*; *How long you think you'll stay friends*.

Ask students to work in pairs to tell each other about a close friend. You could model this activity by telling students about a close friend of yours.

Recorded reading text 47

The reading text is recorded as an extra audio track that can be exploited for various purposes.

Use the audio in this lesson to help students identify where the words and phrases that come before examples are. Give students a sound or action for each word or phrase (*like*, *such as*, *for instance*; e.g., a clap for *like*). Play the track before Exercise 3b and ask students to do the sound or action when they hear the relevant example words or phrases.

MOVE BEYOND

Ask students to do the **Move Beyond** task on page 72.

Homework

Ask students to write a short text about a close friend of theirs, based on the prompts in the extra activity. Ask students to give examples to illustrate their friend's special qualities. In the next class, have students read their texts aloud in pairs or small groups.

GRAMMAR First conditional with *if/unless*

Talk about possible situations in the future *Page 39*

STAGE	TIME	FOCUS
GET STARTED		Talk about Murphy's Law and introduce the first conditional form.
READ AND LISTEN		Read and listen to a conversation about who a girl wants to invite to her birthday barbecue.
STUDY		Use the conversation to complete examples with the first conditional with *if/unless*.
PRACTICE		Transform sentences in the first conditional so that they have the same meaning. Complete first conditional sentences in a conversation.
WRITE AND SPEAK		Write your ideas about friends and relationships and discuss them in pairs.

Get started

Ask students if they have ever heard of Murphy's Law. Write the following words on the board in a random order and ask students to make a complete sentence that expresses the idea behind Murphy's Law.

will / can / If / wrong, / anything / wrong / go / it / go / .
(If anything can go wrong, it will go wrong.)

Explain this law in other words (*if there is any possibility that something will go wrong, it will go wrong*) and give a couple of examples: *If you're early, the bus is late. If you're late, the bus is early.*

Write these sentence beginnings on the board and ask students to work in pairs to complete the examples of Murphy's Law: *If you wear something expensive*; *If you drop a piece of toast*; *If you are doing something dumb*; *If you go out in your worst clothes*; *If you try to stand in a shorter line.*

Elicit answers from different pairs around the class. Invite volunteers to create further examples.

MOVE BEYOND FOR TEACHERS

Murphy's Law

Murphy's Law was born at Edwards Air Force Base in 1949. It was named after Captain Ed Murphy, an engineer working on an air force project. He was frustrated with a technician and famously remarked, "If there is any way to do it wrong, he will."

READ AND LISTEN Grammar in context

1 48

- Refer students to the photo and ask them to describe what is happening. (*Two students/friends are talking.*)
- Play the track for students to read and listen to find out who Olga wants at her birthday barbecue.

ANSWER / AUDIO SCRIPT 48

Tim, Dan, and Bea
See Student's Book, page 39, for audio script.

STUDY

2

- Focus students on the grammar explanations and ask them to complete the examples from the conversation in Exercise 1.
- Choose students to read the grammar explanations and example sentences aloud.
- To further explain the first conditional with *if/unless*, divide the board into two halves. Write *POSSIBLE SITUATION* on the left side and *RESULT* on the right side. Then write, in the left column, two possible situations: *If I study, ...* ; *Unless we finish quickly, ...* .
- Explain that the *if* clause describes a possible situation. Highlight that we use the simple present in the *if* clause.
- Point out that we can use *unless* instead of *if* with an affirmative verb to mean "if not," so the example on the board means "If we don't finish quickly."
- Complete the sentences on the right: *I will pass the exam*; *we'll be late*. Analyze the grammar, pointing out that we use the simple future with *will* + base verb in the result clause. Alternatively, we can use *may* or *might* + base verb depending on how certain we are of the result.
- Refer students back to the conversation to find another example of the first conditional. (*If I invite Tim, he'll probably argue with Dan.*)

ANSWERS

talk invite

Extra activity

Students may need more controlled practice with the first conditional form before doing Exercise 3. Write these sentences on the board and ask students to work in pairs to fill in the blanks with the correct form of the verbs in parentheses:

1 If he ______ late (arrive) again, the trainer ______ (be) angry.
2 You ______ (fail) if you ______ (not study) for your English exam.
3 Unless you ______ (do) your homework now, you ______ (be) stressed.
4 I ______ (be) late unless the bus ______ (come) soon.

ANSWERS

1 arrives; will be 2 will fail; don't study 3 do; will be
4 will be; comes

PRACTICE

3

- Focus students on the pairs of sentences and point out that they have to mean the same thing. Invite two students to read the first sentence and the example aloud. Ask students to complete the second sentence in each pair and remind them to use no more than three words.
- Encourage students to compare their answers in pairs before you check them as a class.

ANSWERS

2 you don't send 3 if he can't 4 Unless you invite
5 unless we clean 6 if people don't

4 ▶49

- Ask students to read the conversation and choose the correct options to complete it.
- Play the track for them to listen and check their answers.

ANSWERS / AUDIO SCRIPT ▶49

1 won't 2 's 3 says 4 will 5 might say 6 'll stop
7 're 8 will stop

See Student's Book, page 41, for audio script.

Extra activity

Ask students to work in pairs to practice reading the conversation aloud, paying attention to sentence stress and rhythm.

If you feel it would be useful before students read the conversation aloud, do some choral drilling and/or back-chaining to practice the rhythm (see Teaching Tips, *Vary drilling techniques*, page 30).

Fast finishers

Ask fast finishers to look at the text on page 38 and find as many examples as they can of first conditional sentences.

WRITE AND SPEAK

5

- Ask students to work individually to complete the sentences with their own ideas.

6

- Divide the class into pairs to take turns reading their sentences from Exercise 5 aloud. Encourage students to say whether they agree or not and to explain why.
- Invite students to read some of their sentences aloud for discussion as a class.

Homework

Ask students to write a first conditional chain of at least five sentences. Each sentence must begin with the idea expressed in the second half of the previous sentence. Ask students to help you build an example on the board; for example, *If I bring an umbrella, it won't rain. If it doesn't rain, I won't get wet. If I don't get wet, I'll wear my new coat. If I wear my new coat, my mom might be happy. If my mom's happy, I may get a nice dinner. If I get a nice dinner, I'll sleep really well. If I sleep really well, I'll have a good day tomorrow!* In the next class, ask several students to write their sentences on the board. Ask the class to help make any necessary corrections.

LISTENING AND VOCABULARY Back from the future

Use stress and intonation to help you understand Page 40

STAGE	TIME	FOCUS
GET STARTED		Recycle words to describe a good friend and think about words to describe the worst friend ever.
SPEAK AND LISTEN		Look at a picture and predict the situation. Listen to a podcast to see if your predictions were correct. Use stress and intonation to help you understand (listening subskill).
WORK WITH WORDS		Match extreme adjectives to their definitions.
REACT		Imagine you're 34 years old and describe your situation, what you look like, and how you feel.

Get started

Draw a picture of two smiling faces on the board and write *Good Friends* next to the picture.

Write this sentence as a word snake (with no space between words) under the face and ask students to find five important qualities in a close friendship: G*ood friends accept you the way you are, tell the truth, share your ideas, are generous with their time, and can keep a secret.*

Draw a picture of a mischievous face and write *Worst Friend Ever* next to the picture.

Divide the class into pairs to make a word snake with five undesirable qualities. Ask students to exchange their word snakes with another pair for them to figure out the five undesirable qualities. Ask students to discuss in groups of four which undesirable quality is the worst. Choose different students to report on the discussion in their group.

SPEAK AND LISTEN

1

- Refer students to the picture. Divide the class into pairs to discuss the questions.
- Choose different students to share their ideas.

2a

- Ask students to read the tips in the HOW TO box. Invite a volunteer to read them aloud.

2b 50

- Play the track for students to listen to a podcast and check their predictions in Exercise 1.

ANSWERS / AUDIO SCRIPT 50

A 34-year-old woman woke up with a memory problem and thought she was 15 again. In the picture, we see her looking at herself in the mirror. The mirror shows how she really looks, and the teenager looking in the mirror shows how she thinks she looks.

Victor: Hi, this is Victor Sanchez.
Linda: And this is Linda Frantum. Welcome to this week's episode of *Stranger than Fiction*, the podcast that looks at some amazing real stories.
Victor: So what's this week's story, Linda?
Linda: Let me start with a question. What would you do if you woke up one morning and you were 34 years old?
Victor: I'd be furious! I love being 15! But that's impossible.
Linda: Naomi Jacobs thought this had happened to her.
Victor: I don't understand.
Linda: Her story starts when she woke up one morning and didn't recognize where she was. So she called out to see who was there, and she didn't recognize her own voice. But things got really scary when she found the bathroom. When she looked in the mirror, she was shocked to see her own face – she looked ancient. She looked exhausted too, with huge black bags under her eyes.
Victor: That's awful. If that happened to me, I'd be terrified. But I still don't understand.
Linda: She was suffering from a really rare condition when your brain deletes all your recent memories. So it's like going back in time to before you had those memories. Naomi was 34, but when she woke up, she really thought she was 15.
Victor: That's unbelievable! So did she get her memory back?
Linda: She did, but it took a long time. And she had to learn about a whole new world. Just imagine how you'd feel if somebody told you that you were actually a mother with a young child. And, if you didn't know what a smartphone was, or how to use the internet.
Victor: It's hard to imagine. That really is a fascinating story.
Linda: Yep. Life really can be ... stranger than fiction!

3

- Ask students which tips in the HOW TO box they used to help them in Exercise 2b and encourage them to check them.

4 50

- Play the track again for students to listen and choose the correct options.
- Encourage them to compare their answers in pairs before you check them as a class.

ANSWERS / AUDIO SCRIPT 50

1 is 2 didn't hear 3 recognized 4 an unusual
5 didn't remember 6 slowly
See Exercise 2b for audio script.

WORK WITH WORDS

5

- Ask students to match the underlined adjectives in the podcast excerpts to the definitions.
- Encourage them to compare their answers in pairs before you check them as a class.

ANSWERS

1 very good or surprising 2 very angry
3 very surprised (in a negative way) 4 very old 5 very tired
6 very big 7 very bad 8 very scared
9 very hard to believe 10 very interesting

Extra activity

Read this short text aloud and ask students to raise their hands (or clap) to stop you every time you say *very* + adjective. Do not read the extreme adjectives in parentheses. These are examples of adjectives that students could use to replace the adjectives you read. Invite students to suggest an extreme adjective as a replacement each time they clap or raise their hands.

I'm going to tell you a very interesting (fascinating) story. It's about a very old (ancient) man and his very bad (awful) experience. I think you are going to say this story is very hard to believe (unbelievable), but it is true. He was feeling very tired (exhausted) on his daily walk in the park, so he decided to sit down on a park bench. He was very surprised (shocked) when the bench started to move. Under the bench there was a very big (huge) man who was very angry (furious) that someone was sitting on it. At first, the very old (ancient) man was very scared (terrified), but then he said, "Oh my goodness me – it's George, my long-lost son!" That is the end of this very surprising (amazing) story.

If there is time at the end, read both texts aloud to show students the difference and encourage them to use extreme adjectives in their writing.

6 51

- Play the track for students to listen and repeat the adjectives from Exercise 5.

AUDIO SCRIPT 51

amazing furious shocked ancient exhausted huge awful terrified unbelievable fascinating

Extra activity

Ask students to add *really* or an extreme adverb of degree to the podcast excerpts in Exercise 5. Then ask them to work in pairs to read them aloud, exaggerating the extreme adjective to practice emphatic stress (e.g., *absolutely amazing real stories*).

You could point out that stress can also be used on the adverb of degree. Alternatively, stress could be used to emphasize the extreme adjective without the need to use an adverb of degree.

7a

- Refer students back to the adjectives in Exercise 5 and ask them to write three true sentences with different adjectives.

7b

- Divide the class into pairs to take turns reading their sentences aloud to their partner. Encourage them to ask at least one question about each sentence. Before they start, invite two students to read the model conversation aloud.

REACT

8

- Ask students to imagine being in Naomi's situation. Divide the class into pairs to ask each other the questions.
- Choose different students to share their answers.

MOVE BEYOND

Ask students to do the **Move Beyond** task on page 72.

Homework

Ask students to write a short text about The Worst Friend Ever using as many extreme adjectives with *really* and extreme adverbs of degree as they can. Ask them to read their texts aloud to a partner at the beginning of the next class. Partners must say "stop" every time they hear an extreme adjective and must define it by saying *very* and the appropriate adjective.

GRAMMAR Second conditional

Talk about imaginary situations in the present and future *Page 41*

STAGE	TIME	FOCUS
GET STARTED		Race against the clock to recycle regular and irregular past tense forms.
READ AND LISTEN		Read and listen to a conversation about the type of parents two friends think they would be.
STUDY		Read grammar explanations about the second conditional and complete examples.
PRACTICE		Recognize and produce the target language in written exercises.
SPEAK		Exchange opinions and compare ideas about imaginary situations.

Get started

Divide the class into pairs to think of a verb in the simple past tense (not the past participle), either regular or irregular, for each of the letters of the alphabet. Set a time limit of five minutes and give regular updates on the time remaining.

Divide the board into five sections, A–E, F–J, K–O, P–T, and U–Z, and invite students to come up to the board and write the past tense verbs they have for one of the sections.

Recycle the pronunciation of regular simple past forms (i.e., /t/, /d/, and /ɪd/) and check their spelling by inviting the class to point out any words that need correcting.

READ AND LISTEN Grammar in context

1 52

- Refer students to the picture and ask them to describe it. Ask: *How does he feel? What is he thinking?*
- Ask students to read and listen to the conversation and decide what type of parents Raj and Kim think they might be.
- Elicit answers from different students around the class.

ANSWERS / AUDIO SCRIPT 52

Kim would be more easygoing than her parents. Raj would be very strict.
See Student's Book, page 41, for audio script.

STUDY

2

- Point out to students that the verbs in orange in the conversation in Exercise 1 are in second conditional sentences.
- Ask them to read the grammar explanations and complete the examples.
- Check answers as a class.

ANSWERS
had; wouldn't Would would; wouldn't

Extra activity

Give students further practice using the second conditional by asking them some questions about unlikely or imaginary situations. Ask: *What would you do if you won the lottery?* Develop some of their ideas by making follow-up questions out of their answers; for example, *If you bought a new car, what kind of car would you buy?*

Write some other examples on the board and elicit answers; for example, *If you lived on Mars, what would you eat? If you were an animal, which animal would you be? If you didn't live in this country, where would you like to live?*

Make sure students answer with the correct form.

Encourage students to think of three questions in the second conditional to ask their partner. Have them ask and answer the questions, paying attention to the form.

Extra activity

To give students extended practice with the second conditional form and the pronunciation of *'d*, ask students to make a chain around the classroom of second conditional clauses.

Write *If I had a million dollars, …* on the board and ask a student to finish the sentence in his or her own words; for example, *I'd travel around the world.* The next student takes the second clause from the first student's sentence and changes it to the first clause of another sentence to continue using this clause; that is, *If I traveled around the world, I'd go by ship*, etc.

Some other starting sentences could be: *I'd be happy if …* ; *If I lived in another country, …* ; *If I had more money, …* .

PRACTICE

3

- Ask students to match the two parts of the sentences.
- Check answers by choosing different students to read the complete sentences aloud.

ANSWERS
2 b 3 e 4 f 5 c 6 a

Extra activity

Give students 30 seconds to memorize the sentences in Exercise 3. Divide the class into pairs to take turns testing each other. One student closes his or her book and the other student reads the first part of the sentence aloud to see if his or her partner can remember the ending.

4

- Ask students to consider the sentences in Exercise 3 and say whether they are true for them. If they aren't, invite students to change them to make them true.
- Circulate and monitor, helping students with any difficulties.

5

- Ask students to complete the sentences with the correct form of the verbs in parentheses.
- Encourage them to check their answers in pairs before you check them as a class.

ANSWERS
1 woke 2 would / 'd live 3 had 4 would / 'd spend; were 5 could; would / 'd go 6 would give; won

6

- Ask students to write questions for the sentences in Exercise 5.
- Draw students' attention to the example question.

ANSWERS

2 Where would you live if you could study in another country?
3 If you had a special talent, what would you want to be?
4 What would you do on the extra day if there were eight days in a week?
5 If you could travel back in time for a day, where would you go?
6 What would your family do if you won the lottery?

7a 53 PRONOUNCE

- Ask students to read the instructions carefully.
- Play the track for them to listen and underline the stressed words or phrases in the sentences.

ANSWERS / AUDIO SCRIPT 53

A: If you <u>woke</u> up with <u>superpowers</u>, <u>what</u> would you <u>do</u>?
B: I'd <u>fly</u> around the <u>world</u>.
C: I wouldn't do <u>anything</u>. I'd go <u>back</u> to <u>sleep</u>.

Extra activity

Ask students to practice saying the conversation in pairs. Encourage them to put more emphasis on the stressed words to reproduce the rhythm of English speech.

7b 54

- Play the track for students to listen and repeat the sentences, paying attention to their rhythm.

AUDIO SCRIPT 54

See Exercise 7a for audio script.

SPEAK

8

- Divide the class into pairs to ask and answer the questions in Exercise 6, giving reasons for their answers.
- Circulate and monitor, helping students as necessary.

Homework

Ask students to use their imagination to write second conditional sentences using these beginnings: *I'd buy a new computer*; *I'd go to the party*; *If I didn't feel so sick*; *I'd go to the beach*; *If dolphins could speak*; *I would be rich*.

At the beginning of the next class, have students compare sentences and decide which are the most imaginative.

Decide what's important to you

Page 42

STAGE	TIME	FOCUS
GET STARTED		Make a human knot to introduce the topic of decision making and how our decisions affect others.
SPEAK AND READ		Read an activity sheet and discuss a student's answers, what you think she is like, and which options she may choose.
DO		Do the activity sheet and discuss the choices you made with your partner.
REFLECT		Reflect on deciding what is important for you in different areas of life and why making choices can be difficult.
EXTEND		Talk about the choices you might make in the future concerning your studies and work.

LIFE SKILLS

DECIDE WHAT'S IMPORTANT TO YOU

In this lesson, students work on decision making – the process of choosing what to do by considering different options and thinking about their consequences. Decision making becomes increasingly important during adolescence, as teenagers become more autonomous and encounter more choices with less and less parental or teacher support. The choices teenagers make affect their own lives and the lives of others as well.

Get started

Invite six to eight volunteers to come to the front of the class. Ask them to get into a circle and reach across to take the hands of two different people standing on the other side of the circle, but they can't hold hands with the person next to them. When everyone has grabbed hands, you have a human knot. Now challenge students to undo the knot without letting go of each other's hands. Remind participants to take their time and make sure no one gets hurt. Ask students: *What did you do to undo the human knot? How did you make sure no one got hurt?* Tell students that today they are going to be looking at making choices.

SPEAK AND READ

1

- Refer students to the photo and invite them to say what Claire looks like and what they think she's like.
- Focus students on Claire's answers and, after they have read them, encourage them to choose two adjectives from the box to describe her.
- Ask them to compare their chosen words in pairs before you elicit some of them as a class.

2

- Divide the class into pairs to talk about Claire's answers and say which options they think she'll choose in Activity 2 and explain why. Draw students' attention to the expressions in the PHRASE BYTES box and encourage them to use these in their answers.
- Choose different students to share what they think Claire's reasons may be with the class.

DO

3

- Ask students to do Activity 1 on the activity sheet.

4

- Give students 30 seconds to do Activity 2 so that they don't have too much time to reflect.

5

- Divide the class into pairs to explain their choices. Ask students to explain to each other why they made these choices and if there are any choices they would change.

REFLECT

6

- Focus students on the REFLECTION POINT and elicit whether they agree or not.
- Lead a class discussion of the questions, choosing different students to share their answers.

EXTEND

7

- Ask students to repeat the procedure they used in Exercises 3, 4, and 5 for these new questions.
- Choose different students to share their answers and develop a class discussion of the jobs they want to do.

Extra activity

As a class, brainstorm other areas where students will have to make decisions (e.g., *money*, *relationships*, *health*, *where to live*). Discuss what types of decisions they may have to make in the future and which ones are the most critical.

Homework

Ask students to write a sentence for each of these instructions.

Describe a decision that you made a few years ago.
Describe another decision that you made more recently.
Describe a decision that you've made that's been good for you.
Describe a decision that you've made that's been bad for you.

At the beginning of the next class, put students into pairs to ask each other questions about the decisions they've made.

SPEAKING Do you mind?

Make and react to requests

Page 43

STAGE	TIME	FOCUS
GET STARTED		Talk about personal possessions and recycle *lend* and *borrow*.
SPEAK		Discuss who you would talk to if you needed something and what that person's reaction would be.
LISTEN		Listen to a conversation where someone makes requests to different people and note the reactions to these requests. Practice making, accepting, and refusing requests in formal and informal situations (speaking subskill).
ACT		Prepare informal and formal conversations making and reacting to requests in different situations.

Get started

Write this famous old saying on the board: *Neither a borrower nor a lender be*. Ask students if they have heard of this expression and if they know its origin. (It is a quote from Shakespeare's *Hamlet*, Act 1, Scene 3, written in 1602.) Ask what students think the meaning may be (*it's smarter to neither lend nor borrow things, especially money*) and if they have a similar expression in their own culture.

Write this list of objects on the board: *toothbrush, umbrella, homework, cell phone, MP3 player, clothes, pen*.

Ask students if they would be prepared to lend them to someone close to them or someone they don't know very well or if they would never lend them to anyone. Discuss their reasons.

Write *Would you … ?* and *Can I … ?* on the board and ask students to complete the questions using *borrow* and *lend* + noun. If necessary, remind students that the person with the item lends it and the person without the item borrows it. Ask students to work in pairs to practice using the structures in short conversations with their partner. (See Teaching Tips, *Lend or borrow?*, page 25.)

SPEAK

1

- Refer students to the situations and ask them to think about who they would talk to and what the person would probably say in each situation.
- Divide the class into pairs to read the situations and discuss the questions. Set a time limit of three minutes.
- Choose different students to share their answers.

LISTEN

2 55

- Have students close their books. Play the conversation for them to listen and decide who Leo talks to in each situation and who says "no" to his requests.
- Ask students to read the conversations to check their answers.
- Choose a student to say the answers.

ANSWERS / AUDIO SCRIPT 55

In the first conversation, Leo talks to his dad. His dad says he can drive him to the festival, but he can't come to get him afterward.
In the second conversation, Leo talks to Jack, and Jack says, "Sure."
In the third conversation, Leo talks to Mr. Gibb. Mr. Gibb says he can't drive Leo home, but he can use his phone.

Leo: Dad, can you drive me to the festival?
Dad: All right. But you'll have to wait 20 minutes.
Leo: No problem. Can we take Jack too?
Dad: OK.
Leo: Thanks. And can you come and get me later?
Dad: Sorry, I can't. Mom needs the car tonight.

Leo: Jack, could you lend me some money for a drink?
Jack: Sure.
Leo: And do you mind if I use your phone to call Kate?
Jack: No, go ahead.
Leo: Thanks.

Leo: Mr. Gibb, could I ask you a favor?
Mr. Gibb: Of course.
Leo: Would you drive me home, please? My dad can't come and get me, and I think I missed the last bus.
Mr. Gibb: I'm sorry, but there's no space in the car.
Leo: OK. Would you mind if I used your phone to call my mother?
Mr. Gibb: No, of course not. Here you go.
Leo: Thank you.

3 55

- Ask students to complete the conversations with the words in the box.
- Play the conversation again for students to listen and check or complete their answers.

ANSWERS

See underlining in Exercise 2.

4

- Ask students to choose the best option for formal situations, using the conversations to help them.

ANSWERS

1 Could/Would 2 Say 3 Would 4 Of course
5 I'm afraid …

5 ▶56

- Play the track for students to listen and repeat.

AUDIO SCRIPT ▶56

1 **Leo:** Can you drive me to the festival?
Dad: All right.
Leo: Can we take Jack too?
Dad: OK.
2 **Leo:** Could you lend me some money?
Jack: Sure.
Leo: Do you mind if I use your phone?
Jack: No, go ahead.
3 **Leo:** Could I ask you a favor?
Mr. Gibb: Of course.
Leo: Would you drive me home, please?
Mr. Gibb: I'm sorry, but there's no space in the car.

ACT

6 ▶57

- Divide the class into pairs to prepare a formal and informal conversation. Before they start, play the track with the expressions in the PHRASEBOOK box and encourage students to use these.
- Invite students to present their conversations to another pair for them to say who's talking in each conversation and whether it's formal or informal.
- Invite volunteers to present their conversations to the class.

Homework

Ask students to write formal and informal requests with one of these words or phrases in each sentence: *a ride home*, *your calculator*, *$10*, *window*, *salt*.

In the next class, ask students to read their requests aloud to a partner to say whether the request is formal or informal and then accept or refuse appropriately.

WRITING A poem about true friends

Use a dictionary *Page 44*

STAGE	TIME	FOCUS
GET STARTED		Write an acrostic poem and recycle vocabulary related to friendship.
SPEAK AND READ		Talk about poems with a partner. Read a poem about friends and answer questions. Read tips on how to use a dictionary (writing subskill).
PRACTICE		Use a dictionary entry to help answer questions about the word *tear*.
DISCUSS		Talk about best friends.
WRITE		Write a poem about best friends using specific phrases.
SHARE		Exchange your poem with other students and discuss it.

Get started

Ask students to write an acrostic poem with the name of a close friend. Explain that acrostic poems are easy to write. They should write the name of their close friend in capital letters down the left side of the page. They then think of a word that begins with each capital letter to describe their friend. Show the class an example; for example:

J olly
O rganized
E asygoing

As students finish, ask them to read their acrostic poems aloud to a partner to see if their close friends have similar or different qualities. Invite several students to read their poems aloud.

SPEAK AND READ

1

- Divide the class into pairs to answer the questions.
- Choose different students around the class to answer the questions and try to develop a discussion of poetry and famous poets students know and have read. Find out if anyone has ever written a poem.

2

- Focus students on the poem and give them time to read it.
- Then ask them to answer the questions.
- Ask students which lines they agreed with. Ask them if they liked the poem and why or why not.

3a

- Ask students to read the tips in the HOW TO box. Invite a volunteer to read them aloud.

3b

- Ask students to read the poem again and answer the questions.

ANSWERS

1 Students' own answers
2 *brother* rhymes with *other*

PRACTICE

4

- Ask students to use the dictionary entry and the tips in the HOW TO box to help them answer the questions.
- Encourage students to compare their answers in pairs before you choose different students to read their answers aloud.

ANSWERS
1 a noun   2 the third definition   3 with *here*

DISCUSS

5

- Ask students to work in pairs and talk about their best friends, saying what their friends do for them as true friends.
- Tell them to find similarities or differences in the things they like about their best friends.
- You may need to monitor and give them some extra questions; for example, *How much time do you spend with your best friend? Do you think it's important to be able to laugh with your best friend? Does your friendship reflect any of the ideas in the poem? What is the difference between your best friend and other friends?*
- As with any discussion, try to close the activity before you feel students are running out of things to say.

WRITE

6

- Explain that students are going to write their own poems about best friends using the starter phrases (in green) from Exercise 2.
- Choose different students to read each step in the box aloud and check that they all understand what is required of them.
- Make sure you have dictionaries or computers available for students to refer to as they write, and remind them to use the tips in the HOW TO box. Set a time limit of 15 minutes for writing.

Alternative procedure
Some students may find it a challenge to generate ideas for their poem. If you think this is the case, you could offer them the option to write their poem in pairs. Although some students will prefer to work individually, others may find collaboration more motivating for this task.

SHARE

7

- Display students' poems around the room and invite students to move around and read as many poems as possible.
- If your class situation makes it difficult to display the poems, have students work in pairs or small groups to share their work.
- Encourage students to make a note of any lines they particularly liked in their classmates' work and ask them to share these with the class.

Homework

Ask students to research a poem in their own language or in English and copy a short section of the poem into their notebooks. If the poem is in their own language, ask students to find an English translation. If this is not possible, ask them to write down the essential ideas in the poem. At the beginning of the next class, ask students to work in pairs to read their poems aloud. Tell them to say whether they liked their partner's choice and to explain why or why not.

VOCABULARY People and relationships

1

- Ask students what the acronym *VIP* stands for (*very important person*) and invite them to tell their partner who the VIPs are in their own lives.
- Encourage students to match the people and the relationships on the flyer to the definitions. Tell students there is one word in the box that isn't used (*parents*).
- Encourage students to compare their answers in pairs before you check them as a class.

ANSWERS
1 old friends 2 girlfriends/boyfriends 3 relatives
4 online friends 5 enemies 6 close friends
7 teammates 8 neighbors 9 classmates
10 acquaintances 11 guests 12 friends of friends

Extreme adjectives

2

- Refer students to the pictures and ask them to describe the people. Elicit what type of person students think each one is.
- Ask them to complete the adjectives in the description of the picture. Point out that the first and last letter of each adjective are given. (See Teaching Tips, *Adjectives ending in* -ed *and* -ing, page 29.)
- Choose different students to read the text aloud, sentence by sentence, to check answers.

ANSWERS
1 huge 2 ancient 3 terrified 4 furious
5 fascinating 6 exhausted 7 shocked 8 awful
9 amazing 10 unbelievable

GRAMMAR First conditional with *if/unless*

3

- Explain to students that they are going to read some online comments about possible situations.
- Ask students to use the first conditional form to complete the comments.
- Circulate and monitor students and stop midtask if you feel that you need to review the form of the first conditional.
- Check answers as a class.

ANSWERS
1 will miss 2 go 3 respect
4 won't have 5 don't send 6 will / 'll be

Second conditional

4

- Write this rule on the board: *We use the first / second conditional to talk about things in the present or the future that are imaginary, impossible, or not likely to happen*. Ask students to choose which option is correct (*the second conditional*).
- Encourage students to give some examples of second conditional sentences.
- Explain that students are going to read an online discussion.
- Ask students to complete the messages in the discussion.
- Check answers as a class.

ANSWERS
1 would 2 left 3 Would 4 found 5 'd take
6 would never know 7 wouldn't 8 were

Extra Resources

Go to the Teacher's Resource Center at mee2.macmillaneducation.com for:

- the Speaking section of the Progress Check 3&4;
- a downloadable project linked to Units 3–4;
- downloadable audio and audio scripts for the Student's Book and Workbook;
- videos and video scripts;
- extra vocabulary at two levels of difficulty;
- extra grammar at two levels of difficulty;
- culture lessons, with full teacher's notes;
- a life skills lesson, with full teacher's notes;
- Speaking Database materials;
- the *Move Beyond Level 5* wordlist;
- tips for using the Grammar Database;
- and more!

Go to Workbook pages 116–127 for further practice material.

PROGRESS CHECK 3&4

Preparing for the Progress Check

Vocabulary review

- Ask students to write the letters of the alphabet, A–Z, down the left side of a page. Explain that for each letter, you want them to write a word that is related to music. Students work alone initially, and after about a minute, they can compare notes with a partner. After a total of two minutes, ask how many words they have found. Reassure them that they will not find a word for every letter, but some letters will have more than one word (e.g., *opera* and *orchestra*). Go through the alphabet, asking students to tell you the words they have found for each letter.
- To continue with the topic of music and to review adverbs of degree, ask some *Do you like … ?* questions about different types of music. These can include classical, piano music, rock, pop, and jazz, as well as any other types that your students will know. Prompt with follow-up questions to elicit adverbs of degree; for example, *How much do you like it? What do you think of [singer's name]?* Continue the discussion until students have used a range of adverbs of degree, reminding the class that they should expect to find them in the Progress Check.
- Divide the class into pairs to review the vocabulary for people and relationships. Give them two or three minutes to see how many items they can remember and write down. Students then look at the **Words & Beyond** section on page 72 to see if there was anything they missed. Ask different students around the class to give you examples of old friends, online friends, acquaintances, enemies, etc. These can be people they know or fictional characters from TV, books, or movies.
- Ask students to look again at Exercise 5 on page 40. In pairs, students take turns using the extreme adjectives in sentences. You could start by giving them the following example: *I had an amazing time at the party on Sunday.*
- After two or three minutes, get feedback by prompting the class with questions such as *Who can tell me something amazing? When was the last time you were furious? Tell me something you find/found fascinating*.

Grammar review

- Divide the class into pairs and ask them to look back at the grammar pages (pages 29, 31, 39, and 41). The grammar for this Progress Check is as follows:
  - Unit 3: Verbs followed by gerunds or infinitives; Comparison of adverbs
  - Unit 4: First conditional with *if/unless*; Second conditional
- To review verbs followed by gerunds or infinitives, divide the board into two columns. At the top of the left column, write *-ing*. At the top of the right column, write *infinitive*. Ask pairs to decide which student will write each form, and encourage them to write short sentences as examples of the form. For example, Student A could write *I <u>don't mind</u> <u>helping</u> in the house.* Student B could write *I'm going to learn <u>to skate</u>.* Allow five minutes before asking how many sentences each pair has made. Ask students to read their sentences aloud and, as they do so, write the verbs on the board in the correct columns.
- To review comparison of adverbs, write a list of regular and irregular adverbs (e.g., *loudly*, *beautifully*, *well*, *hard*, *badly*, *fast*, *carefully*, *long*) on the board and ask students to say comparative sentences with them. Prompt with sentences such as *I can sing beautifully* to elicit, for example, *I can sing more beautifully than you*. Continue in this way until students have used all the different comparative forms.
- For the Unit 4 grammar, set a time limit of five minutes and ask pairs to write two examples of first conditional sentences and two of second conditional sentences. Ask students to read sentences aloud. Write a variety of these on the board, making sure to include a first conditional with *if*, a first conditional with *unless*, and a second conditional.
- For a little extra practice with the second conditional, ask students to think of hypothetical questions to ask other students. Begin by asking one student: *How would you feel if you had to move to another country?* The student answers (e.g., *I'd be very excited*). The same student then asks someone else a different question, and they continue like this until everyone has spoken.

Optional warm-up activities

READ Exercise 1

- Tell students that they are going to practice reading quickly. Give them up to one minute to look at the people's profiles and find what kind of music each person likes.
- After a minute, ask them to tell you what they have found. Point out that they can expect to find what the people dislike, as well as what they like, in this kind of task.
- Explain that they will have to read the reviews to decide which album would be suitable for each person but that this will be easier because they will now know what they are looking for.

LISTEN Exercise 2

- Remind students of the importance of reading ahead before they listen.
- Since students have recently studied stress and intonation (on page 40), ask them to practice saying the sentences in the exercise aloud. Write the following on the board: *I help people with their problems. I write letters for an advice column. I tell people how to be happy.*
- Point out that students will probably hear something similar to one of these sentences in answer to item 1.
- Read the sentences aloud with a natural stress/intonation and ask several students to repeat. Point out that there are many different ways to stress a sentence, but most people stress the nouns and verbs more.
- Try a variety of different ways of reading the sentence aloud, stressing different words. You could stress the word *people* in the first sentence and ask the class what they think that might suggest (*I help <u>people</u> and <u>not animals</u>*). Mention that it is unusual to stress articles, prepositions, etc. You could reinforce this with another example – this time stressing the word *with*. Then ask what it would imply if the pronoun *their* were stressed (*I help people with <u>their</u> problems and <u>not my/your/our</u> problems*).
- Ask the class to practice items 2–5 in this way with a partner. After a few minutes, ask for suggestions and discuss how the sentences change when different words are stressed.

WRITE Exercise 3

- Students sometimes have difficulty thinking of ideas about what to write. Encourage them to try to put themselves in the position suggested in the task and imagine they are that person.
- Ask students to look at the excerpt from their aunt's letter and to think about the main points they need to address. Elicit the following: *What do you like doing? Who are your friends? Are you studying hard?*
- Divide the class into pairs and ask them to write down some of the things they could write for each sentence. They do not have to write complete sentences.
- Then ask students to suggest where in their letter they would address each point (suggestions are given in parentheses below).
  It's been so long since I saw you. (perhaps just a passing comment in the opening of the letter)
  Write and tell me about yourself. (the general content of the letter)
  What do you like doing? (1st main point)
  Who are your friends? (2nd main point)
  Are you studying hard? (3rd main point)

PROGRESS CHECK 3&4

Doing the Progress Check

READ

1

- If you have decided not to do the full warm-up, give students a minute or two to read the people's profiles. Then prompt them with some simple questions; for example:
  - *What kind of music does Kylie like?* (pop and music from the charts)
  - *Does Danny like pop?* (Yes, but he prefers American rock or folk music.)
- Go through the **Test-Taking Tips**, making sure students understand the different strategies that they can choose from in order to do this kind of task.
- Remind students to be careful of negatives in the reviews. They might understand *fond of* where it actually says *isn't fond of*, for example.
- Allow 15 minutes for this section.

ANSWERS
1 D 2 G 3 E 4 H 5 F

LISTEN

2 (58)

- If you have decided not to do the full warm-up, refer students back to the work on stress and intonation that they covered on page 40. Ask them to listen carefully and to use these techniques to help them understand.
- Go through the **Test-Taking Tips** for the listening task, reminding students that these tips will help them.
- Encourage students to spend a minute or two predicting what they might hear.
- Point out that they will hear everything twice. One suggestion in the **Test-Taking Tips** is to eliminate any wrong answers when they listen for the first time. Encourage students to find a strategy that works for them.

ANSWERS / AUDIO SCRIPT (58)
1 A 2 B 3 C 4 B 5 B
Belinda Vine: My name's Belinda Vine, and I write for a weekly magazine for teens. I have a regular section called "Ask Belinda." Basically, people write to me with their problems and I give them advice. Maybe I should also tell you what I *don't* do. I don't tell people what to do. I make suggestions. I say what I would do if I were in their situation. Ultimately, people have to make their own decisions.
Also, people really think that we write the problem letters. We don't. If someone doesn't want their name to appear in the magazine, then we'll invent a name. But we don't invent their problems. We don't need to. At the magazine, we receive hundreds of letters and messages each week.
Most of the problems we receive are about relationships. Maybe a teen's having problems with a boyfriend, a girlfriend, a close friend, or a relative. I often think that writing down a problem on a piece of paper or online can be very helpful. Sometimes you can see things much more clearly when you write them down. Here's an example. This is a message I received today by email. Let's see ...
"Dear Belinda, I'm 14 and my best friend is ignoring me. We usually do everything together, but now she won't talk to me or even look at me. I feel awful. What can I do? Kate."
So if I decided to answer Kate's letter, I'd probably start by asking her some questions. How long have you known your friend? Has anything happened recently? For example, has your friend started to hang out with other people? Even though we often think we are the problem, very often the problem has nothing to do with us.
I'd also probably suggest giving her friend some space. In situations like this, it's often good to find something else to do. If you spend all your time thinking about the problem, you'll only get more upset. If you start doing other things, however, you'll quickly be able to see what's really important to you.
But the best way to solve a problem is to talk about it. We often think no one will understand us if we tell them a problem. That's simply not true. Problems usually won't go away unless you talk about them. I should know. I've had this job for more than 10 years now.

WRITE

3

- Spend a few minutes going through the task with students and eliciting who they have to write to and what their letter must include.
- Remind them that they should address all the points in the letter excerpt.
- Explain that they shouldn't spend too long on their beginnings and endings. Suggest that they begin and end with something straightforward such as *Dear Aunt Joan, ... Love, [name].*
- Finally, remind students of the word limit and the importance of checking their own spelling, grammar, etc.

MODEL ANSWER
Dear Aunt Joan,
Thank you for your letter. I like doing a lot of things, but my favorite hobby is swimming. At school I go swimming twice a week. However, I much prefer going to the beach with my friends.

I'm in a swimming club, and my teammates are all good friends. We often go out together to the movies or to have something to eat.

I'm studying hard for my tests, but there are so many other things happening, it's difficult to concentrate.

I hope you're well. If you come to the USA, will you come and visit us?
Love,
[*name*]

After the Progress Check

Optional game

This game, called *Snowman* (see Games, page 29), follows up on the vocabulary from Units 3 and 4.

- Ask students to look at the **Words & Beyond** pages for Units 3 and 4 (pages 71–72). Encourage them to memorize as many words as possible in three minutes.
- Students take turns coming to the board and challenging the class using vocabulary from Units 3 and 4.
- Choose a volunteer (Student A) to come to the board first. Student A draws the required number of blanks – one for each letter of the word – on the board. Student A can then choose which students suggest letters.
- Individual students guess which letters are in the word. If they are right, Student A writes the letter in the correct place. If that letter is not in the word, Student A writes it on a different part of the board.
- Student A continues to ask other members of the class until someone guesses the word. Whoever guesses the word first scores a point. However, if no one has guessed correctly by the time there are five wrong letters on the board, Student A gets the point.
- Continue with Student B, and so on.

Feedback and extension

READ

- Review the items one at a time, reminding students that the reviews should contain a paraphrase of what is written in the people's profiles; for example, item 1 (*Kylie is a big fan of pop music, especially songs in the charts*) matches to D (*The album from boy band OneStep is even better than last year's debut album. It includes this week's number one hit "New Acquaintance."*).
- Ask students where they found the answers each time. If they got an answer wrong, make sure they understand why.
- Emphasize to students the importance of reading English, either online or in magazines, etc. The more they can read, the better it will be for them. Students with an interest in music might already be reading about their favorite bands, etc. Encourage them to use the internet to learn more through the medium of English. Students can easily access lyrics, either through dedicated sites online or from lyrics that often appear alongside music videos. If students have a favorite song, encourage them to find the lyrics and bring them to class, with the song. You could then spend part of a lesson discussing the way the songwriter has used English in the lyrics.

LISTEN

- Divide the class into pairs. Hand out photocopies of the audio script – one for each pair of students. Ask students to find the part of the audio script that gives the correct answer to each question. Discuss these sections, asking different students to read them aloud with the correct stress and intonation. This will help the class understand that tone of voice often plays a part when choosing the right answers.
- You should also draw attention to sections where there are distractors, pointing out that the wrong answers sometimes appear in the audio script, but the speaker says something that shows that it is incorrect. For example, *People really think that we write the problem letters. We don't.* (question 1, option B)
- As an extension activity, students could act out the role of a TV or radio advice columnist. Give students five minutes to write a fictional problem, similar to what they heard in the listening section. The problems could be about relationships or related to schoolwork, technology, etc. They should add a fictional name at the bottom of their problem. If students finish early, they can write a second problem.
- Gather all the problems into a pile and ask for some volunteers to give advice. Divide the problems among the volunteers and ask them to choose which problem they want to address.
- Tell the volunteers they can begin with *We have an email from [name], who …* . The volunteer should then describe the problem and offer advice.
- There should be enough problems for other students to take a turn. Keep going for as long as students are willing to volunteer.

WRITE

- For feedback with Exercise 3, ask students to focus on where they lost credit (and what they need to remember for next time). Answer any questions and make sure that students understand why they have been marked down in each case. Reassure them that it is perfectly natural to make mistakes in writing but that they need to make an effort to avoid making the same mistakes each time.
- To extend the work students have done on writing (especially if there were a lot of problems), assign a similar writing task for homework (see below).
- Write the task on the board and ask students to complete it for the next class. Use this task as an opportunity to correct any mistakes that they may have made with the letter in the Progress Check. Point out that there is little difference in style between this email and the letter they wrote.

Homework

Write up this task in a style similar to Exercise 3 in the Progress Check.

Read part of an email from your cousin in the USA.

> *I don't know very much about you. Write and tell me something about yourself. What kinds of things are you interested in? Do you enjoy studying? What do you do in your free time?*

Now write an email reply, answering the questions.

Write 90–100 words.

MOVE BEYOND FOR TEACHERS

Different types of music

The reading text in this Progress Check is about different types of music. Ask students to search online for more information about two different types of music. Suggest some genres for them to choose from, such as hip-hop, punk, indie, blues, country, folk, jazz, reggae, etc., or get them to choose their own.

They should aim to find and note down the main points about each of the two types of music and, in the next class, to report back to the rest of the class. Remind them that they can use comparative adverbs (e.g., *Rock musicians play louder than folk musicians*) or extreme adjectives (e.g., *This type of music has a fascinating history*).

UNIT 5 FIVE SENSES

IN THE PICTURE Can you feel it?

Talk about how we use our senses *Pages 48–49*

STAGE	TIME	FOCUS
GET STARTED		Play *Snowman* to introduce the title of the unit and recycle pronouncing the letters of the alphabet.
WORK WITH WORDS		Recycle parts of the body. Associate sense verbs and nouns with each of the five senses. Listen to sentences to say which sense is being described. Practice saying consonant combinations. Watch a video and describe the scene using the sense verbs.
SPEAK		Write about things you love or hate and talk about them with a partner.

Get started

Ask students to keep their books closed. Play a game of *Snowman* (see Games, page 29) to introduce the title of the unit, *Five senses*.

WORK WITH WORDS

1a and 1b RECALL

- Divide the class into pairs. Allow three minutes to do both tasks.
- First, ask students to write the names of parts of the body for as many letters of the alphabet as they can.
- Then ask different students which words they can match to the five icons in Exercise 2a.
- Ask students to do the **Work with Words** task on page 73.

SUGGESTED ANSWERS

Exercise 1a
ankle arm back chest ear eye elbow finger foot hand knee leg mouth neck nose shoulder teeth throat thumb toe tongue

Exercise 1b
1 ear 2 eye 3 hand, finger, thumb 4 nose
5 mouth, teeth, tongue

2a

- Refer students to the names of the five senses in the box and ask them to write them next to the correct icons.

2b 59

- Play the track for students to listen and check.
- Play the track again for students to listen and repeat.

ANSWERS / AUDIO SCRIPT 59

1 hearing 2 sight 3 touch 4 smell 5 taste

3a

- Ask students to match the verbs in the box to the five senses in the table in Exercise 2a. Don't confirm the answers at this point.

3b 60

- Play the track for students to listen and check their answers.
- Play the track again for students to listen and repeat.
- Elicit which of the sense words in Exercise 2a can also be verbs (*touch*, *smell*, *taste*).

ANSWERS / AUDIO SCRIPT 60

1 hearing – hear, listen, sound 2 sight – look, see, watch
3 touch – feel, touch 4 smell – smell 5 taste – taste

Extra activity

Ask students to write their own example sentence for each of the following verbs: *hear*, *listen*, *look*, *see*, and *watch*; for example, *I heard a noise outside my bedroom. What kind of music do you listen to?* (See Teaching Tips, See, look, *or* watch *and* hear, listen, *or* sound, page 25.)

Extra activity

Ask students to add vocabulary relating to the senses to the table in Exercise 2a; for example, in column 4, *Smell*, they could write *odor*, *fragrance*, *perfume*, *scent*, etc. Under *Sight*, they could write *vision*, *appearance*, *stare*, etc.

4 ▶61

- Refer students to the photos and explain that they will hear 10 sentences and should match each of them to one of the photos.
- Play the track for students to listen and match. Point out that some of the photos will be matched to several sentences.

> **ANSWERS / AUDIO SCRIPT** ▶61
>
> 1 a 2 e 3 c 4 d 5 b 6 a 7 c 8 a 9 a 10 d
>
> 1 I can't hear anything apart from amazing music.
> 2 **A:** What do you think of this one?
> **B:** Wow! That smells fantastic.
> 3 It's so hot here and that water looks so cool.
> 4 It's so good not wearing shoes. The grass feels so soft under my feet.
> 5 I like Mexican food. This tastes *really* good.
> 6 There's so much to see in the city. It's huge.
> 7 I love watching the ocean. It's so blue under the sky.
> 8 There's so much traffic. Everything sounds so noisy here.
> 9 I like listening to music while I walk. It's relaxing.
> 10 Sometimes I lie on the grass and imagine I can touch the clouds in the sky.

5 ▶62

- Ask students to use the verbs in Exercise 3 to complete the sentences.
- Play the track for students to listen and check.

> **ANSWERS / AUDIO SCRIPT** ▶62
>
> 1 feels 2 sounds 3 smells 4 see 5 looks 6 tastes 7 hear 8 touch 9 watching 10 listening
>
> See Student's Book, page 48, for audio script.

Extra activity

Play a memory game in groups. Model the activity with the class first. Ask the first student to say a phrase with one of the sense verbs (e.g., *I see the blue ocean*). The next student must repeat what the first student said, *She sees the blue ocean*, and add another phrase, such as *I hear the waves*. The third student must repeat what the first two students have said (e.g., *She sees the ocean. He hears the waves*) and add another one (e.g., *I look at the sky*). Any students who forget a phrase are out of the game. The last student to remember all phrases correctly is the winner.

6a ▶63 PRONOUNCE

- Play the track for students to listen to the words, paying particular attention to the underlined consonants in the first two words.
- Play the track again for students to listen and underline the consonant combinations.

> **ANSWERS / AUDIO SCRIPT** ▶63
>
> smell taste sound strong grass text message sky hand soft

6b

- Remind students that the underlined letters are all groups of consonants pronounced together. Ask them if they find any of these consonant combinations difficult.
- Play the track several times for students to listen and repeat the words.
- Encourage them to practice saying the words slowly in pairs, focusing on any that they find particularly difficult.

7 THE MOVING PICTURE ▶

- Explain to students that they are going to watch a video and that they should imagine they are in each scene.
- Ask students to say something for each scene using the sense verbs.

8

- Elicit the five senses from the class. Then elicit the sense verbs they have been practicing. Remind students that some sense verbs can also be nouns.
- Ask students to choose the correct option to complete each of the sentences.
- Choose different students to read their answers aloud.

> **ANSWERS**
>
> 1 smell 2 sound 3 taste 4 sight

SPEAK

9

- Give students a minute to reflect and write the names of things they love or hate to complete the sentences.
- Divide the class into pairs to read their sentences to each other. Encourage them to say whether they feel the same way.
- Invite some students to share one interesting thing about their partner with the class.

Extra activity

Ask students to write another sentence to explain the reason why they love or hate each thing in Exercise 9. Refer them to the sentences in Exercise 5 to help as a model for their answers.

MOVE BEYOND

Ask students to do the **Move Beyond** task on page 73.

Homework

Ask students to find a picture of a city or a landscape in a magazine or on the internet. Encourage them to imagine they are there and to write a description of the scene using as many sense verbs and nouns as they can. In the next class, have students work in small groups and read their descriptions to each other. When they have finished reading their descriptions, have them tell their groups which scene was their favorite.

READING Fragrance fact file

Use pictures to help you understand *Page 50*

STAGE	TIME	FOCUS
GET STARTED		Discuss personal experiences and opinions and recycle vocabulary related to the five senses.
SPEAK AND READ		Name perfumes and fragrances and talk about products that use fragrances. Read a text on facts about fragrances. Discuss tips on how to use pictures to help you understand a text (reading subskill).
REACT		Discuss surprising facts about fragrances and whether they should be banned in some public places.

Get started

Elicit the names of the five senses. Ask students which senses they think are the most and least important and ask them to explain their reasons in a brief class discussion.

Write these sense words and questions on the board and ask students to write one more question for each of the senses.

Sight: *What's your favorite color?*

Taste: *What food didn't you like when you were young, but do now?*

Smell: *Can you remember a smell that takes you back to your childhood?*

Touch: *What don't you like to touch?*

Hearing: *What sounds don't you like?*

Divide the class into pairs to discuss these questions and take turns asking and answering their own questions. Choose different students to share their answers with the class.

SPEAK AND READ

1

- Ask students to brainstorm things that smell nice. Elicit answers from around the class (e.g., *a rose*, *perfume*, *freshly cut grass*, *Mom's cooking!*).
- Divide the class into pairs to answer the questions. Set a time limit of two minutes for this.
- Invite different students to share their ideas with the class.

2a

- Ask students to discuss why looking at pictures and text titles before you read a text can help you understand the text.
- Refer students to the tips in the HOW TO box to see if they thought of the same tips. Invite volunteers to read the tips aloud.

2b

- Before students start to read, ask them to look at the text and pictures quickly in order to answer the questions.
- Ask students to discuss their answers in pairs before you elicit ideas from the class. Note that this is a prediction exercise, so there is no one right answer for each question. Accept any logical answers.

3 64

- Ask students to read the text to decide if each sentence is correct or incorrect. Don't play the audio at this point. It is an extra feature, and a suggestion for using it in class is included at the end of the lesson.
- Ask students to correct the incorrect sentences.
- Encourage students to compare their answers in pairs before you check them as a class.

ANSWERS

1 I (The very first perfume was incense made from burning wood or plants.)
2 C
3 I (The world's first perfume maker was a woman named Tapputi. She lived in Mesopotamia.)
4 I (The first unisex fragrance appeared in 1994.)
5 I (More than 4,000 ingredients are used in the fragrance industry.)
6 C

4

- Ask students which tips in the HOW TO box they used to help them in Exercises 2b and 3 and encourage them to check them.

Fast finishers

Ask students to find words in the text to match these definitions: *a scientist who studies chemistry* (chemist); *something often burned at religious ceremonies* (incense); *something we use to make a room smell nice* (air freshener); *affected by an allergy* (allergic); *to say officially that you must not do something* (banned).

REACT

5

- Divide the class into pairs to discuss the questions.
- Invite different students to share and explain their point of view. Try to develop a class discussion.

Recorded reading text 64

The reading text is recorded as an extra audio track that can be exploited for various purposes.

In this lesson, use the audio for checking Exercise 3. Stop the track at each point to ask if the answer is correct or incorrect. Where it is incorrect, elicit the correct answer.

MOVE BEYOND

Elicit what a caption is. Then refer students to the explanation given. Focus students on the pictures in the text and ask them to write captions using information from the text.

Homework

Ask students to write a list of smells they associate with living in an apartment or a house (*cooking*, *pets*, *laundry*, *trash*, etc.) and say which smells are pleasant or unpleasant. In the next class, invite students to share their ideas with the class.

GRAMMAR Passives (past, present, and future)

Use the past, present, and future passives to talk about senses

Page 51

STAGE	TIME	FOCUS
GET STARTED		Play a game to recycle vocabulary related to the five senses and pre-teach key words for this lesson.
READ		Read a text about a girl's breakfast and discuss the effect of a cold on your taste buds.
STUDY		Read grammar explanations about past, present, and future passives and complete examples.
PRACTICE		Complete a news story and sentences with the correct passive form of the verbs. Rewrite sentences using the passive form.
SPEAK		Compare information about food consumption in your country and discuss how people will eat food in the future.

Get started

Play a game of *Double Your Bet.* Ask students to work in pairs to decide if the statements below are true or false. Explain that each pair has 100 points to bet on true statements. They can distribute their points as they like, but they must spend all their points and write down how they have spent them. Explain that true statements double the points they bet. However, if they get it wrong, they lose twice the points they have bet.

When they have finished betting, tell students which of the statements are true and ask them to total up the bets to see who won the game.

Statements:

The idea of there being five senses was conceived by Homer, the Greek philosopher. (False – It was Aristotle.)

Ten thousand taste buds can be found inside our mouths. (True)

Fish have the most highly developed sense of taste. (False – Insects do.)

In general, girls have more taste buds than boys. (True)

Taste is the weakest of the five senses. (True)

Dogs have noses that are up to 100 times more sensitive than ours. (False – It is thought that dogs' noses are 2,000 to 100 million times more sensitive than ours.)

People who suffer from anosmia cannot smell at all. (True)

People who have hyperosmia are very sensitive to taste. (False – They are very sensitive to smells.)

In the USA, there is a National Sense of Smell Day in April. (True)

There are five basic kinds of taste. (True – sweet, salty, sour, and bitter)

READ Grammar in context

1

- Refer students to the picture and ask them to describe what is happening. (*A teenage girl is about to eat an egg on toast.*) Elicit whether students had a similar breakfast this morning.
- Invite students to read the text about Molly's breakfast and answer the question at the end of the text.

ANSWER

When you have a cold, your nose is blocked and you can't smell the food. Without your sense of smell, the food tastes different.

STUDY

2

- Focus students on the grammar explanations and ask them to complete the examples, using Exercise 1 to help them.
- Go through the explanations with the class, choosing different students to read the example sentences aloud to check the answers.

ANSWERS

are were 'll be won't be Are was

Extra activity

Students may need more controlled practice with the passive form before doing Exercise 3. Ask students to find examples of past, present, and future passives in the text and write them in their notebooks. Drill the affirmative, negative, and question form for each example.

ANSWERS

Past passive

Visual messages were / weren't sent to her brain / Were visual messages sent to her brain?

When all the messages were / weren't received by the brain / Were all the messages received by the brain?

She was / wasn't given the OK / Was she given the OK?

Present passive

Some cells that are / aren't found in the nose / Are some cells found in the nose?

The taste buds are / aren't located on the tongue / Are the taste buds located on the tongue?

Future passive

She will / won't be given eggs again / Will she be given eggs again?

She will / won't be given the OK by her brain / Will she be given the OK by her brain?

PRACTICE

3

- Focus students on the news story and ask them to complete the text with the future passive form of the verbs in parentheses. Before they start, point out the example.
- Encourage students to compare their answers in pairs before you ask for a volunteer to read the completed news story aloud.
- Invite students to say whether they would like to go to the new fast-food restaurant *Sixth Sense* and why or why not.

ANSWERS
2 won't be allowed 3 will be served 4 will be given
5 Will people be told 6 won't be shown

4

- Ask students to complete the sentences with the correct passive form of the verbs in parentheses. Before they start, draw students' attention to the example.
- Encourage students to compare their answers in pairs before you choose different students to read their answers aloud.

ANSWERS
2 were chosen 3 are sold 4 are often rejected
5 will be left 6 is grown; will be lost

5

- Focus students on the first sentence and the example answer and go over the transformation with the class.
- Ask students to rewrite the remaining sentences using the passive form of the verbs in blue.

ANSWERS
2 A product is often chosen because of the photo on the packaging.
3 However, when the food is prepared, it can look very different.
4 A lot of complaints are received by companies each year.

Alternative procedure: less confident classes
If students are still unsure about how to change an active sentence to passive, explain that they should follow these steps:

- Make the object of the active sentence the subject of the passive sentence.
- Form the passive using the correct tense of the verb *be* and change the active verb to its past participle.
- Make the subject of the active sentence the object of the passive sentence (although the subject can sometimes be omitted because it is unnecessary).

Fast finishers
Ask fast finishers to look at the text on page 50 and find as many examples as they can of passive sentences.

SPEAK

6

- Divide the class into pairs to compare the information given in Exercises 4 and 5 with the situation in their own country.
- Invite students to discuss how they think people will eat in the future. Encourage them to try to include the passive form in their discussion.
- Choose different students to explain their opinions and try to develop a class discussion to end the activity.

Homework

Ask students to write three breakfast menus: a healthy breakfast, an unhealthy breakfast, and a breakfast that will be eaten in the future. Encourage students to read their menus aloud to a partner at the beginning of the next class and discuss who has invented the healthiest, unhealthiest, and most futuristic breakfast.

LISTENING AND VOCABULARY The power of color

Follow a conversation *Page 52*

STAGE	TIME	FOCUS
GET STARTED		Recycle vocabulary related to colors to introduce the topic of the lesson.
SPEAK AND LISTEN		Talk about words you associate with different colors. Read about and practice tips on how to recognize words and phrases that help you follow a conversation (listening subskill). Listen to an interview about the National Color Wheel and find out how culture affects your choice of color.
REACT		Discuss which color reflects the way you are feeling now and your favorite color.
WORK WITH WORDS		Find out the meaning of color idioms and expressions. Discuss experiences related to color idioms and expressions.

Get started

Write the following list on the board: *A suit for an interview, A cell phone, Chocolate, The building we are in, Nail polish, A motorcycle, The walls in your bedroom, A sports car.*

Divide the class into pairs to discuss which color is the best for each item on the list.

Invite different students to come up and write the colors they have talked about on the board. Discuss why students chose the same, similar, or different colors as a class.

SPEAK AND LISTEN

1a

- Ask students to think of what they associate with each color in the box and to write the first word they think of.
- Invite students to compare their ideas in pairs before you discuss the color associations as a class.

Fast finishers
Ask students to categorize the colors as "warm" (orange, red, yellow …) or "cool" (blue, gray, green, silver …).

1b

- Focus students on the color wheel and ask them to find the colors given in the box that are on the wheel.
- Ask them to work with a partner and take turns pointing to a color.

2a

- Ask students to read the tips in the HOW TO box. Invite a volunteer to read them aloud.

2b ▶65

- Tell students that they are going to listen to an interview with Amy Shore about the National Color Wheel. Before they listen, ask them to read the list of topics.
- Play the track for students to listen and number the topics in the order they are mentioned.

ANSWERS / AUDIO SCRIPT ▶65

a 3 b 4 c 2 d 1

Host: So, Amy, tell us about the National Color Wheel.
Amy: Well, basically, we're asking people to visit our website at www.nationalcolorwheel.org so that they can take part in our National Color Wheel survey.
Host: What do people have to do to take part?
Amy: It's very simple. They just have to look at our color wheel and choose the color that represents the way they feel and then choose their favorite color.
Host: So what's the purpose of the survey?
Amy: Well, we're doing the survey in order to make people think about the importance of color in their lives, and to discover the nation's favorite color. The thing is, our lives are full of colors, from the colors of the clothes we wear to the colors of our walls at home. But how much do we really know about what those colors mean?
Host: I imagine you'd get different results in different countries. I was reading on your website about how colors mean different things in different cultures.
Amy: That's right. These days we often assume that everyone on the planet is exactly the same. But the way we all relate to colors shows how different we are. For example, in the West we associate the color white with peace, while in China it means death. We associate the color green with nature and the environment, while in some parts of the world, especially countries with jungles, it means danger.
Host: I associate green with Ireland, but that's probably because I'm part Irish.
Amy: That's another good example. But even though we react to colors in different ways, they have a powerful influence on all of us. We saw this in a similar survey in Manchester. Most of the 20,000 people who took part chose yellow to describe the way they were feeling. Yellow is a happy, sunny color. However, the city's "favorite color" was blue. Curiously, no one chose white or gray as their favorite color.
Host: Fascinating. Well, good luck with the survey.
Amy: Thank you.

3 ▶65

- Play the track again for students to listen and choose the correct answers.
- Encourage them to compare their answers in pairs before you check them as a class.

ANSWERS

1 A 2 B 3 A 4 C

4

- Ask students which tips in the HOW TO box they used to help them in Exercises 2b and 3 and encourage them to check them.

REACT

5

- Divide the class into pairs to look at the color wheel and answer the questions.
- Invite students to discuss as a class whether they chose the same, similar, or different colors.
- Ask students to work in the same pairs and each choose a role, A or B. Refer Student A to the task on page 75 and Student B to the one on page 76.
- When they have finished, do a quick class survey to see if most students said the same colors.

WORK WITH WORDS

6

- Refer students to the list of idioms and phrases and ask them to match them to the definitions.

ANSWERS

1 d 2 c 3 f 4 g 5 h 6 i 7 j 8 b 9 e 10 a

Extra activity

Read these sentences aloud for students to complete with one of the phrases from Exercise 6.

1 *I couldn't see anything in the Sixth Sense restaurant. It was ______ .*
2 *I spent too much over the weekend and now I'm ______ .*
3 *Do you feel all right? You look ______ .*
4 *I find the color gray depressing. It makes me ______ .*
5 *We're waiting to ______ to go on a trip at the end of the year.*
6 *I don't usually eat vegetables, maybe ______ .*
7 *The loud music started ______ and woke me up.*
8 *The results of the survey weren't ______ .*
9 *When I don't want to hurt people's feelings, I sometimes ______ .*
10 *It upsets me when people waste food. It makes me ______ .*

ANSWERS

1 as black as night 2 in the red 3 as white as a sheet
4 feel blue 5 get the green light 6 once in a blue moon
7 out of the blue 8 black and white 9 tell a white lie
10 see red

7

- Divide the class into pairs to make a list of things that make them see red, make them feel blue, are black and white, and only happen once in a blue moon.
- Invite students to share some of their answers with the class.

Extra activity

Tell students some color jokes to see if they can think of the answers. Ask if they find them funny.

What is black and white and "red" all over? (a newspaper – there is a play on words on the homophone *red/read*)

What is black and white and black and white and black and white? (a penguin rolling down a hill)

You could invite students to tell the class any suitable jokes about colors that they know. Encourage them to translate them into English to see if they are funny.

MOVE BEYOND

Ask students to do the **Move Beyond** task on page 73.

Homework

Ask students to write 100 words about important colors in their country and what they represent. At the beginning of the next class, have students work in small groups and compare their ideas.

GRAMMAR (*In order*) *to* ... , *so* (*that*) ...

Talk about the purpose of doing things

Page 53

STAGE	TIME	FOCUS
GET STARTED		Recycle vocabulary from the unit so far and introduce the topic of the lesson.
READ		Read about the story of Braille and say whether young people still use it today.
STUDY		Read grammar explanations of (*in order*) *to* and *so* (*that*) and complete examples from the text.
PRACTICE		Use the target language to complete sentences and a conversation. Write sentences with (*in order*) *to* and *so* (*that*).
SPEAK		Exchange opinions about the five senses and compare your ideas.

Get started

Play a game of *Pictionary.* Divide the class into teams. Ask each team to send a volunteer to the front of the class. Give the students at the front of the class a word or phrase to draw on the board.

As the students are drawing, the first team to correctly call out what it is wins a point.

Repeat this several times with different students. Suggested words and phrases are: *fragrance*, *brain*, *the five senses*, *taste buds*, *traffic*, *color wheel*, *grass*, *survey.*

Invite students to think of other ways that we can communicate words, other than saying them or drawing them. (You could introduce the idea of Braille here, as well as miming words.)

READ Grammar in context

1

- Refer students to the photo and elicit what they think the boy is doing and what the text is going to be about.
- Ask students to read the story of Braille and find out if young people today still use it.
- Choose a student to say the answer.

ANSWER

Not usually. They prefer using electronic screen readers.

STUDY

2

- Read through the grammar explanation with the class. Then ask them to complete the examples, using the story in Exercise 1 to help them.
- Encourage students to compare their answers in pairs before you check them as a class by inviting different students to read the example sentences aloud.

ANSWERS

read they could

PRACTICE

3

- Ask students to read the sentences and choose the correct option to complete them.
- Encourage students to compare their answers in pairs before you choose different students to read the sentences aloud.

ANSWERS

1 so that 2 to 3 in order 4 so that 5 to

Extra activity

Give students 60 seconds to memorize the sentences in Exercise 3. Ask students to work in pairs to take turns testing each other. One student closes his or her book and the other student reads the first part of the sentence aloud to see if his or her partner can remember the rest.

4 66

- Elicit from students whether they know anyone who is color-blind and, if so, how this affects their everyday life.
- Point out that we can use *so* either with or without *that* after it and *to* with or without *in order* in front of it. Ask students to read the conversation between Mike and Jackie and complete it with *to* or *so*.
- Circulate and monitor students, helping if necessary.
- Play the track for students to listen and check their answers. You could stop the track and elicit the answers from different students, asking why they chose that option in order to consolidate usage.

ANSWERS / AUDIO SCRIPT 66

1 so 2 to 3 to 4 to 5 so 6 so

See Student's Book, page 53, for audio script.

5

- Invite students to complete the sentences in their own words using *in order to* / *to* or *so that* / *so*.
- Encourage students to compare their sentences in pairs or small groups.
- Choose different students to read their sentences aloud.

SPEAK

6

- Divide the class into pairs to answer the questions. Before they start, invite two students to read the model sentences aloud.
- Ask different students to share their opinions with the class.

Homework

Ask students to make sentences using *in order to* / *to* or *so that* / *so* and these phrases: *save money*, *learn English*, *study hard*, *not carry a lot of money*, *not get sunburned*, *take vitamins*. In the next class, ask students to share their ideas with the class.

LANGUAGE & BEYOND COMMUNICATE & COOPERATE

Recognize nonverbal communication *Page 54*

STAGE	TIME	FOCUS
GET STARTED		Play a game to recycle vocabulary related to the senses and present words from the lesson.
SPEAK AND READ		Communicate a phrase without speaking to your partner. Read a text about body language and discuss points that you think are true with your partner.
DO		Find examples of body language in the text and demonstrate them.
REFLECT		Reflect on how body language can reveal things about us but is not always accurate.
EXTEND		Create a scene from a silent movie and perform it for the rest of the class.

LIFE SKILLS

RECOGNIZE NONVERBAL COMMUNICATION

Nonverbal communication is important not only in communicating meaning but also in building social relations. The ability to relate well to others is important throughout life, and nonverbal communication plays a key role. Developing the ability to understand and use nonverbal communication can help you connect with others, express what you really mean, navigate challenging situations, and build better relationships at home, at school, and in your future workplace.

In order for students to get better at interpreting nonverbal communication, they should observe people around them and notice how people act and react to each other. Remind students that they should be aware of individual differences and that people from different countries and cultures tend to use different body language signals.

Students can train themselves to use nonverbal signals that match their words and reinforce what they are saying. They can use body language, for example, to convey positive feelings even when they are not actually experiencing them. If they're nervous about a situation (e.g., a job interview or a first date), they can use positive body language to signal confidence even though they're not feeling it.

Get started

Play a game of *Articulate!* Prepare by writing some key words and phrases from the lesson on cards. Divide the class into two or more teams. Explain to students that the objective is to be the first team to correctly guess all the words that their teammates describe in the time given. Point out that all players must take turns taking the top card from the pack and explaining the word to their team. When a team member calls out the correct answer, the next describer quickly takes another card and repeats the process. When the time runs out, each team counts the number of cards that were correctly guessed. Before they start, make the rules clear:

When describing a word, you *must not*:
- Say what letter the word starts with or how many letters it has
- Say the word or any derivative (e.g., if the word is *time*, you can't say *timer* or *timed*)
- Use clues such as "It rhymes with … " or "It sounds like … "

When describing a word, you *can*:
- Choose to *pass* and not play a card, but only once each turn
- Gesticulate, act, and mime (but *not* mouth) the word

Possible words and phrases for cards:

gesture, *face*, *eye*, *movement*, *communicate*, *body*, *to tell a lie*, *stand*, *character*, *hide*, *mirror*, *disgusting*, *smell*, *reveal*, *accurate*, *feel*, *tired*, *quiet*, *hear*, *taste*, *head*, *wall*

SPEAK AND READ

1
- Divide the class into pairs to take turns choosing one of the phrases in the box and communicating it to their partners without speaking to see if they can understand.

2
- Focus students on the text about body language. Ask them to read it and check the points that they believe are true, based on their own experience.
- Ask students to compare answers in pairs before you start a class discussion by inviting different students to say which points are true for them and why.

DO

3
- Divide the class into groups and refer them back to the text to find examples of body language.
- Encourage them to take turns demonstrating the body language described.
- Invite them to demonstrate other suitable examples to see if their partners can interpret them correctly.

REFLECT

4

- Focus students on the **REFLECTION POINT** and elicit whether they agree or not.
- Encourage students to discuss the questions as a class, inviting several different students to answer each question.

Extra activity

Ask students to look back at the article to help them think of at least five ways they can use nonverbal communication to create a good impression.

SUGGESTED ANSWERS

Stand tall with your shoulders back.
Smile and maintain eye contact.
Put your head to one side when you listen.
Mirror your partner's body language.

Extra activity

Ask students to talk about last weekend in pairs. In a less confident class, you could ask students to read a conversation in the book aloud (e.g., Exercise 4 on page 53). Ask them to concentrate on their own and their partner's body language. After their conversation, ask students to give feedback on their partner's nonverbal communication and ask if their partner agrees with their analysis.

Extra activity

Ask students what body language they might use in these situations: *You're at a New Year's Eve party. You are giving a presentation in front of the class. You're having an argument with your friend. You are having an interview for a babysitting job.*

EXTEND

5

- Divide the class into groups to create a scene from a silent movie, following the instructions.
- Circulate and help students with any difficulties.
- Encourage students to rehearse their scene and perform it for other students to describe what happens.

Extra activity

If you have the facilities, play a silent movie for students. Silent movies are excellent for getting students to produce language. You could try Buster Keaton's *Nothing but Pleasure*, Charlie Chaplin's *The Kid*, *The Red Balloon* directed by Albert Lamorisse, or Jacques Tati's *Les Vacances de Monsieur Hulot* and *Jour de Fête*. Alternatively, you could use more modern movies such as *The Artistes* or a Wallace and Gromit film.

Divide the class into pairs or small groups. Explain that one or two students should watch the movie and describe what is happening to the other students, who have their backs to the screen. Ask students to switch places every few minutes. If necessary, write the vocabulary students need on the board as the actions happen.

Homework

Ask students to research cultural differences in hand or facial gestures. Encourage them to write short notes that they can use at the beginning of the next class to talk in groups.

SPEAKING At the pharmacy

Ask for help with words at the pharmacy *Page 55*

STAGE	TIME	FOCUS
GET STARTED		Recycle vocabulary to talk about common illnesses and what you can buy at the pharmacy.
SPEAK		Look at photos of common health complaints and say what is wrong and what the people in the photos should do.
LISTEN		Listen to conversations in a pharmacy where people are asking for products. Practice asking for help when you don't know or understand a word (speaking subskill).
ACT		Role-play a conversation between a pharmacist and a customer.

Get started

Write these jumbled sentences on the board for students to order in pairs. Encourage them to race against each other to try to be the first to unscramble the sentences.

do / do / have / you / when / headache / What / a / you / ?
(What do you do when you have a headache?)
been / recently / sick / you / Have / ?
(Have you been sick recently?)
any / you / Do / have / allergies / ?
(Do you have any allergies?)
to / you / go / pharmacy / do / often / the / How / ?
(How often do you go to the pharmacy?)
buy / pharmacy / can / at / What / you / the / ?
(What can you buy at the pharmacy?)

Invite students to come up and write the sentences in the correct order. Drill the pronunciation of *headache* (/ˈhedeɪk/). Tell students that in the USA another word for *pharmacy* is *drugstore*.

Encourage students to ask and answer the questions in pairs. Choose different students around the class to say what their answers were for different questions. Elicit and write a list of products you can buy at the pharmacy on the board (e.g., *sunscreen*, *antiseptic cream*, *bandages*, *eye drops*) and save this to give students ideas in Exercise 6.

SPEAK

1

- Refer students to the photos and ask: *Do these people look happy? How do you know?*
- Divide the class into pairs to answer the questions.
- Choose different students to share their answers.

LISTEN

2 ▶67

- Play the conversations for students to listen and write down which of the problems shown in the photos is not mentioned in the conversations.
- Encourage students to compare their answer in pairs before you choose a student to say the answer.

ANSWER / AUDIO SCRIPT ▶67

The problem in photo c (headache) is not talked about.

1

Pharmacist: Are you all right?
Adele: I need something for my stomach. I have … I'm not sure how to say it in English. It's a pain.
Pharmacist: You mean a stomachache?
Adele: Yes. Is this the right thing for a stomachache?
Pharmacist: Yes, it is.
Adele: And I don't understand what this means. Can you help me?
Pharmacist: Let me see. Oh … FD&C 6. It's a color they use in the medicine.
Adele: I see. Does this sign mean that it's bad for you?
Pharmacist: It can be bad for some people. Are you allergic to anything?
Adele: No, I don't think so.
Pharmacist: Then you're probably OK.

2

Pharmacist: Can I help you?
Takeshi: Yes. I need some of that spray you put on your skin. I don't know what it's called. It's a special spray for keeping insects away.
Pharmacist: Do you mean insect repellent?
Takeshi: I think so.
Pharmacist: This one is very good.
Takeshi: What does "light fragrance" mean?
Pharmacist: It means the spray has a fragrance, but it's not very strong. Here. Smell it.
Takeshi: Hm. That's not too bad.
Pharmacist: We also have this in a lotion.
Takeshi: What's the difference between the spray and the lotion?
Pharmacist: Just the price. The spray is cheaper.
Takeshi: OK. I'll take the spray.

3 ▶67

- Play the conversation again for students to listen and write the missing words.
- Choose different students to say the answers.

ANSWERS

1 stomach 2 stomachache 3 stomachache 4 skin
5 insects 6 insect

Alternative procedure: more confident classes

Encourage more confident students to try to remember and write in the missing words. Then play the track for them to listen and check their answers.

4a

- Ask students to read the tips in the HOW TO box. Invite two volunteers to read the tips aloud.

4b ▶68

- Focus students on the phrases from the conversations and encourage them to complete any words they can from memory.
- Play the track for students to complete the phrases or check their answers.
- Play the track again for students to listen and repeat.

ANSWERS / AUDIO SCRIPT ▶68

1 sure 2 means 3 called 4 for 5 difference
See Student's Book, page 55, for audio script.

Extra activity

Ask students to read the conversations aloud in pairs.

5

- Ask students to match the phrases in Exercise 4b to the tips in Exercise 4a.

ANSWERS

1 Say that you don't know the word.
2 Say that you don't understand.
3 Say that you don't know the word.
4 Explain what it's for.
5 Ask the other person for more information.

ACT

6 ▶69

- Divide the class into pairs to complete the tasks. Encourage students to use the ideas on the board from the **Get started** activity to help them think of products you buy at a pharmacy. Before they start, play the track with the expressions in the PHRASEBOOK box and encourage them to use these in their role-play. Set a time limit of five minutes to prepare and act out the conversation.
- Ask students to change roles and repeat with another product you can buy at the pharmacy.
- Ask students to present one of their conversations to the class.

Alternative procedure: less confident classes

In a less confident class, ask students to prepare the conversation in written form before doing this as a speaking activity. When students change roles and repeat with another product you buy at the pharmacy, ask them to try to perform the role-play without their written notes.

Homework

Ask students to find three or four pictures of things that they do not know the English word for. Ask them to write about these objects using the expressions in the PHRASEBOOK. At the beginning of the next class, ask students to work in pairs. Ask them to read each description aloud for their partner to guess the picture it refers to. When they have finished, encourage them to find out the names of the things in English.

WRITING A place I really like

Link similar ideas

Page 56

STAGE	TIME	FOCUS
GET STARTED		Play a game to recycle language from the unit.
SPEAK AND READ		Describe a picture and talk about similar places. Read a description to match to the picture. Look at words to link similar ideas (writing subskill).
PRACTICE		Link sentences together to make them more complex.
DISCUSS		Talk about the home of a relative or family friend and say what you do there.
WRITE		Write a description of the home you discussed.
SHARE		Read your description for a partner to listen and draw the place. Compare your description with your partner's picture.

Get started

Play a game of *Three in a Row* (see Games, page 29). To win a square, teams take turns choosing a square and making a correct sentence linking the two items; for example, *Sometimes you can find the same things in the pharmacy and the supermarket*.

pharmacy / supermarket	Braille / electronic screen readers	look / watch
body language / what you say	listen / hear	feel blue / see red
silent movies / Charlie Chaplin	visual messages / taste buds	dictionary / history book

SPEAK AND READ

1

- Divide the class into pairs to look at the photo and describe it and tell their partner about any similar places they know. Before they start, refer students to the expressions in the PHRASE BYTES box and encourage them to use these in their discussion.
- Choose different students to describe the photo and say whether they know a similar place.

2

- Ask students to read the description and say which part of the photo doesn't match.
- Elicit the answer from the class.

ANSWER

The beach does not have sand; it has rocks. There are no hills in the picture.

3a

- Refer students to the tips in the HOW TO box. Invite volunteers to read the tips aloud.

3b

- Invite students to look back at the text in Exercise 2 and underline all the linking words from the HOW TO box.

ANSWERS

Other relatives often come too, so the house ...
The house is in the middle of nowhere, and there aren't any ...
... hills to climb and a forest to explore. There's the ocean as well.
... wind on my face and the sand under my feet. I also love swimming ...
My grandma is not only one of the coolest people on the planet, but she's also an amazing cook.

PRACTICE

4

- Focus students on the sentences and ask them to rewrite them using the words in parentheses to link the ideas. Point out that some will be joined into one sentence, whereas others will still be two sentences.
- Encourage students to compare their answers in pairs before you check them as a class.

ANSWERS

1 There's a park near my house, and I go there once or twice a week.
2 It's not only a good place to meet friends, but it's also a good place to play sports.
3 There are some basketball courts. There's also an area for skateboarding.
4 Once a month there's a market. They have concerts in the summer too.
5 I go there to have fun. I sometimes go there to read as well.
6 You see a lot of different people there. People take their pets there too.

Extra activity

Ask students to work in pairs to write a sentence that describes each of the following words in sensory, descriptive terms: *sand*, *river*, *trees*, *house*, *birdsong*.

Encourage them to use at least two adjectives. Then ask them to note which of the five senses they have described; for example, *I love the feeling of fine golden sand between my toes* (touch/sight).

DISCUSS

5

- Ask students if they think they would like to visit the place described in Exercise 2. Encourage them to give reasons for their answers.
- Ask some more questions related to the text to get them thinking about the content of the description; for example, *Would you like to stay in a house that's in the middle of nowhere? Do you think you'd get bored? / Would you go swimming in the ocean when the water is freezing? / Do you like the feeling of wind on your face and sand under your feet? / Do you like it when there is the smell of cooking or baking in the house? What cooking smells do you like? / Have you ever stayed anywhere scary? Why was it scary?*
- Divide the class into pairs. Tell students to think of the home of a relative or family friend that they like to visit and to describe it to their partner. Ask them to say what they do when they're there.
- Set a time limit of five minutes for this and then choose different students to tell the class what their partner talked about.

WRITE

6

- Tell students that you'd like them to write a description of the home they discussed.
- Advise them to use the description in Exercise 2 as a model.
- Read through Steps 1 and 2 in the box and ask students to give you some examples from Exercise 2. Remind them to use the tips in the **HOW TO** box.
- Ask students to close their books for a minute and elicit the five sense verbs (*see*, *hear*, *taste*, *smell*, *touch*). Tell them to use their senses in their descriptions and to say how the place makes them feel. Ask them which senses the writer uses in Exercise 2 and how the place makes her feel (i.e., *see – hills, forest, ocean, it's dark*; *hear – it's quiet*; *smell – cooking and baking*; *touch – wind on your face, sand under your feet*; *feel – a little scary*).
- Tell them they can open their books and use them as a reference as they write. Set a time limit of 10 minutes for writing.

SHARE

7

- Divide the class into pairs and make sure they have paper, a pencil, and an eraser.
- Explain that you want them to read their description to their partner, who will draw the place in as much detail as possible.
- You could invite a student to the board and demonstrate the task, with the student listening and drawing on the board.
- Encourage students to listen to their partners carefully and to ask them to repeat sections if necessary.
- Ask students to compare their description with their partner's picture and to say how accurate the picture is. Ask them to reflect on how their description could have been better.

Homework

Ask students to write five sentences to connect some of the ideas in the **Get started** activity using *and*, *also*, *too*, *as well*, and *not only* + *but also*. At the beginning of the next class, have students work in pairs and show their sentences to their partners. Encourage them to point out any errors to each other.

VOCABULARY The senses and sense verbs

1

- Divide the class into pairs to look at the words in the box and match them to the five senses (*touch – feel, touch; sight – look, see, sight, watch; smell – smell; hearing – hear, hearing, listening, sounds; taste – taste*).
- Ask students to work individually to complete Casper Wright's introduction to his video game with the words in the box.
- Encourage them to compare their answers in pairs before you check them as a class.

ANSWERS
1 watch 2 sight 3 see 4 listening 5 hearing
6 hear 7 sounds 8 Look 9 touch/feel
10 feel/touch 11 smell 12 taste

Color idioms

2

- Explain to students that they are going to complete the conversation from the video game with colors to make typical English expressions.
- In a less confident class, write the color options on the board: *black, white, red, blue, green*.
- Divide the class into pairs to complete the conversation by writing a color in each blank.
- Choose different students to read their answers aloud to check them as a class.
- Invite students to read the conversation aloud in pairs.

ANSWERS
1 black 2 blue 3 white 4 black 5 white 6 red
7 green 8 red 9 blue 10 blue

GRAMMAR Passives (past, present, and future)

3

- Write a scrambled past passive sentence on the board for students to order; for example, write *invented Marconi The was by radio* (The radio was invented by Marconi) and elicit from students which tense this sentence is in and how we form the passive.
- Explain that the text is an encyclopedia entry and ask students to complete it with the passive form of the verbs in parentheses.
- Choose different students to read the text aloud, sentence by sentence, to check answers as a class.

ANSWERS
1 was created 2 was inspired 3 was interviewed
4 will be used 5 will be connected 6 was reported
7 is played 8 will be remembered

(*In order*) *to …* , *so* (*that*) …

4

- Ask students to read the SensaWorld rules and complete them using *in order to / to* or *so that / so*.
- Circulate and monitor as students are doing the task. If you feel they are having difficulty, stop them midtask and do a quick review of how we use *in order to / to* and *so that / so*.
- Check answers as a class.

ANSWERS
1 in order to / to 2 so that / so 3 in order to / to
4 in order to / to 5 so that / so 6 so that / so

Extra Resources

Go to the Teacher's Resource Center at mee2.macmillaneducation.com for:

- midterm tests;
- downloadable audio and audio scripts for the Student's Book and Workbook;
- videos and video scripts;
- extra vocabulary at two levels of difficulty;
- extra grammar at two levels of difficulty;
- CLIL lesson, with full teacher's notes;
- a life skills lesson, with full teacher's notes;
- Speaking Database materials;
- the *Move Beyond Level 5* wordlist;
- tips for using the Grammar Database;
- and more!

Go to Workbook pages 128–139 for further practice material.

PROGRESS CHECK 5

Preparing for the Progress Check

Vocabulary review

- Draw a table on the board with these headings: *The senses* and *Color idioms*.
- Invite students to come to the board and write vocabulary items under each heading. For each item, check that everyone understands the meaning. The lists do not need to be complete.
- With several items in each column, refer students to the vocabulary in **Words & Beyond** on page 73. Encourage them to call out any items that they missed. Students can then go through the Progress Check and see how many of the items they can find.

Grammar review

- To remind the class of the grammar they have studied in the previous unit, start a "race," where students check the book and tell you the main grammar points from Unit 5. Write these on the board, asking for example sentences as students call them out. The grammar for this Progress Check is as follows:
  - Unit 5: Passives (past, present, and future); (*In order*) *to* … , *so* (*that*) …

Optional warm-up activities

READ Exercise 1

- For students who are unfamiliar with this type of task, spend a few minutes reading through the questions and the options, pointing out that in this reading activity the texts are in the form of notes or notices.
- Direct students to the text in question 1 and ask the following questions:
  What type of text is this?
  Where would you expect to find it?
  Who would read it?
- Elicit that this is a sign in a public place and that people might read it if they were going into a store, for example.
- Then ask students to look at the question and the three answer options. Ask them to find references in the text; for example, *Option A says all animals can come in with their owners, but the text says no dogs or other animals are allowed, only guide dogs*; *Option B mentions dogs but not guide dogs*; *Option C mentions dogs and blind people, so C is the correct answer.*
- Go through the other texts, asking the questions above about the kind of text, where you might find them, and who might read them. Students will then tackle the remainder of the questions with more confidence.

LISTEN Exercise 2

- Listening to a conversation can be more difficult than listening to a monologue because students have to remember who says what. With that in mind, refer students back to page 52, where they learned how to follow a conversation.
- Ask the class to tell you what audio type they are going to listen to here (*a conversation between two people*) and what the subject of that conversation is (*the sense of smell*). Remind students to use the instructions and exercise items to help them predict what they are going to hear.
- Spend a few minutes looking at the true-false items and asking students to tell you what they are likely to hear. Prompt by asking: *If sentence 1 is false, what might be true?* (Ellen says she doesn't like / hates the smell of strong fragrances. / Ellen says she likes the smell of weak fragrances.)
- Repeat for the other sentences and elicit possibilities similar to the following:
  2 Ellen wants to get something at the pharmacy so that Ken feels better.
  3 Ken doesn't have a strong sense of smell. / Ellen has a strong sense of smell.
  4 There's a faint smell of cheese.
  5 Ken doesn't agree / doesn't think that the shopping center smells bad.

WRITE Exercise 3

- Remind students that the blanks usually depend on the grammar that they have studied in the previous two units. Ask students to tell you what grammar they should expect to find in this Progress Check (passives; [*In order*] *to* … and *so* [*that*] … ;
- Ask the class to look at the items in Exercise 3 and, without answering them, to write down which of them tests each of the expected grammar items.

WRITE Exercise 4

- Ask students to look at the bullet points for the writing task and ask them to think about the structure of their email and which structures they will use for each bullet point. Elicit suggestions similar to the following:
  - First bullet point: opening sentence; *I am writing to tell you* …
  - Second bullet point: main body; descriptions
  - Third bullet point: closing comment; *Hope to see you after camp. Your friend, [name]*

Doing the Progress Check

READ

1

- Remind students that these texts are notes or notices that we might find in everyday situations. If you have decided not to do the full warm-up, ask students to tell you what each type of text is (1 – *sign in a public place*; 2 – *email or message to a friend* 3 – *sign at a school*; 4 – *text message*; 5 – *sign in a store*).
- Read through the **Test-Taking Tips** with the class and remind them to look for words and phrases in the text that correspond to those in the answer options.
- Allow 5–10 minutes for this section.

ANSWERS
1 C 2 B 3 B 4 A 5 C

PROGRESS CHECK 5

LISTEN

2 70

- If you have decided not to do the full warm-up, encourage students to spend a minute or two looking at the questions and predicting what they might hear.
- Read through the **Test-Taking Tips** for the listening task, answering any questions students have. Refer students back to the HOW TO boxes on pages 52 and 55.
- Since students will hear the conversation twice, tell them to make sure they don't lose their place in the first listening. Explain that the answers usually appear in the same order as the exercise items, which makes it easier to know what to listen for. If they cannot understand the answer, they should move on to the next item so that they do not miss any answers. They can then use the second listening for checking and filling in any blanks.

ANSWERS / AUDIO SCRIPT 70

1 F 2 T 3 F 4 F 5 F

Ellen: Let's go to the clearance section. They have some jeans on sale.
Ken: There it is. On the other side of the perfume department. Come on.
Ellen: [Starts coughing]
Ken: What's wrong?
Ellen: Fragrances ... I'm very sensitive to strong smells. I just need to get away from the smell.
Ken: Let's go back into the mall. Are you OK?
Ellen: Sorry, strong perfume makes me cough and gives me a really bad headache.
Ken: There's a pharmacy over there ... we could go in to get some ... uh ... something for your headache ...
Ellen: No, it's OK, thanks. I'll be fine in a while ... I just have a really strong sense of smell.
Ken: I have a really good sense of hearing, but I don't notice smell that much.
Ellen: Can you smell that?
Ken: Smell what? I don't smell anything!
Ellen: You don't smell the fish? There's a sushi bar across from us.
Ken: What I smell is coffee from that café ...
Ellen: ... and the cake from the bakery ...
Ken: ... and the popcorn over there ... Mm, I feel really thirsty and hungry now.
Ellen: Me too!
Ken: Mm. This mall is a really smelly place. Let's go eat!

WRITE

3

- Remind students that this type of task is often grammar based. They should expect to see examples of the grammar that they have studied in Unit 5.
- Remind students that the meaning must be the same in both sentences and that they should check their spelling when they have finished.

ANSWERS

1 smells
2 have been received
3 in order
4 feels

4

- If you have decided not to do the full warm-up, spend a few minutes going through the task with students and eliciting who they have to write to and what their message must include (the three bullet points).
- Remind them that this type of task calls for a friendly, conversational style.
- Encourage them to use color idioms as well as senses and sense verbs.
- Finally, remind students of the word limit and the importance of checking their spelling, grammar, etc.

MODEL ANSWER

Hey Josh,
I'm writing to tell you about the great time I am having at summer camp. So far, we have explored the woods, made a huge bonfire, and toasted marshmallows to make delicious S'mores. Today, we got the green light to participate in a multi-camp archery competition. Can't wait to tell you more about it. See you when I get back.
Your friend,
Alex

After the Progress Check

Feedback and extension

READ

- Review the questions one at a time and explain to students that they are going to focus on the wrong answers.
- Divide the class into pairs and ask them to find reasons why each of the wrong answers is inappropriate.
- After a few minutes, discuss as a class what students have found. They should mention some of the following answers.

ANSWERS

1 A It clearly says, "No entrance with dogs or other animals."
  B Dogs with their owners are only permitted if the dogs are guide dogs and their owners are blind.
2 A *Hearing* is correct because Cheri is talking about listening, but she goes on to talk about eating food, not smelling it.
  C While the word *beautiful* could be used for sight; neither smell nor touch are introduced in the text.
3 A The text does not refer to this year.
  C The words *not ever* are not used.
4 B Not mentioned or implied.
  C The frowning face symbols don't suggest excitement.
5 A/C The sign gives specific days and hours that the pharmacist will be available.

LISTEN

- Hand out photocopies of the audio script – one for each pair – and ask students to find where they made mistakes.
- Ask pairs to underline the sections of the conversation where they found the answers.
- Some students find listening tasks very hard. Try to encourage students who have had difficulty and stress that these tasks tend to get easier with practice.
- If the class made a lot of mistakes in the exercise, play the audio again, pausing at relevant points for students to process the information they have heard.

WRITE

- Students who had difficulty with Exercise 3 need to focus on the grammar points from the unit (see the grammar review above). Write one or two example sentences on the board and then divide the class into small groups to come up with more examples for each point. If necessary, ask students to write more sentences for homework.
- For students who had difficulty with Exercise 4, do a similar task, building up a model on the board. Write the following, asking different students for ways to fill in the blanks to describe a situation to a friend:

  Hi Julie,
  I am writing to tell you about ....
  So far, ...
  Today, we ....?
  See you soon
  Your friend

- When the model is complete, ask other students to suggest alternatives. You could then erase the previous suggestions and fill in the blanks with new ones.

MOVE BEYOND FOR TEACHERS

Read in English

Remind students that any kind of reading they do in English will help them, including signs, notes, invitations, and instructions wherever they can find them. Short texts like those in the Read section of the Progress Check are sometimes used in exams. Some sites have online tests that students can do for extra practice.

WORKBOOK AUDIO SCRIPT

Unit 1

Track ▶75

Page 84, Exercises 2 and 3

GEMMA: Hey, Mark! What are you so happy about? It's cold and rainy and there's nothing to do.
MARK: I'm leaving tomorrow to go to Mexico for four days. Hello sunshine!
GEMMA: That's sorta far to go for four days.
MARK: Yeah, but it's a special occasion. My family is going for a wedding. My cousin Rafa is getting married.
GEMMA: So, when d'ya leave?
MARK: Early tomorrow morning. Our flight's at 6:00.
GEMMA: Ugh! Are you ready?
MARK: What d'ya mean?
GEMMA: D'ya have your passport and stuff? Is your suitcase packed?
MARK: Um, no. I always do things at the last minute. I don't need much – a couple of T-shirts. That's all.
GEMMA: I dunno. I think it's kinda cold there right now. It's January, you know, not July. You need to take a sweater.
MARK: Well, I guess you're right. I'll take a sweater.
GEMMA: And d'ya think you're ready for the math test when you get back on Monday?
MARK: Test? What test?
GEMMA: Mark, I think you need to pack your math book too.

Track ▶76

Page 84, Exercise 6

1
GEMMA: Hey, Mark! What are you so happy about?
2
MARK: Yeah, but it's a special occasion.
3
GEMMA: Do you have your passport and stuff?
4
GEMMA: I dunno. I think it's kinda cold there right now.

Track ▶77

Page 87, Exercises 1 and 2

1
DAN: Hi! Pete and I are going to the movies tonight. Would you like to come?
JIM: I'm sorry, but I can't come. I'm going to a party with Rachel.
DAN: That's too bad. Another time!
2
LEA: Hi, Mac. I'm having a barbecue on the beach for our class.
MAC: Great! When is it?
LEA: It's on Saturday afternoon. Can you come?
MAC: Sure, I'd love to. I'm free that afternoon.
3
ANN: Jane and I are going on a day trip to New York next Saturday. Would you like to come with us?
LORI: That sounds fantastic. I'd love to. Thanks for inviting me.
4
RON: Hi, Sam. I'm inviting some people out for pizza tonight. Are you free?
SAM: Sorry. I'd love to come, but I can't. I'm going to a concert with my brother.

Track ▶78

Page 87, Exercise 4

CARLA: Hi, Lucas. I'm trying to organize a surprise birthday party for Tina. Would you like to come?
LUCAS: That sounds like fun. I'd love to. When is it?
CARLA: We're thinking of having it after school tomorrow at four o'clock. Can you come then?
LUCAS: Oh, sorry. I'd love to, but I have to babysit my little brother tomorrow afternoon.
CARLA: That's OK. We can have it on Wednesday. Are you free then?
LUCAS: Sure, Wednesday sounds great.
CARLA: Fantastic! Meet at my house on Wednesday at four o'clock. Don't be late!

Track ▶79

Page 87, Exercise 5b

Circled words with /e/: friend, get, net, then, twenty
Underlined words with /eɪ/: age, baby, date, paint

Unit 2

Track ▶80

Page 96, Exercises 2a and 3

Message 1
JANIE: Hi, Brian! It's 7:30. So early on a Monday morning! We're on our way to the airport to fly to the Bahamas for a festival, and we're sitting in a traffic jam on the highway. We've been here for half an hour, and we haven't moved at all. I think a bus has broken down. It's hot, and I'm bored. What a terrible start to our trip. Oh, better go – I think we're starting to move ... finally.

Message 2
JANIE: Hey. It's eleven o'clock, and we're at the airport. And guess what? The plane's delayed. They say it's because of bad weather, but the weather looks nice outside. We have to wait for two hours! Ugh, the place is really packed – there are people everywhere! At least Dad gave me some money to buy a magazine to read.

Message 3
JANIE: So it's still Monday – 5:00 in the afternoon – but the good news is we're on our way! Our flight was canceled, so we got our car from the parking garage and drove to the Port of Miami. We got a cruise ship to the Bahamas, and we're sailing all night. We should arrive in the Bahamas at seven o'clock in the morning. I'm so excited!

Track ▶81

Page 99, Exercises 3 and 4

1
TEEN 1: I'm meeting my friend. She's on the flight from Lima. Where's arrivals?
AGENT 1: That's upstairs.
TEEN 1: Sorry, I didn't hear that.
AGENT 1: Upstairs. You need to wait outside the Customs area for her.
TEEN 1: Thank you!
2
TEEN 2: I'm traveling on the 9:30 flight to Buenos Aires. Is it on time?
AGENT 2: You should check the times on the screen. It's updated every two minutes.
TEEN 2: Where's that?
AGENT 2: It's over there, past check-in.
TEEN 2: Can you please say that again?
AGENT 2: Yes. Go past check-in.
TEEN 2: OK. Thanks!
3
TEEN 3: Excuse me. I'm taking the flight to New York. Where's passport control?
AGENT 3: Oh, you need to go to check-in first.
TEEN 3: Really? Where's that?
AGENT 3: It's downstairs and to your right.
TEEN 3: Could you **repeat** that, please?
AGENT 3: Downstairs and to your right.
TEEN 3: Thank you very much!

Track ▶82

Page 99, Exercise 6

bag	bike	shampoo
departure	passport	toothbrush
passenger	hairbrush	toothpaste
baggage	plane	boat

Words with /b/: bag, baggage, bike, boat, hairbrush, toothbrush
Words with /p/: departure, passenger, passport, plane, shampoo, toothpaste

Unit 3

Track ▶83

Page 108, Exercises 3 and 4

HOST: So, tell us about you and your band.
ELISA: I'm Elisa from Café Negro.
HOST: What kind of music does your band play?
ELISA: Oh, mostly pop, and some rock too.

HOST: OK. And what instruments do you play?
ELISA: I play piano. Susana plays guitar and Ana's on the drums. Lupita is our singer. She's terrific.
HOST: So, when did you start playing with the band?
ELISA: Uh, at school in 2010.
HOST: Who inspired you to play music?
ELISA: I had a great music teacher at my school. When I was 10 years old, he taught me to play different instruments, and he encouraged me to find one that I really loved and stay with it. It's fun to practice when you find an instrument that's right for you.
HOST: How many songs have you recorded?
ELISA: Three. You can download them all. And of course I'm writing more songs for the band.
HOST: And what do you like best about playing music?
ELISA: Playing with my friends! It's so much fun to play and sing together.
HOST: Well, good luck in the future.

Track 84

Page 108, Exercises 5 and 6

HOST: Tell everyone a little bit about yourself. Like, what instrument do you play and what music do you like?
RICARDO: I'm Ricardo, and I play guitar. I play mostly folk music. I especially like love songs.
HOST: It sounds like you've been playing for a while. When did you start learning?
RICARDO: As for instruments, I started learning how to play the guitar about five years ago. My uncle is a folk singer and he inspired me to learn how to play. I sing a little too, but not very well. I didn't start singing until last year. But now that I'm writing my own songs, I want to be able to sing well.
HOST: So, you're writing songs? How many have you recorded?
RICARDO: I've written a lot, but I haven't recorded many songs. In fact, last month I recorded my first one, called "Dark Hearts."
HOST: What do you like best about playing music?
RICARDO: People often ask me what I enjoy about playing guitar. I guess it's bringing music into people's lives. I think music makes people feel happy.
HOST: It certainly does. Let's hear another song.
RICARDO: Sure.

Track 85

Page 111, Exercise 2

1
AMITA: Hey, Malike, how was your trip to Bali with your family?
MALIKE: Oh, we had a really fantastic time. On the last day we saw this traditional Balinese dancing. My mom said they danced more gracefully than any ballet dancer she's seen.
AMITA: Really? Why are they so good?
MALIKE: A lot of people say it's because they learn to dance with their hands when they're very young. Because they hear music from such an early age, they have this totally amazing sense of rhythm.
AMITA: What was your opinion?
MALIKE: I thought the dancing was great, but I really loved the costumes. They were so colorful and beautiful. Some people think they look a little strange, but I don't care what other people think. I loved them.

2
AMITA: So, tell me more about this dancing. What kind of music do they dance to?
MALIKE: They dance to the gamelan.
AMITA: Gamelan? What's that?
MALIKE: It's a kind of traditional band with instruments like drums, strings, and flutes. My brother thought they were cool, but my dad hated it because it was too noisy!
AMITA: And what about you? What did you think?
MALIKE: Well, I don't really have an opinion. I was so busy watching the dancers, I don't really remember what the music was like.

Track 86

Page 111, Exercise 4b

Words with /ɔ/: audience, audition, caught, song, thought
Words with /ɑ/: concert, confidence, costume, modern, opera

Unit 4

Track 87

Page 120, Exercises 2a and 2b

1
TEEN BOY: Did you go to the party with Peter?
MARIA: No, I didn't go with Peter. I went with Ed.

2
TEEN BOY: Are you coming over at four o'clock?
MARIA: No, I'm not coming over at 4:00. I'm coming over at 5:00.

3
TEEN BOY: Is that girl your sister?
MARIA: No, she isn't my sister. She's my cousin.

4
TEEN BOY: Did you order hamburgers at the restaurant?
MARIA: No, I hate hamburgers. But I love hot dogs.

Track 88

Page 120, Exercise 3

BEA: You look stressed.
SELMA: I'm not stressed. I'm tired.
BEA: Why's that?
SELMA: Pete called me. And not in the afternoon, but late at night.
BEA: Did he have a problem?
SELMA: Yes, he needed help with homework.
BEA: Math homework or English homework?
SELMA: Both!
BEA: But why is he calling anyone so late? I'd be kind of mad!

Track 89

Page 120, Exercises 4 and 5

KAREN: Hi, Steve.
STEVE: Hey, Karen! What's up?
KAREN: Not much ... You know, I saw Jordan's friend yesterday ... oh, what's his name ... the tall dark-haired guy?
STEVE: You mean Brad?
KAREN: Yeah. I have a terrible memory for names. I can remember faces but not names.
STEVE: You know, Anna, my cousin? She can remember people she's seen – even just once in a big group. She can even remember acquaintances from when she was five years old. It's a special ability. People like Anna are called "super recognizers."
KAREN: That's amazing. Is she like those people who can remember everything they've read or every picture they've seen?
STEVE: I don't think she can remember everything she's ever read, but she remembers faces!
KAREN: Wow! Imagine going up to someone in a store and saying "Hi! I saw you in a museum in Atlanta six years ago!" They'd think you were crazy.
STEVE: Gosh, yes! I don't know if I'd like to be like that. But Anna says it can be very useful. For example, super recognizers work with the police to find criminals in large groups of people, like at soccer games when fans cause problems.
KAREN: I never knew that! I'd be happy if I could just remember people's names! Who was Jordan's friend again?

Track ▶90

Page 120, Exercise 6

1 I'm so angry.
2 I'm so angry.
3 I'm so angry.

Track ▶91

Page 120, Exercise 7

1 John can remember everything.
2 John can remember everything.
3 John can remember everything.

Track ▶92

Page 123, Exercise 4

1
A: Excuse me. We're here on vacation. Would you take a picture of us, please?
B: Of course ... Smile!
2
A: We don't have a menu on our table. Would you mind if we borrowed yours for a moment?
B: Not at all. Here you are.
3
A: I'm going out tonight. Do you mind doing the laundry?
B: Sorry, I'm afraid I can't. I'm going out too.
4
A: I have to go to the library. I won't be long. Can you tell Mom that I'll be back in time for dinner?
B: All right.
5
A: You have some great ideas for your essay. Do you mind if I use some of them?
B: Sorry, but you should think of your own.

Track ▶93

Page 123, Exercise 5b

SARA: Ron, what are you doing here?
RON: It's Marty's computer. He's having problems with it.
SARA: Can I ask you a favor?
RON: OK. Go ahead.
SARA: It's my laptop. Would you check it for me? I can't get online.
RON: OK. No problem.
SARA: Thanks, Ron. You're a star! Oh, another thing – I dropped my hair dryer, and it won't work now. Could you look at that too?
RON: Sure. I'll do that after the laptop.
SARA: Thank you so much! What would we do without you?
RON: That's what friends are for!
SARA: Oh, one final thing. I can't get a signal on my new phone. Can you fix that?
RON: Sorry, I'm afraid I'm no good with phones.
SARA: That's OK. Do you mind if I borrow your phone to call Debbie?
RON: Not at all. Here you are!

Track ▶94

Page 123, Exercise 7

1
A: If you fixed my phone, what would it cost?
B: If I fixed your phone, I'd do it for free.
2
A: If you had to go on stage, how would you feel?
B: If I had to go on stage, I'd feel confident.
3
A: If your teacher made a mistake, what would you do?
B: If my teacher made a mistake, I'd point it out.

Unit 5

Track ▶95

Page 132, Exercise 2b

1
FEMALE 1: Although I don't usually like wearing yellow, this jacket looks good on me.
2
MALE 1: There are times when I don't really want to go out. For example, when I've had a long day at school.
3
FEMALE 2: I couldn't download the music I wanted. The thing is, I need a special program and we don't have it.
4
MALE 2: Tom's waiting outside for me even though I told him to meet me in the classroom.
5
FEMALE 3: It isn't hard to check your messages on a cell phone. Basically, you need to go to voicemail and it's all there.

Track ▶96

Page 132, Exercises 3 and 4a

HOST: So, Tony, what's the documentary tonight about?
TONY: Basically, it's about a girl, Stella, who has a really strange problem – although some people say it's not a problem, it's an ability.
HOST: And what is this problem – or ability?
TONY: Well, the thing is, it isn't easy to explain. It's called synesthesia – and don't worry, I'm not going to ask you to spell it! Basically, it's when our senses get a little confused.
HOST: You're right. I am a little confused!
TONY: OK. For example, people with synesthesia sometimes see colors when they hear different things – like words or music. When Stella listens to music, she sees silver and gold. The colors she sees depend on the type of music and the instruments.
HOST: That's amazing. It definitely sounds more like an ability.
TONY: Yeah – but imagine if that happens all the time. It's a very powerful feeling and not always a positive one. And some people see colors when people are speaking to them. This happens to one man on the show, Luke. He says that people's words are red when they're angry or blue when they're not telling the truth. Basically, his head is always full of confusing colors.
HOST: Wow. Scary! It's strange, but sometimes words have colors for me too. When I think of the days of the week – Monday is red, Tuesday is blue ... maybe I'm synes ... whatever you said.
TONY: Maybe you need to see a doctor!
HOST: Um, well, anyway, about the documentary. It's at 7:30. I hope you can join us.

Track ▶97

Page 132, Exercise 5b

Although most people today think of pink for girls and blue for boys, you might be surprised to learn that this is a fairly new idea. Sure, it would be really weird to see a three-year-old boy dressed in bright pink today. However, in Victorian times, that wouldn't have been so strange at all! Back then, for instance, parents dressed their children in colors like pinks, blues, and whites. Even though it sounds strange now, boys in Victorian times wore dresses too – just like the girls! However, things have changed a lot since then.

Track ▶98

Page 135, Exercise 3

1
A: Good morning. I need something for my skin. I sat in the sun too long. I'm not sure how to say it in English.
B: You mean you got sunburned?
A: Yes. Is this the right thing for my problem? I don't know what it's called.
B: That's sunscreen. It protects you from the sun. You need this one if you're already sunburned.
A: Thank you very much for your help.
2
A: Hello. I want to buy some insect repellent. What's the difference between this one and this one?
B: This one is a liquid that you put on your skin, but this one's a spray.
A: It says "For external use only." I don't understand what this means. My English isn't very good.
B: It means you can put it on your skin, but you can't eat it.
A: It's only for your skin?
B: That's right.
A: OK, I'll take the spray.

Track 99

Page 135, Exercise 4

A: Good morning. What can I get you?
B: I'd like a cup of coffee and one of those … I'm not sure how to say it in English.
A: You mean cookies?
B: Yes, please, a chocolate one. And some eggs for breakfast, please. What's the difference between sunny-side up and eggs over easy?
A: Sunny-side up means the eggs are cooked only on one side. Eggs over easy are cooked on both sides.
B: OK, thank you. Then I'd like the eggs over easy, please.
A: Is that for here or to go?
B: I'm sorry, I don't understand what that means.
A: Do you want to eat and drink here in the café or take it with you?
B: Here, please.

Track 100

Page 135, Exercise 5b

Beginning of word: grass, school, speak, street, throat
End of word: sound, attend, fact, help, pink

WORKBOOK ANSWER KEY

UNIT 1

VOCABULARY 1

Page 80

1 **1** parent **2** young adult **3** teenager **4** senior **5** college student **6** middle-aged person **7** child **8** baby

2 **1** parent **2** child **3** baby **4** middle-aged person **5** senior **6** teenager **7/8** college student / young adult

3 Emily is a child. Grandma/Grandpa is a senior. Mom/Dad/Aunty Patty is middle aged. Mom/Dad is a parent. Nico is a child. Angelica is a teenager. José is a baby.

4 **1** get **2** get **3** vote **4** retire **5** graduate **6** leave **7** go **8** have **9** go **10** get

5 **1** driver's license **2** graduate **3** college **4** get a job **5** have children **6** retire

READING

Page 81

1 **1** all **2** information **3** beginning **4** words

2 **1** 5,000+ **2** romantic **3** places **4** blacksmith's shop **5** get married **6** *Star Trek*

GRAMMAR 1

Page 82

1 **1** She **2** do not/don't **3** He **4** Do **5** Yes **6** does **7** 'm **8** 're **9** isn't **10** are **11** Is **12** isn't **13** are **14** Why

2 **1** e **2** d **3** f **4** b **5** a **6** c

Page 83

3 **1** retire **2** 's making **3** organize **4** are watching **5** never wear **6** stay

4a

Stative verbs: believe, know, like, need, remember, want

Action verbs: celebrate, dance, do, enjoy, paint, prepare

5 **1** **Do you need** some help with that project?

2 He doesn't want to study physics next year because **he prefers** biology.

3 Freddie **doesn't want** to go to college when he graduates from high school.

4 **I'm saving** money right now to go on vacation next year.

5 Jess **is getting** ready to go out right now.

6 How often **do you visit** your grandparents?

6 **1** knows **2** doesn't speak **3** 'm enjoying **4** exercise **5** 'm not studying **6** isn't improving

7

1 talk **2** 'm riding **3** ride **4** are / calling **5** 's driving **6** 're passing **7** need **8** See

8 **1** Do you like Indian food?

2 What are you doing?

3 Does your brother play soccer?

4 Does your teacher usually give a lot of homework?

5 Where are Amy and Sue going?

6 What time does history class start?

LISTENING

Page 84

1 **1** d'ya **2** yeah **3** stuff **4** can't **5** um

2 A, B, F

3 **1** Mexico **2** the weekend/four days **3** wedding **4** 6 o'clock **5** T-shirts **6** January **7** a sweater **8** a test/a math test

4 **1** sort of **2** kind of **3** don't know **4** yes **5** you **6** going to **7** things **8** What do you mean?

5 **1** That's sort of far to go for four days.

2 What do you mean?

3 I think it's kind of cold there now.

4 I don't know.

5 So, when do you leave?

6 **1** Hey **2** Yeah **3** stuff **4** stuff **5** dunno **6** kinda

7 **1** I **2** I **3** C **4** C **5** I **6** I

VOCABULARY 2

Page 85

1 **1** cotton **2** enormous **3** square **4** valuable **5** plastic **6** colorful **7** tiny **8** unusual

2 **1** valuable **2** useful **3** antique **4** old-fashioned **5** special **6** colorful

3 **1** amazing wooden **2** old white **3** tiny silver **4** small traditional **5** old cotton **6** long pink

Words & Beyond

4a

secondhand: used / not new

doll: a child's toy that looks like a small person or baby

wooden: made out of wood

identical: exactly the same as something else

packaging: the paper/plastic that covers a new product before it's opened or used

4b **1** doll **2** secondhand **3** wooden **4** identical **5** packaging

5 **1** turned **2** ceremony **3** stuff **4** diving

GRAMMAR 2

Page 86

1 **1** We **2** didn't **3** Did **4** were **5** wasn't **6** wasn't **7** Were **8** were **9** going

2 **1** was pouring **2** were preparing **3** didn't want **4** was waiting **5** found **6** was dancing

3 **1** called **2** Were you watching **3** wasn't watching **4** was working **5** was listening **6** Did you get **7** did you send **8** sent **9** wasn't working **10** was working **11** noticed **12** didn't change

4 **1** listened **2** bought **3** was shopping **4** spoke **5** was **6** came **7** was dancing **8** fell **9** hurt

SPEAKING

Page 87

1 **1** C **2** D **3** A **4** B

2 **1** but I can't come **2** That's too bad. **3** Great! **4** Sure, I'd love to. **5** That sounds fantastic. **6** I'd love to come, but I can't.

3 **1** R **2** A **3** A **4** R

4 3, 2, 7, 6, 5, 4, 1

5 **Circle:** friend, get, net, then, twenty
Underline: age, paint, date, baby

WRITING

Page 88

1 **1** a heading **2** questions **3** notes

2 **1** What, where, and when was it?

2 What happened? Who was there? What did I do?

3 Why was it special? What do I remember about it?

3 Underline: A really special day for me was my brother's wedding last summer. (Ana…dress.)

Circle: The whole day was fantastic, but best of all, now I have a very special sister-in-law.

Page 89

5 Answers will vary.

1 What, where, and when was it?

2 What happened? Who was there? What did I do?

3 Why was it special? What do I remember about it?

Life Skills

1 They are organizing an end-of-year party.

They need to find out who is coming, reserve a table at a restaurant, decide on a menu, get decorations, think about music.

2 **1** b **2** b **3** b **4** b

3 Answer will vary.

VOCABULARY REVIEW

Page 90

1 **1** 1, 3, 2 **2** 2, 1, 3 **3** 3, 1, 2 **4** 2, 1, 3 **5** 3, 2, 1

2 **Across** **1** parents **2** retire **3** crown **4** celebration **5** doll **6** election
Down **7** ritual **8** license **9** ceremony **10** university **11** job

3 **opinion:** useful, valuable, unusual, old-fashioned, traditional

size: enormous, tiny

shape: square

age: antique

color: colorful

material: wooden, cotton

GRAMMAR REVIEW

Page 91

1 **1** you're sharing **2** How's it going? **3** get **4** don't argue **5** cooks **6** are you doing **7** I'm just watching **8** Do you want **9** we're decorating

2 **1** 'm looking **2** 'm preparing **3** need **4** 'm studying

3 **1** invited **2** got **3** was running **4** happened **5** fell **6** cut **7** needed **8** was carrying **9** came **10** started

4 **1** I; While I was waiting for the movie to start, I bought some popcorn. **2** I; I'm sorry Mrs. Rivers, but I don't understand what we have to do for homework. **3** C **4** I; Right now we're celebrating our soccer team's victory. **5** C **6** C

UNIT 2

VOCABULARY 1

Page 92

1 **Across** **1** ship **5** helicopter **7** bus **8** bike **Down** **2** plane **3** taxi **4** motorcycle **5** horse **6** truck

2 **1** ride **2** fly **3** drive **4** drive **5** sail **6** ride

3 **1** hairbrush **2** toothpaste **3** toothbrush **4** visa **5** sleeping bag **6** passport **7** boarding pass **8** suitcase **9** shampoo **10** backpack **11** wallet

4 **1** scissors **2** wallet **3** shampoo **4** suitcase **5** a toothbrush **6** a hairbrush

5 **1** c **2** d **3** f **4** e **5** a **6** b

6a Flying to a different country: hairbrush, toothpaste, toothbrush, visa, passport, boarding pass, suitcase, shampoo, wallet
Staying at a hotel: hairbrush, toothpaste, toothbrush, suitcase, shampoo, wallet
Going camping: hairbrush, toothpaste, toothbrush, sleeping bag, shampoo, backpack, wallet

READING

Page 93

1 **1** headings **2** layout **3** pictures **4** weblinks **5** beginning **6** goal

2 Text A 3 Text B 1 Text C 2

3 Text A: instruct Text B: persuade Text C: inform

4 **1** C **2** C **3** I **4** C **5** I

5 **1** A **2** A, C **3** C **4** C **5** B

GRAMMAR 1

Page 94

1 **1** have **2** 's **3** have **4** hasn't **5** I've **6** Where

2 **1** ever/never **2** exact time **3** already/just/yet

3a **underline:** 've just arrived; 've never watched; hasn't called; hasn't forgotten, 've been, 've already bought; Have you received

b for 15 minutes; since last night

4a

base verb	Past participle
be	been
wait	waited
travel	traveled
buy	bought
read	read
write	written
speak	spoken
catch	caught
do	done
make	made

4b be, buy, read, write, speak, catch, do, make

Page 95

5 **1** for **2** since **3** for **4** since **5** for **6** since

6 **1** I've never stayed in an expensive hotel.
2 Have you swum in the ocean yet?
3 He's just unpacked his suitcase.
4 I've already been in the pool three times.
5 Have they ever traveled to Europe?
6 Our plane hasn't taken off yet.

7 **1** just **2** already **3** never **4** yet **5** ever **6** for

8 **1** I haven't called Paul for two weeks.
2 Have you spoken to Kenny about the party?
3 We've bought tickets for the concert on Wednesday.
4 Sally's just gotten her grades.
5 Which of these books have you read?
6 The teacher hasn't given us any homework!
7 Where have you been until now?
8 We've just won the World Cup!

9 **1** 've been **2** 've eaten **3** 've spoken **4** hasn't gone **5** has made **6** have you done

10 **1** Yes, I've just left.
2 I've already checked.
3 No, I've never been (to China).
4 No, she hasn't gotten her results yet.
5 I've had a pet dog for five years.
6 I've lived in California since 2005.

11 **1** I've lost my passport.
2 We've already eaten
3 The taxi has arrived.
4 The weather has changed.
5 I've spent all my money.
6 I've failed my driving test.

LISTENING

Page 96

1 **1** listen for the main ideas **2** listen for specific information

2a **A:** Message 1, **B:** Message 3, **C:** Message 2

2b **1** negative **2** negative **3** positive

3 **Message 1:** 1 7:30 a.m. 2 Bahamas 3 highway (in the car, in traffic) 4 half an hour (30 minutes)
Message 2: 1 11:00 a.m. 2 airport 3 bad weather 4 2 hours
Message 3: 1 5:00 p.m. 2 cruise ship 3 7:00 a.m.

4 **1** half an hour **2** highway **3** bad weather **4** two **5** ship **6** night

VOCABULARY 2

Page 97

1 **1** seat **2** departure **3** arrival **4** reservation **5** distance **6** flight **7** connection

2 **1** flight **2** reservation **3** distance **4** departure **5** connection **6** arrival

3 **Across:** **2** destination **3** passenger **5** seat **Down:** **1** fare **2** delay **4** route

4 **line:** a group of people politely waiting to do something
trip: when you go somewhere and come back again
voyage: a long journey, usually by ship
journey: the act of traveling from one place to another
passport control: the area where your documents are checked
gate: a part of an airport where you get on or off a plane
homesick: missing home when you're in another place
check in: the act of showing your ticket and giving your luggage to the staff at the airport
crew: the people who work on a plane or ship
customs: the place where your luggage is sometimes searched
take off: to begin to fly a plane in the air at the beginning of a flight
land: to guide a plane safely back to the ground at the end of a flight

5 **1** crew **2** line **3** take off **4** homesick **5** gate **6** trip **7** customs **8** land

GRAMMAR 2

Page 98

1 **1** d **2** e **3** a **4** c **5** b

2 **1** is going to land **2** You'll definitely **3** We're meeting **4** is likely to be **5** You'll get **6** I'm going to ask

3 **1** does your plane leave **2** are you getting **3** Are you going to eat **4** Will you need **5** Are you likely to recommend **6** Is anybody meeting

4 **1** 'm going to have **2** 'm playing **3** 'm going to relax **4** is **5** 'll definitely watch **6** are likely to come **7** 'll probably go **8** starts

5 **1** 'm going to meet **2** 'll probably watch **3** is likely to win **4** 'll definitely be **5** will probably score **6** aren't likely to lose

SPEAKING

Page 99

1 **1** Sorry, I didn't hear that.
2 Could you repeat that, please?
3 Can you please say that again?
4 Sorry, I don't understand.

2 1 Gates 1-29 **2** Customs
3 Departures **4** Passport control
5 Arrivals **6** Check-in
3 Departures, Gates 1–29
4 Conversation 1: Sorry, I didn't hear that.
Conversation 2: Can you please say that again?
Conversation 3: Could you repeat that, please?
5 1 I'd like to check in **2** Can I have
3 Here you are **4** are you checking
5 I have **6** your carry-on bag **7** boarding pass **8** gate number is it **9** Gate 15
10 a good flight
6

/b/		/p/	
toothbrush	boat	toothpaste	shampoo
hairbrush	baggage	passport	passenger
bike	bag	plane	departure

WRITING
Page 100
2 1 d **2** c **3** f **4** h **5** e **6** b **7** a **8** g
3 1 Right now **2** for 10 years
3 every summer **4** every day
5 Yesterday **6** seven days ago **7** since then **8** Tonight **9** at 4:15 p.m. **10** next year
4 1 they come here, Marianne and I go walking and climbing **2** we're really enjoying, we're staying **3** parents have had **4** we were walking **5** I saw
6 they're taking us…dinner, I'm taking the plane **7** I'll definitely come back

Life Skills
Page 101
1 Kate was at Union Station in Chicago. She was trying to buy some tickets.
2 The station was very crowded, and Kate was uncomfortable being so close to other people.
3 Answers will vary.

VOCABULARY REVIEW
Page 102
1 1 sleeping **2** first **3** carry-on **4** sharp
5 college **6** passport **7** boarding
8 driver's
2 1 passenger – the others are all age related
2 toothbrush – the others are all things you need to get into places
3 route – the others are all types of transportation
4 homesick – the others can all describe objects
5 fare – the others are things you go on
6 backpack – the others all go into a backpack
7 suitcase – the others are all places at an airport
8 vote – the others all happen on a plane
3 Across: 3 teenager **5** cotton
7 colorful **9** reservation **11** scissors
12 baby
Down: 1 antique **2** connection
4 documents **6** trip **8** departure
10 money
4 1 useful **2** square **3** old-fashioned
4 middle-aged **5** trip **6** destination
7 route **8** seat

GRAMMAR REVIEW
Page 103
1 1 I'm working; I'll definitely be able to
2 doesn't want; doesn't have
3 has worked; loves **4** are you going; Are you likely to be **5** are building; is driving **6** Have you seen; were listening
2 1 How long have you been home?
2 I've just gotten back. **3** My plane landed at 11:30 this morning.
4 Did you have a wonderful time in China? **5** I've never enjoyed a trip so much. **6** I saw some pictures of the Great Wall yesterday **7** thought about you! **8** While I was walking along the Great Wall **9** My phone hasn't worked since last Thursday.
3 1 has been a teacher for
2 go jogging / jog every day **3** 's likely to rain
4 've just seen **5** while I was eating/ having **6** met Tom six months ago
4 1 has left; will take **2** are waiting; has landed **3** have found; were drinking
4 is landing; will arrive **5** have not boarded; will miss

Unit 3
VOCABULARY 1
Page 104
1 opera **2** drums **3** trumpet **4** singer
5 guitar **6** conductor **7** orchestra
8 violin **9** flute **10** musician
2 1 rock **2** performance **3** jazz
4 hip hop **5** audience **6** musician
7 venue **8** opera
3 1 a conductor **2** the concert
3 a band **4** audience **5** musician
6 hip hop
4a 1 concert **2** venue **3** drums
4 audience **5** performance **6** singer
7 musicians **8** band

READING
Page 105
1 1 part **2** similar **3** before **4** after
5 mean
2 and 5

Noun	Verb
audience	host
conductor	listen
range	moaned
spotlight	sing
standard	
Adjective	**Adverb**
classical	beautifully
fantastic	well
annual	nervously
upside down	

3 1 yes **2** a review
4 1 Eurovision Song Contest
2 Saturday **3** Denmark **4** Austria
6 1 a **2** b **3** b **4** b **5** b **6** a **7** a **8** a

GRAMMAR 1
Page 106
1 1 to go **2** to play **3** to buy
4 to become **5** to go **6** performing
7 listening **8** being **9** watching
2 1 b, c, e **2** a, b, d
3 1 drum/drumming, plan/planning, sit/sitting, stop/stopping, swim/ swimming **2** become/becoming, create/ creating, hope/hoping, take/taking, write/writing
4 Verbs followed by infinitive: decide, hope, inspire, learn, plan, want, would like
Verbs followed by gerund: don't mind, enjoy, imagine, practice
Verbs followed by both: like, forget, hate, love, prefer
5 a Incorrect: 1, 2, 5, 6, 8, 9, 10
b 1 being **2** to play **5** to play **6** to play
8 seeing **9** to be **10** to meet

Page 107
6 1 moving **2** to teach **3** playing
4 to go **5** traveling **6** to get
7 1 being **2** to be or being **3** being
4 to be **5** being **6** to be **7** to be **8** to be
9 to be **10** to be **11** being **12** to be
8 1 to watch **2** to join **3** listening or to listen **4** to come **5** making **6** to win
7 to write **8** to see
9 1 I don't mind helping you. **2** You should learn to speak Spanish yourself!
3 I decided to learn the guitar instead.
4 I'm not planning to go until 9:00 p.m.
10 1 to start **2** watching **3** going **4** to get **5** waiting **6** not to record
11 1 I forgot to write down the assignment. **2** I prefer listening to folk rather than jazz. Or, I prefer to listen to folk rather than jazz. **3** I don't mind finishing the typing for you. **4** I can't stand listening to heavy metal music.
12 1 forget to send **2** hope to see
3 enjoyed swimming **4** decided to buy

LISTENING
Page 108
1 1 Read **2** Decide **3** listen **4** write
3 1 kind of music **2** instruments
3 inspired you (to play music)? **4** songs have you recorded
4 5 (some) rock **6** piano **7** (at school) in 2010 **8** three **9** playing with friends
5 10 folk **11** guitar **12** about five years ago **13** my uncle **14** bringing music into people's lives (making people happy)
6 1 I play mostly folk music. **2** As for instruments, I started learning how to play the guitar about five years ago.

3 I sing a little too, but not very well.
4 In fact, last month I recorded my first one. 5 People often ask me what I enjoy about playing guitar.

VOCABULARY 2

Page 109

1 **1–2** pretty, fairly **3–4** really, very
5–8 extremely, incredibly, totally
2 **1** incredibly **2** really **3** a little
4 totally **5** a pretty **6** really **7** extremely
8 a little **9** a lot **10** totally
3 **1** extremely **2** incredibly **3** a little
4 really **5** a little **6** incredibly

Words & Beyond

4 **1** stage **2** gesture **3** audition
4 confidence **5** convey **6** talent
7 criteria **8** focused

GRAMMAR 2

Page 110

1 **1** harder **2** more beautifully
3 the quickest **4** the most beautifully
5 fast **6** carefully **7** worse **8** better
2 **1** the fastest **2** harder **3** the most creatively **4** worse **5** the highest
6 the earliest **7** more powerfully
8 better **9** the most confidently
10 farther
3 **1** The audience shouted more loudly for Anna than for Mark.
2 Kevin swam the fastest in the competition.
3 I didn't do as well in math this year as I did last year.
4 My friend paints more beautifully than many professional artists.
5 Greta danced better than the other dancers in the audition.
6 Freddy sings the worst in the whole school!
4 **1** higher **2** the hardest **3** more beautifully **4** as well as **5** faster
6 better **7** as well as
5 **1** Can you paint as creatively as Max?
2 You need to learn to write more neatly.
3 At the audition, Oliver performed the most confidently. **4** Isabel can't run as fast as Nicola because she's only 13.

SPEAKING

Page 111

1 **1** A **2** B
2 **1** lot of people **2** your opinion
3 thought **4** people think **5** don't care
6 about **7** you think **8** have an opinion
3 **Asking for an opinion:** What was your opinion? And what about you? What did you think?
Giving an opinion: I thought … I don't care what other people think … I don't really have an opinion.
Presenting other people's opinions: A lot of people … Some people think …

4

/ɔ/	/ɑ/
audience	concert
song	opera
caught	modern
audition	costume
thought	confidence

WRITING

Page 112

1 **1** but **2** although **3** even though
4 however
2 **1** Although **2** but **3** However, **4** but
5 However, **6** Even though
3 **1** Although / Even though **2** However
3 Even though / Although **4** However
5 but **6** Although / Even though
4 **1** I; The composer Beethoven was deaf, but he wrote some amazing classical music. **2** C **3** I; I'd like to be a singer, but I get nervous in front of an audience. **4** C **5** C **6** I; The band is very famous in Europe, but no one has heard of them in the USA.

Life Skills

Page 113

1 He's painting his room.
Possible answers:
2 Dan didn't stay on task. He finished one wall, but he got distracted by his friend, his music, and his hunger.
3 Buy enough paint before you begin. Eat before you start and have food at your house. Invite some friends to help you paint. Listen to music while you paint.

VOCABULARY REVIEW

Page 114

1 **Across:** **5** tradition **6** visa **7** orchestra
10 enormous **11** ceremony
Down: **1** valuable **2** ritual **3** colorful
4 passenger **8** drum **9** folk
2 **1** customs **2** scissors **3** shampoo
4 opera **5** adult **6** trumpet **7** trip
8 passport **9** toothbrush **10** helicopter
11 route **12** election

GRAMMAR REVIEW

Page 115

1 **1** Where do you like to listen to music?
2 Are you going to watch the concert on television?
3 Where were you going when I saw you this morning?
4 Have you ever learned how to play an instrument?
5 How long have you liked rock music?
2 **1** decided **2** listening **3** don't
4 to play **5** being **6** to borrow
3 **1** longer **2** harder **3** quicker/more quickly **4** as well as **5** worst **6** best
4 **1** d **2** a **3** f **4** b **5** e **6** c
5 **1** Susie speaks English as fluently as Kyle.
2 Nick is diving the best in the competition.
3 I'm meeting Matthew after school today.
4 Helena has played the drums for six years.
5 I've never been to Paris before./I haven't been to Paris before.
6 We would like to take a vacation in Maine this summer.

Unit 4

VOCABULARY

Page 116

1 **ambitious:** having a strong wish to be rich and successful
generous: willing to be more kind, helpful, or giving (with money, for example) than most people
sensitive: being aware of and responding to other people's feelings.
creative: describes a person who can think of a lot of new ideas
competitive: wanting to win in whatever you do
cheerful: looking happy and positive
brave: not afraid of danger or difficult things
polite: not saying unkind or rude things
rude: not polite; a person who says or does things that might upset or anger other people
2 **1** generous **2** sensitive **3** creative
4 ambitious **5** competitive **6** cheerful
3 **1** enemies **2** neighbor **3** classmates
4 relative **5** guest **6** acquaintance
4 **1** old friends **2** teammates **3** online friends **4** close friends
5 **A** Mrs. Mendoza; **B** Rita; **C** Lucia;
D David; **E** Emma

READING

Page 117

1 **1** like **2** such as **3** For example
4 For instance **5** headings **6** first
2 **1** I'm very shy with people I don't know, such as acquaintances.
2 My neighbor is really generous. For example, last week he lent me his MP3 player.
3 My cousins share a lot of things, such as clothes and books.
4 Diego and I are very different. For instance, I love soccer/tennis but he prefers tennis/soccer.
3 **1** b **2** d **3** a **4** c
4 **1** Julieta and Mia **2** Rodrigo **3** Vi
4 Alex **5** Julieta and Mia **6** Alex

GRAMMAR 1

Page 118

1 **1** present **2** *will, may, might* + base verb **3** present **4** *will, may, might* + base verb
2 **1** I **2** C **3** I **4** C **5** C

3 **1** He thinks they might miss the movie. **2** Greta **3** Enrique's parents will be angry and his dad will have to take Greta to the movie. **4** No **5** He's going to leave in five minutes if she's not ready.
4 **1** A **2** A **3** A **4** A **5** B

Page 119
5 **1** If my sister doesn't wake me up early tomorrow, I'll be happy.
2 We'll meet after school unless our class finishes late.
3 Harry has tennis practice this morning unless it rains.
4 If you don't want to go shopping, I'll go by myself.
5 If you forget your key, the neighbor will let you in.
6 My brother will give us a ride unless there's a problem with his car.
6 **1** calls **2** comes **3** don't get **4** makes **5** don't talk **6** find
7 **1** If I get home early, I'll take the dog for a walk. **2** Unless I can earn some more money, I won't be able to go to Lisbon. **3** I'll wear my new dress if I go to Georgia's party. **4** If we win this game, we'll be in the finals of the competition. **5** My cousin will give me some advice if I ask her for help. **6** Jonas won't talk to me again unless I apologize.
8 **1** *What will you do if she says no? If she says no, I'll probably cry.* **2** What will you do if you miss the train? If I miss the train, I'll catch the bus. **3** Who will you invite to play soccer if Tom doesn't come? If Tom doesn't come, I'll invite Mark. **4** Where will Dave and Mike stay if they go to Tokyo? If Dave and Mike go to Tokyo, they'll stay with Yuko. **5** If Beatriz visits you, where will you take her? If Beatriz visits us, we'll take her to the theme park.
9 **1** don't go **2** will get **3** talk **4** don't accept **5** will be **6** invite **7** explain **8** will respect **9** doesn't understand **10** won't be

LISTENING
Page 120
1 **1** important **2** stressed **3** feelings **4** up **5** down
2a **1** Peter, Ed **2** 4, 5 **3** sister, cousin **4** hamburgers, hot dogs
3 stressed, tired; afternoon, night; math, English; late; mad
4 **b** someone they know with a special ability
5 **1** I **2** I **3** C **4** I **5** C **6** I
6 **1** I'm, b **2** so, a **3** angry, c
7 **1** Ann, c **2** can, b **3** everything, a

VOCABULARY 2
Page 121
1 **1** amazing, d **2** terrified, e **3** furious, b **4** shocked, h **5** ancient, i **6** exhausted, g **7** huge, c **8** awful, j **9** unbelievable, a **10** fascinating, f
2 **1** amazing **2** furious **3** exhausted **4** huge **5** awful **6** shocked

Words & Beyond
3 **1** ambitious **2** generous **3** sensitive **4** creative **5** competitive **6** cheerful **7** brave **8** polite **9** rude

GRAMMAR 2
Page 122
1 **1** simple past **2** would **3** simple past **4** would
2 **1** an imaginary **2** simple past **3** would **4** can **5** first or second
3 **1** had; would buy **2** changed; would miss **3** would be; called **4** were; would drive **5** would understand; spoke **6** would move; had
4 **1** What would you do if you got lost overseas? **2** What would you do if you lost your homework? **3** Where would you go if you could travel anywhere?
4 How would you feel if you couldn't answer any questions on a test?
5 **A** 2; If I lost my homework, I'd tell the teacher. **B** 4; If I couldn't answer any questions on a test, I'd feel stressed. **C** 1; If I got lost, I'd ask someone for directions. **D** 3; If I could travel anywhere, I'd see the pyramids.
6 **1** could go **2** 'd visit **3** started **4** could take **5** stopped **6** 'd visit **7** had **8** 'd fly **9** had **10** could take **11** let **12** 'd fly

SPEAKING
Page 123
1 **1** Could/Can **2** Can/Could **3** help **4** Do **5** Would
2 **1** ✓ **2** ✓ **3** ✗ **4** ✓ **5** ✓ **6** ✗ **7** ✓ **8** ✓
3 **Circled:** Would you mind helping me with this problem, please? Do you mind if I leave early today? Would you mind if I borrowed your dictionary? Of course. I'm afraid … No, go ahead. Not at all.
Underlined: Can/Could I borrow your phone? Can/Could you give me a ride, please? OK. All right. Sure. Sorry, I can't.
4 **1** Would **2** course **3** borrowed **4** Not **5** Do **6** I'm afraid I can't **7** Can you **8** All **9** Do
5a **a** Would you check it for me?
b Do you mind if I borrow your phone to call Debbie?
c Can I ask you a favor?
d Can you fix that?
e Could you look at that too?
b **1** Can I ask you a favor?
2 Would you check it for me?
3 Could you look at that too?
4 Can you fix that?
5 Do you mind if I borrow your phone to call Debbie?

WRITING
Page 124
1 **1** b **2** a **3** d **4** c **5** e
2a frank 3; bear 2c; lie 1b; relay 4
3a **1** fly – sky **2** city – pretty
3 cruise – choose **4** bored – afford
5 flight – sight **6** trip – ship
7 friend – lend **8** plane – train
4 **1** simple **2** no **3** no **4** no
5 friends and relatives **6** cities and sights, different cultures, and people
7 eat wonderful food and take a lot of pictures **8** happy and relaxed

Life Skills
Page 125
1 She has to decide what she's going to do during next week's vacation. She decides to stay home and go to soccer practice, and then go away with her parents for a couple of days.

VOCABULARY REVIEW
Page 126
1 **A** 2; connection **B** 4; heavy metal **C** 5; traditional **D** 3; stage **E** 1 patient
2 **1** huge **2** online **3** friendships **4** acquaintances **5** friend **6** reminds **7** celebrations **8** stuff **9** homesick **10** miss **11** distracting **12** focused
3 **Across:** **4** valuable **8** retire **10** suitcase **11** rhythm **12** reservation
Down: **1** wallet **2** venue **3** line **5** scissors **6** classmates **7** passenger **9** audition

GRAMMAR REVIEW
Page 127
1 **1** invites **2** won't get **3** will land **4** were **5** told **6** agree
2 **1** take **2** 'll be **3** wear **4** were **5** 'd explain **6** doesn't understand **7** wouldn't worry **8** cared
3 **1** have you been **2** joined **3** chatting **4** to join **5** to practice **6** Do you have **7** more confidently **8** better **9** 's calling **10** you'll be **11** wants
4 **1** We won't have the party outside if it rains. **2** Jas writes more neatly than Mason. **3** I hope to travel overseas after my exams. **4** While the band was playing, many people in the audience left. **5** We're likely to be late, so let's meet inside the restaurant.
6 I don't mind rock music, but I prefer heavy metal.

Unit 5

VOCABULARY
Page 128
1 **1** shoulder **2** neck **3** hand **4** face **5** back **6** leg **7** knee **8** toe **9** foot
2 **1** touch, hand **2** taste, mouth **3** smell, nose, hearing, ear

3a **1** touch **2** taste **3** smell **4** sight **5** hearing **6** hearing **7** hearing **8** touch **9** sight
3b **1** feel **2** taste **3** smell **4** see, look **5** listen **6** hear, sound **7** hear **8** touch, feel **9** watch, see
4 **1** watch **2** tastes **3** sounds **4** smells **5** hear **6** feels **7** see **8** look **9** listen

READING
Page 129
1 **1** Before **2** visuals **3** connection **4** style **5** when
2a **1** a **2** b **3** b, c, e
3 **1** I **2** C **3** C **4** I **5** I **6** C
4 **1** a **2** b **3** a

GRAMMAR 1
Page 130
1 **1** are **2** isn't **3** subject **4** was **5** weren't **6** will/'ll **7** won't **8** be
2a **1** no **2** the action **3** no
2b **1** don't know **2** not as important as **3** not very obvious
3 **1** P **2** P **3** A **4** P **5** A **6** P **7** A **8** A
4 were taken, was opened, were brought together, is written, was damaged, will be repaired, will be sent back, was built, it's known for
5 Present passive: is written, it's known for; Simple past passive: were taken, was opened, were brought together, was damaged, was built; Future passive: will be repaired, will be sent back

Page 131
6 **1** Too much food is thrown away these days. **2** Most food is bought in supermarkets. **3** The pizza was delivered one hour after I ordered it. **4** In the future, more vegetables will be grown in people's gardens. **5** We were told by the manager that the restaurant was closing. **6** Some of the best products are made by small companies.
7 **1** made **2** was launched **3** isn't delivered **4** is fitted **5** is controlled **6** travels **7** was designed **8** will take off
8 **1** is served **2** is delivered **3** were taken **4** isn't cooked **5** are given **6** is built **7** are given **8** will be opened
9 **1** This delicious sauce was first made in Vietnam. **2** Then it was produced by David Tran, an immigrant, in Los Angeles in the 1980s. **3** It was mixed in buckets at home and driven to customers in Tran's van. **4** The hot sauce was named Sriracha. **5** Today it is loved by people of all nationalities. **6** The sauce is used by famous chefs and restaurant chains for many meals. **7** More than $60 million of Sriracha is sold each year by David Tran's company. **8** The sauce's recipe won't be shared with anyone.

LISTENING
Page 132
1 **1** an important point **2** examples **3** contrasting information
2a **1** Although **2** For example **3** The thing is **4** even though **5** Basically
2b **1** Even though **2** For instance **3** Basically **4** although **5** The thing is
3 a
4 **1** I **2** I **3** C **4** I **5** C **6** C
5a **1** Although/Even though **2** However **3** For example/instance **4** Although/Even though **5** However

VOCABULARY 2
Page 133
1 **1** once in a **blue** moon **2** see **red** **3** get the **green** light **4** as **black** as night **5** out of the **blue** **6** tell a **white** lie **7** as **white** as a sheet **8** be in the **red** **9** **black** and **white** **10** feel **blue**
2 **1** j **2** b **3** f **4** a **5** c **6** d **7** h **8** e **9** g **10** i
3 **A** g **B** h **C** e **D** i **E** b

Words & Beyond
4 **1** potato chips **2** pale **3** tongues **4** complaints **5** ban **6** pharmacist

GRAMMAR 2
Page 134
1 **1** buy a skateboard **2** I can buy a skateboard **3** play in a band **4** I could play in a band
2 **1** to **2** so that **3** so that **4** in order to **5** in order to **6** so that
3 **1** c **2** b **3** e **4** f **5** d **6** a
4 **1** On order to/To **2** In order to/To **3** So that **4** so that **5** In order to/To **6** So that **7** so that
5 **1** We met at the café so that we could have a good talk. **2** I organized a party in order to celebrate Javier's birthday. **3** I studied hard in order to do well on the test. **4** We took one small piece of luggage so that we could check in more quickly. **5** I'm taking an online English course to improve my listening and grammar skills.

SPEAKING
Page 135
1 **1** I'm not sure how to say it in English. **2** Does that mean … ? **3** I need something for … **4** Is this the right thing for … ? **5** I don't know what it's called. **6** What's the difference between … ? **7** I don't understand what this means. **8** I need some of that … **9** It's for …
2 **Explaining what you need:** I need something for … ; It's for … ; I'm not sure how to say it in English.; I don't know what it's called. ; I need some of that …
Asking for help: Does that mean … ?; I don't understand what this means.; Is this the right thing for … ?; What's the difference between … ?
3 **1** need something **2** how to say it **3** Is this the right thing for **4** what it's called **5** What's the difference **6** what this means **7** It's only for
4 Correct order: 1, 10, 7, 4, 3, 6, 5, 8, 9, 2
5a **Beginning of word:** grass, school, speak, street, throat **End of word:** attend, fact, help, pink

WRITING
Page 136
1 **1** and **2** as well **3** after **4** end **5** true
2 **1** and **2** also **3** too **4** also **5** also **6** as well
3 **1** We always go camping, and I love sitting outside listening to the birds singing.
2 I not only like to go sightseeing, but I also like to visit the places that local people go to.
3 We usually go to the park. We go to see our relatives in the city as well.
4 My cousins always come on vacation with us. My aunt and uncle sometimes come with us too.
5 My friends and I rent a small house in the mountains, and we go walking every day in the fresh air.
6 I not only stay at home for my vacation, but I also do nothing for a week. It's so relaxing!
4 **1** and **2** Not only **3** also **4** also **5** as well / too **6** as well / too
5 **1** C **2** D **3** A **4** B

Life Skills
Page 137
1 She was at a basketball game. She was talking to Mendi.
2 She stood close to Gina. She had her arms folded. She kept her eyes down while they were talking.

VOCABULARY REVIEW
Page 138
Parts of the body: nose, hair, back, eyes, face, knee, shoulder
Appearance: good-looking, wavy, small, straight, blonde, tall
Sense verbs: sound, smell, touch, hearing, watch
2 **1** sheet **2** back **3** blue **4** hard **5** night **6** common
3 **1** sensitive **2** competitive **3** ambitious **4** furious **5** blind **6** homesick **7** enormous **8** valuable
4 **1** shocked **2** senior **3** extremely **4** toothpaste **5** flute **6** relative **7** invisible **8** venue **9** stuff **10** Secret word: complaint

GRAMMAR REVIEW

Page 139

1 **1** were invented **2** are made **3** drank **4** are **5** think **6** is claimed **7** will continue **8** will be sold

2 **1** I watched the documentary so that I could learn more about memory. **2** Sam gets better grades than his brother because he works harder. **3** I took an extra English class this semester in order to communicate with people during my trip to the USA. **4** Janice talks more loudly than anyone I know!

3 **1** I can see more clearly with these new glasses. **2** I wanted to visit the new pizza place, but it was closed. **3** Sam enjoys streaming new music in her spare time. **4** You must listen more carefully in class. **5** I was inspired to start writing because of my love of books. **6** Ben speaks Spanish better than anyone in our family.

4 **1** b **2** d **3** f **4** c **5** a **6** e

5 **1** not likely to **2** 're planning to go **3** 'd like to **4** forgot to send **5** better than **6** If you

Macmillan Education
4 Crinan Street
London N1 9XW
A division of Macmillan Publishers Limited

Companies and representatives throughout the world

ISBN 978-1-380-00780-3

Written by Anna Cole and Michael Terry

Go Beyond First published 2015
First edition entitled *Beyond* published 2014

Designed by EMC Design Ltd.

Cover design by EMC Design Ltd.

On-body design by Dynamo Studio, Co.

Full acknowledgements for illustrations and photographs in the facsimile pages can be found in the *Move Beyond* combined Student's Book/Workbook.

Printed and bound in China

2021 2020 2019 2018 2017
10 9 8 7 6 5 4 3 2 1